Joseph Simms

Human Faces, What They Mean.

How to read personal character

Joseph Simms

Human Faces, What They Mean.
How to read personal character

ISBN/EAN: 9783337370152

Printed in Europe, USA, Canada, Australia, Japan

Cover: Foto ©Thomas Meinert / pixelio.de

More available books at **www.hansebooks.com**

HUMAN FACES,
WHAT THEY MEAN!
HOW TO READ PERSONAL CHARACTER,

BY

JOSEPH SIMMS, M.D.

ISAAC PITMAN, Esq.,
Inventor of Modern Phonetic Short-
Hand Writing.

EARL OF SHAFTESBURY,
A Highly Benevolent Face.

This Book is Illustrated by upwards of 200 Engravings,
AND
Contains Several Hundred Signs of Character, Forming an Original System and Classification of Physiognomy.

MURRAY HILL PUBLISHING COMPANY,
129 East 28th Street, New York.
1887.

PRESS OPINIONS REGARDING DR. J. SIMMS' LECTURES AND BOOKS.

AUSTRALIA.—MELBOURNE PRESS.—" Physiognomy is an interesting theme when treated by a master like Dr. Simms' who has devoted his life to it. Hence a large audience assembles nightly at the Athenæum to listen to the subject."—*The Herald*, 11th October, 1882.

" The hall was crowded in every part, and hundreds were unable to gain admittance. Dr. Simms has a very telling way of impressing a truth, with a witticism or a joke, hence an evening passes quickly and pleasantly at his lecture."—*The Age*, 3rd October, 1882.

" At the Athenæum last evening Dr. Simms delivered his sixty-first and closing lecture in Melbourne to a large and well-entertained audience."—*The Argus*, 21st March, 1884.

" These lectures are fraught with fun and instruction, presented in a didactic and agreeable manner."—*The World*, May 8, 1883.

" Dr. Simms is a skilled and practical physiognomist, and teaches how to read the human face and its indications of character."—*Telegraph*, June 9, 1883.

" This gentleman's able expositions of physiognomy are the most scientific and practical ever given in this city."—*Bulletin*, Melbourne, October 13, 1883.

SYDNEY PRESS.—" The lecture was highly instructive, as are all of Dr. Simms' lectures. The entertaining character readings of faces of living citizens are remarkable proofs of physiognomic science.—*Daily Morning Herald*, September 1, 1881.

" There are few platform speakers whose success has been so pronounced in almost every part of the world. . . . The entertainment being, as usual, provocative of great amusement."—*Evening News*, Sydney, Australia, Dec. 12, 1883.

" Dr. J. Simms gave his 67th and closing lecture to a crowded audience of attentive ladies and gentlemen. It was the most scientific, ablest, and best lecture ever given on those subjects in Sydney. No other lecturer has been able to draw such large audiences to scientific pay lecturers for so long a time with continued interest. He has proved himself a most masterly practical physiognomist."—*Daily Telegraph*, Sydney, December 15, 1883.

" Last evening Dr. Simms closed his sixth and last series of lectures in Sydney with the 67th lecture. The closing discourse was an able and entertaining one to a crowded audience. The lectures have throughout been attended by large and interested audiences."—*The Sydney Morning Herald*, December 15, 1883.

" Dr. J. Simms, the great physiognomist, who has a world-wide reputation, delivered his 67th and closing lecture here to a crowded audience last Friday evening, with the ablest discourse heretofore delivered in this city. We agree with the *Pictorial World* of London, ' that Dr. Simms is known as a most skilled practical physiognomist,' and wish him many more hearers in his useful career."—*The Bulletin*, 22nd December, 1883.

" Dr. Simms gave the closing lecture of his course of ten lectures in the Methodist Church, Ann street, last night, when the subjects were treated in an instructive and amusing manner. The lecture which evinced careful and extensive reading and original thought, made plain some of the great primal laws of nature which lie at the base of all human progress. This lecture was the ablest and most entertaining of the series, all of which have been well attended."—*The Brisbane Courier*, Queensland, July 29, 1881.

NEW ZEALAND.—" Dr. Simms does not practice any of the charlatanism usually adopted by phrenologists or mesmerists, his lectures are elegant and amusing, devoid of low jokes or puns, and can be listened to with interest."—*The New Zealand Herald*. Auckland, March 17, 1881.

" We are convinced that there have been a few natural Physiognomists who could read character correctly from the facial lineaments ; Zopyrus, Lavater, and Dr. J. Simms, belong to this limited and favoured class. Dr. Simms has been lecturing more than a quarter of a century to crowded houses."—*Evening Star*, Auckland, New Zealand, March 18, 1881.

" Last evening Dr. Simms gave a lecture, the closing one of his instructive and amusing course, in the Congregational school-room. Large audiences have given undivided attention to these lectures, which have been original and edifying. Dr. Simms is a wonderful reader of the human face."—*The Press*, Christchurch, N. Z., May 14, 1881.

" Dr. J. Simms is undoubtedly the most eminent physiognomist and lecturer on character ; this public examinations are astonishingly accurate, and his lectures are very learned, ingenious and humorous. His lectures have drawn large audiences here, and have been able unfoldments of scientific physiognomy in a popular manner. The entire course has been a success, and cannot fail to be that in any intelligent community where the lectures are heard."—*The Observer*, Auckland, New Zealand, March 26, 1881.

" Dr. Simms seems to be master of his profession, for, without touching the head, by a lighting survey of the face, he described character very accurately."—*Morning Herald*, Dunedin, New Zealand, May 26, 1881.
[Continued on page 240.]

An Original and Illustrated
PHYSIOLOGICAL
AND
PHYSIOGNOMICAL CHART.
By J. SIMMS, M.D.

J. B. PORTA.   J. G. LAVATER.
NATURAL PHYSIOGNOMISTS.

THIS work was prepared by its Author with the design to provide the subjects of his examinations with a permanent record of their Mental, Moral, and Volitive dispositions, and to furnish them with all necessary information and advice respecting their choice of occupations, and of companions for life. It also contains valuable directions for the cultivation and restraint of every physical and intellectual power, with medical counsel relative to the proper means to be employed in the recovery and preservation of health.

THIS WORK PRESENTS
A New and Complete Analysis and Classification
OF THE
TEMPERAMENTS OR FORMS OF MANKIND,
And Designates a great number of Faculties heretofore unrecognised, the Physiognomical Signs of which have Never Before Been Discovered.

In this Chart every power is marked upon a scale of from one to twelve, an extended gradation which enables the Examiner to reach every extreme, and to assign its relative position to every important modification of character.

Read and learn "The lore which wig-crowned History scorns," but which is Eternally fixed by the Immutable Laws of Nature.

FIRST EDITION PUBLISHED AT GLASGOW, SCOTLAND, IN 1873.

REVISED AND REPRINTED IN 1882.

IMPROVED AND REPRINTED IN 1887.

Entered, according to Act of Parliament, in the year 1872, by J. SIMMS, M.D., *in Stationers' Hall, London.*

Entered, according to Act of Congress, in the year 1872, by J. SIMMS, M.D., *in the Office of the Librarian of Congress at Washington.*

COPYRIGHT BY J. SIMMS, M. D., 1886.

INTRODUCTION.

PHYSIOGNOMY is the art, or science by which the characteristics of the mind are discovered in the general configuration of the body, and particularly in the features of the face. The present book is a revised and enlarged edition of a Physiognomical Chart which I published some time since in the United States, and which was, as far as I am aware, the first, of the kind, that has ever been presented to the public. The face of man is like the face of a clock, which by definite external signs reveals the workings of the inward machinery. I have said that these signs are definite, yet, as a clock would tell the hours in vain to one who was ignorant how to interpret the movements of its hands, so the human countenance would vainly represent the character to those who were unable to decipher its emblematic writing. Hence the value of a reliable system of Physiognomy to aid the instinctive, but often mistaken judgments which all men immediately form as to the character of those whom they meet.

Physiognomy like all other sciences, has been developed slowly. Aristotle attempted in the fourth century before Christ to place it on a systematic footing before the ancient world. Galen, Cicero, Seneca. Pliny, and Quintilian all wrote upon this theme, but the advance of the science is chiefly due to the moderns—especially to J. Baptista Porta who in the early part of the seventeenth century pursued some valuable investigations which were based upon a comparative view of the faces of men and of the lower animals, and to the great and good Lavater. The "Physiognomical Fragments" which were published by the latter made him extensively known, yet they are so deficient in method, and often so much at fault in the application of rules which their author founded upon his own experience, that they are now regarded as possessing but little scientific value

The term Physiognomy, which is derived from two Greek words, that signify "to know nature," points us, by its etymology, to the proper method to be pursued in its study. He only who is a wide and close observer of the faces, forms, and characters of men, and of the lower animals, or who is familiar with the conclusions attained by reliable investigators who have studied nature in this field, can hope to become an expert in physiognomy. For the assistance of those who have been unable to extend their observations by travel, or who are naturally deficient in observing power, I shall in a few months publish a work entitled "Nature's Revelations of Character" in which I shall present a new, and, as I believe, advanced analysis and classification of the powers of the human mind and body, together with the physiognomical signs by which every faculty is disclosed.

Although Physiognomy has not heretofore been satisfactorily developed as a complete science, it is, in many of its elements, constantly, and successfully applied in the details of practical life, and inwoven into the axioms of society, and literature. The early poets always assumed the closest connection between the character, and the personal appearance of the heroes they described. It is related that Zopyrus, an Athenian physiognomist, after examining the features of Socrates, declared that he was by nature addicted to gluttony and drunkenness—

an impeachment which was admitted by the great moral teacher who confessed that it had taxed his powers of self-command to the utmost to restrain his native tendency to these animal excesses. Caius Tranquillus Suetonius, in his "Lives of the Twelve Cæsars" informs us that Titus, when emperor of Rome, inquired of a physiognomist by the name of Narcissus whether Brittanicus would succeed to the imperial crown, and that Narcissus, after an examination of the prince pronounced that judgment with respect to him which has since been confirmed by history.

In this chart will be found a description, and exposition of the various *forms* which, in a greater or less degree, enter into the physical structure of every individual, and which are the signs, if not the authors of his mental characteristics. It also contains much valuable sanitary advice, together with a definition of all the intellectual faculties, and rules for their cultivation or restraint as the peculiarities of the case may require. Any person who has had his chart marked by a competent examiner may, by the careful and persistent observance of these rules, strengthen the good, and correct the evil qualities of his nature until he has developed a healthy and harmonious organization. In nearly twenty years of close observation of, and reflection upon the mental and physical powers of the human family I have assured myself that, owing to an imperfect analysis, the number of our faculties has been hitherto underestimated. Accordingly, in the present chart, I have named, described, and vindicated these overlooked powers, and I therefore claim that this is the most complete, and hence the most scientific anthropological record which has yet appeared. It is also of great practical service, inasmuch as it designates the occupations in which the subjects of examination are adapted to succeed, as well as the mental and physical characteristics which should distinguish their matrimonial partners. Both in business and in marriage the most ruinous blunders are constantly being made by men and women who consume their lives labouring hopelessly in occupations for which they are wholly unfitted by their organization, or who wreck their connubial happiness, and the healthfulness of their offspring by unsuitable marriages. All this may be avoided by following the scientific directions given in this chart.

Man can perform, suffer, and enjoy more than any other creature. With firm steps—with body erect, and head heavenward he walks forth a representative on earth of the Supreme Intelligence of heaven. He looks forward, and lives in the future—around him and exists in the present—is cast down, and looking backward takes the retrospect of the past. He moves as on the wings of the wind, his power enabling him to compass both sea and land. He unites flexibility and strength, courage and gentleness, repulsion and attraction, vivacity and repose. Borne by the volatile steam he rides secure on the waves of the ocean, or flies over the cold iron along the valleys chasing the deer round the foot of the mountains. He stands upon the sands of the Atlantic and snatching the lightning from the clouds sends it, freighted with meaning, to where the Pacific waves kiss shores of gold. Such, and so wonderful is this unparalleled creature, this universal microcosm. Where can he find a subject of contemplation so interesting or so instructive as himself? But to the successful study of human nature Physiognomy furnishes an almost indispensable assistance. He who has fully mastered its laws may read, as in a book the occult secrets of his own organization and, with a glance, become intimately acquainted with every passing stranger.

THE FORMS OF THE HUMAN BODY.

"We are all the slaves of our organism."--*Emerson*.

THE question of human responsibility, involved as it is in the metaphysical subtleties, yet pregnant with the weightiest practical interest, has ever been the vexed inquiry of speculative theology. But although I am somewhat attracted to this perplexing field, by the subject I am about to discuss, I shall not, here, attempt its exploration. I shall leave the metaphysicians to solve the question, whether mind is the result of physical organization, or physical organization the result of mind; or to what extent they both act, and react upon each other. In this work, strictly devoted as it is to physiognomical science, it will be sufficient for me to point out those mental and moral characteristics, which, in common experience, are always found in connection with distinctive physical types.

A scientific definition of the types of the human body, as regards the relations and proportions between its various parts, has been attempted even by the earliest writers. Galen and Hippocrates contended that all men could be classed under four *crases* or temperaments, viz. the sanguineous, bilious, melancholic, and phlegmatic. The bilious temperament, according to Hippocrates, is the result of an excess of yellow bile secreted by the liver; the melancholic, of a surplus of black bile produced by the spleen; the sanguineous, of an overplus of blood originated by the heart; and the phlegmatic, of a superabundance of phlegm—a watery fluid consequent upon the action of the brain. The progress of physiological science has shown us that the brain does not, as the Greek physician supposed, originate a watery fluid, and that black bile is not produced by the spleen, nor blood by the heart. Yet, notwithstanding these errors in the details of Hippocrates' system, his classification, as such has been handed down through succeeding ages, and is more or less in favour, to-day. Now I maintain that this ancient system and all the modern schemes which have been founded upon it, are essentially false, because they are not based upon nature, and because their terminology is obscure to any but the scientific student.

I prefer, in the consideration of this subject to discard the word temperament altogether, as liable to grave misunderstanding, and to designate the different classes of men by their different physical *forms*. These forms, which are five in number, I shall consider in the following order:—the Abdominal Form; the Thoracic Form; the Muscular and Fibrous Form; the Osseous or Bony Form, and the Brain and Nerve Form. In this order I follow nature in the manner in which she unfolds the respective powers of mankind. I ascend from that which developes first to that which is latest in maturing, from the lower part of the face and physique to the superior portions, and the same order is maintained throughout the entire classification of this chart. The number of the classes of the signs of the faculties, correspond with the number of forms which the signs and their even combination represent. Every person of course, possesses all of these forms but in the vast majority of instances, they are unequally developed, in which case, the predominating form or forms, by marking the leading characteristic, indicates the class to which the subject belongs.

The abdomen is that part of the body which lies between the thorax and the pelvis, and includes the larger part of the digestive apparatus, and the intestines. The form to which the abdomen gives its name may be morbidly increased by entire freedom from care and study, and excessive indulgence in eating drinking, and sleep. Those in whom it is highly developed have full cheeks, a double chin one or more wrinkles running round the neck, short and irregular wrinkles on the forehead, almond shaped and sleepy eyes, a round pug nose, and general fulness in the abdominal region. They are epicurean in their tastes. prudent, indolent, good-natured, social, and fond of making and of spending money. They are inclined to adipose accumulation and succeed better in the social circle, than in high deliberative or executive functions. The activity of their excernent system gives them the plump and aqueous appearance which is consequent upon an abundance of the vital fluids. Daniel Lambert may be cited in illustration of the abdominal form.

The Thoracic form is highly developed, when the thorax is relatively large. The heart and the organs of respiration are contained within the thoracic cavity, hence mountain air, and mountain climbing ; striking the chest rapidly after a full inhalation ; running ; swimming, and other exercises increase the Thoracic form, by developing the lungs, and stimulating the circulatory action of the heart. Those in whom this form predominates are fond of amusements, pure air and exercise. They are cheerful, and imaginative, but dislike confinement and are usually averse to study. Their muscles are of a fine and rather firm texture, and they have generally a large nose, with expanded nostrils, prominent and wide cheek bones protuberant veins. and moderate or small brain and abdomen. They are peculiarly liable to acute diseases, and especially to inflammatory complaints. Cicero was a good example of this form.

As large bones are not always accompanied by powerful muscles, it is necessary to discriminate between the Muscular and Fibrous, and the Osseous forms. Dr Windship, of Boston, although able to lift 2600 lbs., is a man of small frame-work. The Muscular form is developed by all kinds of energetic and healthful muscular exercise. Those who are distinguished by it, are sensitive and energetic. They possess abundant physical courage, and although comparatively slow to anger, are desperate when exasperated. In the purely intellectual powers, they are seldom gifted, but when urged to practical exertion by love, ambition, rage or fear, there are few obstacles which they cannot surmount. They are elastic and amorous, and when irritated, become destructive. Dr Windship, who is a conspicuous instance of this form, told me that light haired people were the most susceptible of physical development. He is light-haired, and of a sandy complexion. Romulus, Hercules, Achilles, Hector, Ajax. Alexander the Great, William Wallace, and Robert Bruce, all possessed the muscular form. The Spartan legislators paid particular attention to the development of the physique, and to that end ordained that women as well as men should practise running, wrestling, boxing, jumping, swimming, quoit-pitching, and throwing the javelin. To insure a muscular race, they also ordered that all weakly and deformed children should be destroyed immediately after birth. Plutarch informs us that, the better to tone the fibres, the athletic exercises of the Greeks were performed by both men and women in a nude condition. The physical signs of the muscular form are, general breadth of the body, well defined tendons and muscles, heavy shoulders, a broad nose at the base, and a large, short neck. The muscles may be developed by vigorous exercise in the shade, but the growth of the bones is dependent on the influence of sunlight

Those persons strongly characterized by the osseous form, have a sallow or dark complexion, long limbs and fingers, square shoulders, a prominent nose, hollow cheeks and temples, and straight hair. They are ungraceful in their movements, slow in motion and judgment, but very reliable ; awkward in bestowing or receiving a favour. careless in details, and more fond of comfort than display. When this form is supported by a large brain, and general healthiness of organization, it is highly favourable to talent and greatness. Plato, Plutarch, Alfred the Great, La Fayette, Washington, and Lincoln possessed the osseous, in marked, but harmonious combination, with the Brain and Nerve form.

The Brain or Nerve form is shown by various external signs, such as, an uneven or angular surface of skull, sharp features, thin lips and nostrils, wasted physique, an anxious and discontented expression, a relatively small chest and neck, and a relatively large head. Persons of this form are quick in their motions, keenly sensitive to every species of suffering or enjoyment, and peculiarly susceptible to the influence of alcoholic liquors, opium, tobacco, and tea. They are apt to be dyspeptic, irritable, fidgetty, and super-attentive to details They carry too much sail, and they need a great deal of sleep, and healthful food to repair the waste of nature incident to the excitement of their intense lives

The most important lesson which can be derived from the science of physiognomical forms is, that an appropriate and protracted system of education and living may so modify their relative development as to bring them all into that harmonious proportion which is the condition of the highest mental and physical health. A child for instance, in whom the brain and nerve form is unduly ascendant, may acquire the osseous form by drinking calcareous water, and by plain diet, pure air, and light manual labour in the sunlight. All the other forms may be similarly transmuted by appropriate training. The Creator has given perfection of physique to very few of his creatures, but He has arranged the animal economy with such ineffable wisdom and goodness. that all have it in their power to decrease their natural defects, and approximate, at least, to a perfectly harmonious organization. As childhood is the period when human beings are most susceptible to all kinds of educational influences it is evident that parents and guardians are deeply responsible for the healthy combination of forms in the children whose rearing is committed to their care.

FORM No. I.

ABDOMINAL FORM.

The various peculiarities by which we discover the ABDOMINAL FORM, *are sleepy eyes, watery and puffed appearance of the flesh, plump cheeks, large abdomen, one wrinkle round the neck, short wrinkles in the forehead, and a flat, languid expression of the visage.*

1. Possessing no vitality, or so little that you cannot accomplish much, hence you are a worthless member of society.

2. Your mental manifestations are indicative of sensitiveness, perception, intensity, &c., and may be strong and rapid, but you are liable to wear out.

Abdominal Form large.
Hippopotamus, taken from life in the Zoological Gardens in London, England

3. The smallness of your waist is an indication that the nourishing part of your body is weak.

4. You are rather lank and lean, yet you make up in action what you lack in bulk.

5. The abdominal viscera are not sufficiently active to cushion your bones roundly with fat.

6. When exposure is necessary, you can endure the cold, yet you are naturally free from calidity or gelidity.

7. Your absorbents are sufficiently active to sustain the body with care; and you are well balanced in the nutritive and digestive forces.

8. You have certainly a tendency to long life, and are possessed of an abundance of the juices. When you wish to be so, you are companionable.

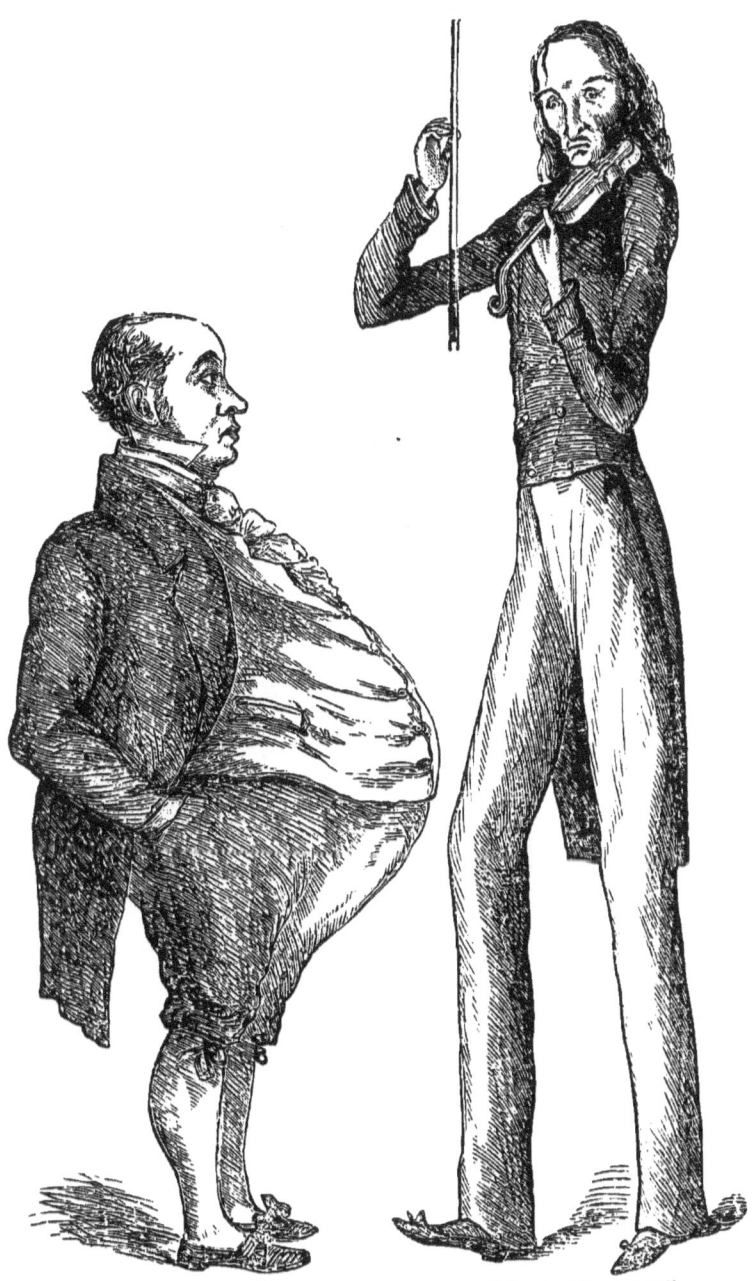

Abdominal Form large.
Nathan Meyer Rothschild,
the money potentate of the world.

Abdominal Form small.
Nicholas Paganini,
the wizard of the bow.

9. The general plumpness of your face indicates good assimilative organs and appropriative powers, with an excellent nourishing apparatus.

10. Your cellular tissue is full to repletion, hence you are apt to be good-natured and social, unless soured by troubles or misfortunes.

11. The excernent system which secretes the fluids from the blood is particularly active in you.

12. You are a sleepy, half-inanimate, gross mass of fat; so much so that it seems to be a burden to you; your structure contains a superabundance of fluids; hence you are fond of ease. Persons of your form rarely, if ever, figure among the illustrious.

A. To Cultivate the Abdominal Form:—Sleep all you can; eat bulky, nutritious food, as much as you can, but only one or two kinds at a meal; take everything easy; eat slowly; masticate well; laugh heartily, but never weep; go up one stair at a time instead of two; and only exercise enough to keep the fluids of the body in motion. Sumptuous and excessive nourishment produces the abdominal form, and gives plump, thick, and round rather than tall figures, so plants which spread much are never very tall. Decambulation, motion, and respiration are hindered by extreme obesity; yet gormandizing, ease, and sleep will make one ventrose and fat.

B. To Restrain the Abdominal Form:—Keep your eyes open and your mouth shut; eat little; sleep little; take your food in a concentrated form; and engage in an occupation demanding thought and great activity. In ancient history we find several accounts of very fat persons being made thinner or more attenuated by certain reducible remedies. Vaseus relates an incident of the King of Spain, the father of Ordonius, who was named Crassus, because he was so greasy and fat. He, becoming wearied and impatient with his load of fat, visited different countries, and finally obtained relief of it by a certain herb which Cardan called bird's-tongue. There is an account in Athenæus of Dionysius, the over-fat tyrant of the Heracleots, who would over-sleep so soundly, that they could not wake him except by pricking him with needles, and he was cured by the application of leeches to his entire body. Fallopius says he saw the skin so incrassated in a very fat man, that he lost his sense by reason of the over-impaction of the nerves. Poor fellow, how fortunate for him that he did not live among the Lacedemonians, where fat people were in disgrace, and punished by the most severe laws made against them. Pliny gave an account of Apronius, who was sometime Consul of Rome, and had a son so fat that he could not walk, until the doctor removed a large quantity of fat from his abdomen.

FORM No. II.

THORACIC FORM.

The manner in which the THORACIC FORM *betrays itself, physiognomically, is by the possession of large nostrils, wide malar bones, full throat, small abdomen, brain, bones, &c.*

1. Having languid and feeble circulation and respiration, the world seems to you to be a whirlpool of luxuriant imaginations.
2. You are deficient in respiration and blood power.

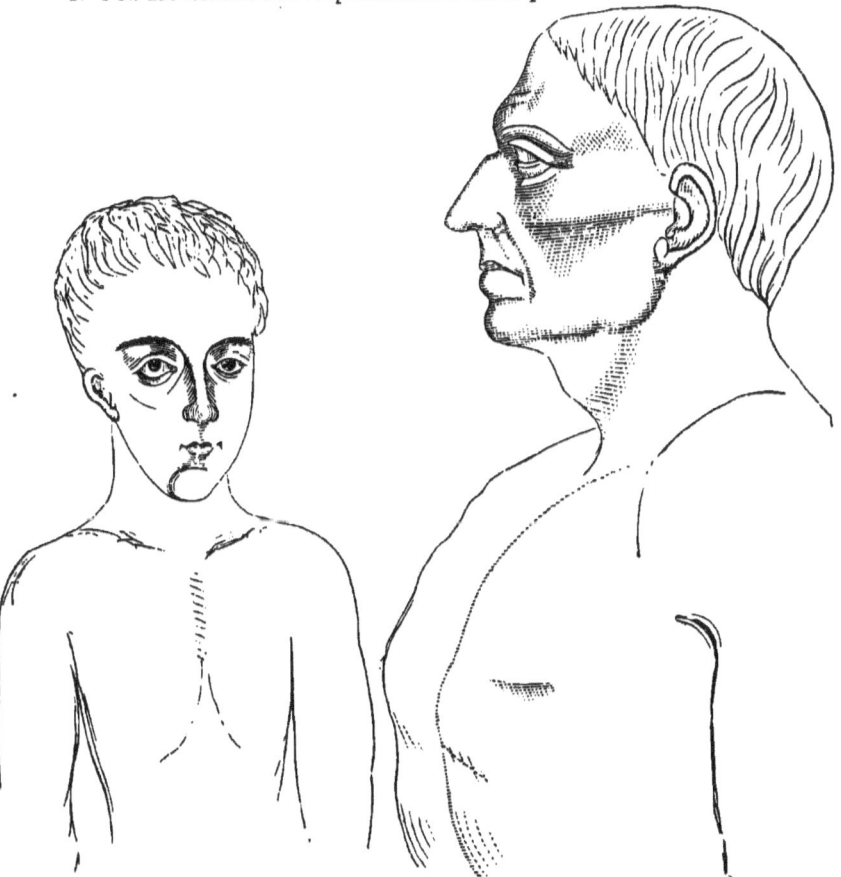

Thoracic Form small.
Edward I., the only son of Henry VIII., whom he succeeded to the throne of England in 1547, and died at the early age of 16 years.

Thoracic Form large.
Cicero, the Prince of orators, who conquered Cæsar by his eloquence, and composed 50 verses in a single night

3. Of hopes and prospective joys, you have very few, and are often surprised and startled.

4. Lacking blood, there is little ardour in your form.

5. You gape and yawn as if but half awake most of the time; you are ill adapted to city life.

6. You are liable to be languid and passive and you will find many superior to yourself in this world.

7. The sympathy of your nature is with out-door air; your health is deteriorated by any in-door business or labour; you are usually possessed of animation equal to your business demands.

8. The blood of your body has a tendency to flow upwards instead of downwards, and you may occasionally feel dizzy from this cause.

9. Though you enjoy physical action very well, yet you could become quite a student with application.

10. Your pathway in life is strewn with bright hopes, which you are ever discovering as you move onward. Your respiration is slow and heavy.

11. Having powerful respiration, you would succeed eminently in active business pursuits, as you possess great energy, and have both strength and courage.

12. Your veins are blue and your pulse strong, regular, and frequent; hence your imagination and perception are quite lively; and you are very passionate and always cheerful.

A. To CULTIVATE THE THORACIC FORM.—Keep in motion; climb hills and mountains; breathe a pure atmosphere night and day; bathe your chest, use friction and gentle pounding; keep your shoulders up; walk erect, and live on a generous diet of animal and farinaceous food, avoiding nerve stimulants. You should live on the mountains, if possible.

B. To RESTRAIN THE THORACIC FORM.—Avoid animal food, beer, ale, porter—all fermented liquors; be almost a vegetarian in diet; live in-doors; inhale less oxygen; but, above all things, keep cool and avoid excitement. Live a sedentary life in the low lands of your native country, and study with that elastic energy which surely conquers circumstances or bodily excesses.

FORM No. III.

MUSCULAR AND FIBROUS FORM.

The broad phiz and physique; short heavy neck; rough, low forehead, broad flat nose; short ear and deep perpendicular wrinkles on the face, are unmistakable indications of a powerful MUSCULAR FORM.

1. Your miserable body is a clog to you; every step you take is a laborious effort.

2. Your limbs seem unbraced, your step halting, your mind fickle, and your fainting effeminacy obtains with few, if any, sturdy people.

3. Weakness, debility, and languor have settled upon your frame, while strength, vigour, and energy should have been your noble characteristics.

MUSCULAR AND FIBROUS FORM.   12

4. Sadly needing strength, it is a pity you do not possess some of those prodigious powers which are lodged in the muscles of the lion.

5. Your muscles are weak, perhaps enfeebled for want of proper exercise when young; or, in later years, you are or have been overworked, perhaps.

6. Your muscular strength cannot be compared to the trunk of an elephant, which (trunk) Cuvier estimates as possessing 30,000 muscles. and with which the elephant can wrench asunder the strong limbs of stout trees. A careful and prudent use of gymnastics would improve your frame.

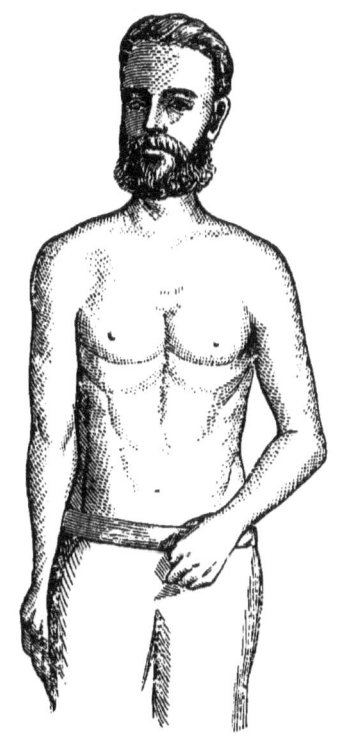

Muscular and Fibrous Form large.
Tom Johnson a notorious champion of England in 1789

Muscular and Fibrous Form small.
Amadeus, King of Spain, second son of King Emmanuel of Italy.

7. The fibrous and muscular structures of your system are fairly well developed.

8. You possess a large amount of fibre, and could lift a heavy load or strike a severe blow.

9. You have great powers of physical endurance, and your muscles and fibres are well developed; yet you are not equal to Romulus, Hercules, Ajax, Hector Achilles, Patroclus, Paris, Asius, Æneas, Sarpedon, Glaucus, or Asteropæus, in physical prowess.

10. Lacking acuteness and the impressional nature, you will not likely become distinguished in the fine arts.

11. You have remarkable tranquillity of mind, and wonderful muscular strength—slow to be aroused, but, when aroused, you will overcome every opposition or obstacle.

12. You are nearly, yet not quite, a solid mass of muscle; you are likely to be a modern Samson in strength, though not, perhaps, inclined to rest on the lap of Delilah, but rather resembling Ulysses.

A. TO CULTIVATE THE MUSCULAR AND FIBROUS FORM.—Procure works on physical culture, such as the "Swedish Movement Cure;" "Physical Perfection," by Jacques; Lewis's "New Gymnastics," &c., and thoroughly practise the advice given in those authorities. Give yourself a thorough gymnastic education; lift, work, play, and keep the muscles working, yet allowing them reasonable rest. But remember that power and endurance of mind as well as health depend much upon the muscles.

B. TO RESTRAIN THE MUSCULAR AND FIBROUS FORM.—It is seldom necessary in this brain-age, in which sensations are appreciated more than common sense; yet if you require more exquisite sensibilities, read and think more, but work and exercise less.

FORM No. IV,

OSSEOUS OR BONY FORM.

Strongly protruding bones in a rough face; sunken eyes; hollow temples; square shoulders; large joints, hands, and feet; spare body, with lean limbs and face; moderate or small head; are the various apparent ways in which the OSSEOUS FORM discovers itself to the observer.

1. The small size of your body is owing to the diminutive size of the bones; you would make a good Tom Thumb, but you are utterly useless for practical life. Get under a glass case at once! you'll look best at home on the mantel-piece.

2. Your skeleton is the most insignificant part of your whole body. Ossification was a long time in completing its work in your system; hence you are not very persistent, and you are liable to softness of the bones or "*Mollities Ossium.*"

3. You are extremely highwrought and your bones are full of gelatine, which gives them and you wonderful elasticity, but you sadly lack the phosphates and also the carbonate of lime which would make you more stable and reliable.

4. Yours is a small and finely moulded form, and to you the coarse drudgeries of life are distasteful; you are liable to rickets, or bone softening, because the secretory organs of your system do not furnish a sufficiency of earthy material.

5. The bones of your structure are not very large; hence your gracefulness is greater than your endurance.

6. Your bones are fine and abound in organic matter and are almost free from anything earthy or inorganic. You may be active, but you are not capable of great projects or continued effort.

Osseous or Bony Form small.
Char'es Stratton, "Tom Thumb."
About three feet in height.

Osseous or Bony Form large.
Abraham Lincoln.
Height about six feet six inches.

7. Your bones are not large, but are sufficiently enveloped in muscle and adipose tissue to give you roundness. Such was Oviedo, the Spaniard, as described by Washington Irving, and the famous historian, Prescott.

8 The Osseous structure of your organization is not excessive neither is it deficient; you are boniform in this respect.

9. You are neither too tall nor too short to use your framework with ease. Should occasion demand it, you can endure grief, trouble, privation, hardship, exposure, and severe physical trials quite well, as did your prototype, Agamemnon.

10. You start slowly in the morning and may be slow towards night, but you are not easily exhausted, being recuperative and singularly positive,—in reality a Diogenes.

11. You have powerful bones and framework, but want freedom and ease of action, being utterly devoid of grace; but in pursuing a project, you are steady and inflexible, as old Draco.

12 You dislike to trouble yourself about trifles; being tall and not particular, you rarely find fault; your bones are very large and you hate the little deceptions and trickeries of fashionable life. In your purpose, you are absolute and emphatically unequivocal; you resemble much the character given to Guy Livingstone by the author of "Thorough."

A. TO CULTIVATE THE OSSEOUS OR BONY FORM:—Take gentle pedestrian and equestrian exercise in the sunlight; let your food be largely fabaceous and of an aperient nature, which will further the spirits upwards and tend to improve the blood and carry off the poison humours which facilitates the circulation of the blood in the extremities and capillaries and attenuates the form. Avoid sweets of all kinds, pastry, tobacco, opium, and all narcotics. Let your drink be pure water impregnated with calcium or lime, if possible. from a spring out of limestone subsoil; but carefully abstain from all kinds of alcoholic liquors, no matter how diluted. Xenophon, understanding this susceptibility of the human form to transformations, and wishing to rear large athletic men, commenced feeding the Persian children upon cardamomums or water cresses, which he said made them grow taller and enhanced their physical prowess Another very important means of elongating the human form is natural heat or caloric. This natural warmth in the body can be supplied and kept up safely only by exercise. Hence too much confinement at school or in sedentary occupations will stunt the growth of children and especially their bones. This will account for the fact that country children who attend school during a small part of the year become larger in stature than those reared in the city. Children should avoid such substances as nitre because it is cold in its nature and lessens the heat of the body, thus retarding bone-growth. A puppy fed upon milk and nitre was kept small and lively. Mercury also, in all its forms, should be avoided, as well as iodide of potassa, with every variety of the alkalies. which are all deleterious to bone-growth by impairing the natural heat of the body Milk, on the contrary, should be used largely, especially by the young, as it nourishes the bones, which never grow so rapidly as when nature furnishes the child or the young with abundance of the lacteal fluid. Hence it is accounted for that children in dairy countries grow taller than those living on bread and flesh without milk. Let it be remembered, however, that milk will not agree with mature persons who are scrofulous or have a tendency to acrid humours. Moderate diet, partaken of at regular or stated times, without excess or stint favours bone-growth. The sunlight tends to promote the growth of the bones. Pliny the elder informs us that in his time in India (about 70 A.D.) where there are no shadows, and generous sunlight, there were men of thirty feet in height.

B. To RESTRAIN THE OSSEOUS OR BONY FORM:—This can be done by a sedentary and studious life in the shade; keep out of the sunlight during your exercise; move off with animation; stir quickly when you work; attend dancing school and polite parties. The consecutive study and shady halls of our colleges would do much to hold in check your growth of bones. Engage in an in-door occupation and spend your leisure hours in lively company, active exercise in the shade, in quiet games, in writing or in reading, and your bones will decrease in thickness and heft, yet not so much in length. I would not wish to recommend living luxuriously or lasciviously, which joined with the effeminate rearing of the young, prevents great bone-growth and noble stature; yet in this fast but small age, if you live as rapidly and foolishly (as is too common) you will restrain bone-growth. Dry nourishment given to children will tend to restrain the stature. As is mentioned in (A) nitre is preventive of growth in the young; and the quantity used in some rural districts to preserve meat and butter has an injurious effect on the growth of the young who consume those articles of diet.

FORM No. V.

BRAIN AND NERVE FORM.

A large head and small body; pyriform face; long wrinkles on the forehead; with sharp features, are the general signs of a predominance of the BRAIN AND NERVE FORM.

1. Dulness and apathy are the great weaknesses which beset you; some persons, for very good reasons, deem you *senseless*.

2. You are obtuse and devoid of sensibility to the touch; have an apathetic and callous nature; and few things in this world affect you.

3. Having little sensitiveness or physical sensibility; you are generally in a semiconscious state, though, to the inexperienced and unsuspecting, you may appear somewhat keen and acute.

4. Romantic ideas, novels, and intensely sensational dramas, you care little for; the prick of a thorn, a cut, or a stroke from a whip, hurts you not so severely as it would one whose nerve sensation was more largely developed.

5. Your sensations are lacking in promptitude and not very vivacious.

6. You are well balanced in that part of your nature which is susceptible of external impressions.

7. Your sentient system is quite under the control of your will.

8. With plain living you can avoid excesses; yet you desire excitement when business will permit.

9. Your nervous power being well developed you have generally much activity.

10. You have excellent nerve-power; but your mind will be likely to debilitate and weaken your body.

11. One having this degree of the Brain and Nerve Form will be intense in feeling, and will suffer and enjoy in extremes.

12. Your life being in your Brain and Nerves, which are almost a solid mass, you become, if hurried, very irritable at times.

Brain and Nerve Form small.
A licentious and brutal flat head Indian man, of Cape Flattery, Washington Territory, America.

Brain and Nerve Form large.
Dr Spraker, President of Wittenberg College, at Springfield, Ohio. He has studied, taught, lectured, and preached all his life

A. To CULTIVATE THE BRAIN AND NERVE FORM:—Lead an active city life, if possible; avoid every pursuit that does not keep your mind in the most intense and vigorous action; attend lectures, debates, sermons; read and study several hours daily, especially the works of American and Irish authors; but never fully gratify your appetite at meals. Eat sparingly of fish, as that edible contains phosphorus which is required to give strength for the brain work. Partake of oatmeal porridge, as it keeps the bowels open and strengthens the brain, thereby giving a clear mind. Gerald Massey, an eminent poet, has learned the advantages arising from using the above recommended articles of diet, and clearly expresses his mind on the subject in the following words:—"There is a deal of phosphorus in oatmeal, and phosphorus is brain. There is also a large amount of phosphorus in fish. Consequently, I never miss having a fish dinner at least once a week, and take a plate of good, thick, coarse, well-boiled Scotch oatmeal every morning in my life." With him, I will say I know the practical benefits of oatmeal and fish, by having eaten both in Scotland.

B. To RESTRAIN THE BRAIN AND NERVE FORM:—Engage in field sports and out-door exercises; practise gymnastics; walk, dance, run, and build up the body with a generous and life-giving diet. Sleep more. But avoid novels, fictitious ideas, and books which excite you, as well as reiterated pleasures. A sedentary and studious habit would injure your health and constantly increase that which you wish to lessen.

THE STOMACH.

THE STOMACH *is the central organ of digestion, which secretes gastric juice by means of innumerable follicles in its internal or mucous coat, the action of which upon the various articles consumed is quite similar to that of prolonged boiling in water.*

Stomach very strong.
David Hume. He could partake of a hearty meal, and immediately apply himself to severe mental labour, without experiencing the least inconvenience.

Stomach weak.
Gustavus III., King of Sweden, who suffered several years with dyspepsia.

1. Being a confirmed dyspeptic, you are liable to heartburn, general lassitude and inertia, while everything you eat gives you pain.

2. The power of nutrition in your system being entirely exhausted, you have become like a worn-out draft-horse. Let your stomach rest and wait for an appetite.

3. Your digestive apparatus alternating between good and poor cause you to be haunted by many ills which all arise from your moderate or feeble digestive powers. Such are, your general state of irritability, peevishness, daintiness, apprehensions and groundless fears.

4. The lank and thin frame you carry about is sufficient testimony that the alveoli and mucous peptic glands have become weak. Hence you do not draw all the nourishment out of the food you consume. You may have ravenous appetite, and yet the food you take is hurried along the alimentary canal undigested. The muscular coat of your stomach is debilitated.

5. There are certain kinds of edibles which disagree with you and cause intumescence or swelling of the stomach, which on this account fails to supply in abundance the materials for the renewal of the body.

6. Your vigour of digestion is only fair, and unless discretion is used, you will suffer. It would be well to cultivate this organ of the body.

7. With due care you need not suffer from indigestion. Bear in mind that all polypes, animalcules, and monads feed slowly and digest well.

8. Your organs of nutrition may remain good if care be taken in eating. Avoid rapidity, be careful in quality, and leave off with an appetite. By following this rule you may secure the famous Thomas Parr's ("Old Parr's") motto—"A long life and a happy one."

9. Your powers of alimentation and assimilation are excellent. You are not liable to pine for the want of materials for growth and renewal, as you can eat the most substantial food with impunity. You love to live well and have strength in your blood. The gastric follicles and peptic glands are healthy, and secrete an abundance of gastric juice; the columnar epithelium of your stomach is healthy and active. Hence your stomach is excellent.

Charles VI., Emperor of West Austria, who died with dyspepsia.

10. As the result of good digestion, you have generally a very good flow of animal spirits. The secernent and absorbent systems are ably performing their respective duties; your body is well nourished.

11. Anything you eat is digested thoroughly, and appropriated properly to the use of each bodily organ; hence you are not liable to become a dyspeptic. You have a superabundance of the materials of nutrition.

12. Your digestion is equal to that of an ostrich or an anaconda; viands never trouble you after they are consumed; your blood is rich in carbon and nitrogen. None perform more thoroughly than you the process of chymification. You may safely adopt the sagacious advice of the sage old king of physicians, Esculapius, "There is not a luxury that is inimical to vitality, if partaken of in moderation and not too frequently."

A. To Cultivate the Healthy Action of the Stomach:—Avoid tobacco, alcohol, and opium, as they retard the metamorphosis of the tissues; eat slowly, coarse dry bread; drink copiously after eating; eat only when hungry; use oatmeal puddings; cast away your care and sorrow; be cheerful at table; laugh and talk much while eating; avoid all condensed food; knead the body opposite the stomach and bowels daily; avoid sitting and sleep much; eat plain food only, in moderate quantities; use stale bread; masticate well and slowly; swallow only small morsels of meat at a time; use no strong purgatives; if possible, always take a *siesta*. Lay aside all anxieties and discontentments; visit places of amusements; exercise in pure air, and above all cultivate a perfect serenity of temper. Allow no savoury and luxurious dishes or gratifying and stimulating drinks to decoy your appetite away from satisfaction to satiety and into immoderate meals. Should you increase the quantity of your food, it should be accompanied with a proportionate increase of exercise that disease may be precluded.

B. To Restrain the Healthy Action of the Stomach:—Never stimulate the appetite; think less of your eating; remember that a gourmand or cormorant cannot be respected among eminent literary characters; eat sparingly; be anxious and studious; you have only to look about you to learn that the world is encumbered with useless devourers; hence try to refrain from adding to their number by your dereliction of surfeit.

THE LIVER.

The liver *secretes bile from the venous blood, and produces, from the blood, animal starch, which is readily converted into sugar.*

1. You do not throw off the bile of the system well; the liver is torpid and you are stupid and inactive of mind and are afflicted with the "blues" nearly all the year round.

2. Your blood is not well relieved of its material for bile. To protect you from sickness, stirring out-door life would be the best preventive.

3. Being subject to become jaundiced, you are liable to headache and low spirits.

4. A fit of anger in your case may cause such a copious and unusual secretion of bile as to ruin your health. Save the liver all the work you can.

5. Rich living, greasy food and sweets will prove highly injurious to you.

6. When the clouds lower and gloomy winds whistle through the leafy arbours you become a trifle blue or low-spirited; by regulating your diet you will be saved from many of these gloomy reveries

7. Quite well balanced, you are, in this organ. Discretion at meals may exempt you from much sickness.

8. The hepatic cells are active and healthy. You will experience little annoyance from torpidity and portal system if you eat sparingly.

9 The bile necessary to chylification is fairly well secreted in your system; though not the best, still you are not liable to abscess of the liver.

10. You are well adapted to feverish climates, as you dispose of the bile of the system well. Headache will seldom trouble you.

11. Your skin is clear and your mind the same; you could live in a warm climate; you have an unusual amount of vis and mental energy, and you are likely to be cheerful.

12. You will be able to live in malarious climates and yet retain good action of the portal and hepatic systems. Your liver ably does its work in secreting the bile, so that you have an overflow of joyful emotions

A. To CULTIVATE THE VIGOUR OF THE LIVER:—In spring-time, eat lightly and sparingly, and only when a good appetite demands food and then only partially satisfy the appetite. Use only the very best lean meats and unbolted wheaten bread.

B. To RESTRAIN THE VIGOUR OF THE LIVER:—Eat more cooling articles and those containing or generating less bile such as vegetables, berries, baked apples, fruits, and all tart and nitrogenous food, there being little carbon or heat in them. Yet these possess as much nutrition as the system requires, for warm weather in temperate and tropical climates.

THE KIDNEYS.

THE KIDNEYS *excern the urea and the surplus fluids of the system from the blood*.

1. Much of the urea of your blood has been left in it. This great weakness of the kidneys unfits you for the intended duties of life.

2. Your blood is impure, and your back is the weakest part of your organization; hence the sharp twinging pains you often feel there.

3. Whisky-drinking would soon cause you to have Bright's disease. Your weakness is in the small of the back; a dull, torpid sensation occasionally creeps over your loins; at other times keen darting pains momentarily shoot across your back between the first *lumbar* vertebra and the crest of the ileum.

4. When awaking in the morning you often experience unpleasant sensations across the part of your back opposite the kidneys.

5. You will be profited if you favour the kidneys by avoiding the strain caused in lifting ponderous objects while not in an erect posture.

6. There is not so much native vigour in these organs as to unbalance their action by dissipation and invite disease. You are somewhat weak across the *lumbar* region of the back.

7. There is fair tone in the cortical substance which is about three-fourths of each kidney. Avoid all venereal diseases by leading a life of virtue, and the kidneys may not complain in their silent way by pains.

8. These glandular organs are none too active in their secretion of urine. If you avoid intoxicating beverages you may pass through life without waxy degeneration or Bright's disease of the kidneys.

9. With due care you may never be troubled with sharp pains in the back. Properly living and carefully guarding against excesses of all kinds will keep you strong in this part of your body.

10. By taking due care, your kidneys will always remain healthy and strong. The feelings of those who complain of a weak back, you can hardly appreciate.

11. No lameness ever afflicts you in the small of the back, day after day you can work in a stooping posture without realising positive injury.

12. These emunctories remove from the blood large quantities of refuse

excrementitious matter; they are highly active and much water is carried through them The urea is faithfully secreted from your blood by your healthy and vigorous organs.
A. To Cultivate the Healthy Action of the Kidneys:—Night and morning wash your back opposite the kidneys with cold water; rub this part briskly, heavily, and thoroughly with the hand fifteen minutes twice every day; avoid stimulants, sexual excess and lying on your back while sleeping; and carefully guard against heavy lifts while stooping.
B. To Restrain the Action of the Kidneys:—Avoid all acid and subacid fruits as they cause excessive urination.

THE HEART.

The heart *is an important organ in the circulation and distribution of the blood.*

1. You are a weak half-inanimate specimen of humanity, and can accomplish very little ; difficulties are, by your feeble spirit, enlarged from molehills to mountains. Your pulse is fluttering and irregular.

2. The surface of your system does not receive a sufficient amount of blood to keep the skin active and healthy, and thus you are liable to affections of the heart.

3. Your circulation is rather poor; your heart is a weak organ rendering you subject to cold extremities, while any over exertion subjects you to palpitation of the heart. Avoid sudden starts and surprises.

4. Your blood force would be more of a barrier to disease, had you more. At times you feel languid and liable to irregular pulse.

5. Your blood is not sufficiently ventilated because it is not sent with sufficient force to the lungs, and surface of your body.

6. Your blood moves rapidly through the innumerable ramifications of the beautiful network of blood-vessels, though not so powerfully as in those of the Thoracic Form.

7. You are exempt from the extremes of weakness or power; but great states of excitement may cause irregular action of your heart.

8. Your circulation is fair; you are not liable to suffer from bloodless extremities or a hot head, if circumstances are favourable, unless you sit much of your time. Daily exercise rapidly the whole body to keep the heart vigorous.

9. Your heart performs well its part, but fear may cause irregular action of this organ. Anger or grief so forcibly affects your heart that it feels as if it would rend it.

10. You feel the vigour and vis of constitutional power; when excited your heart throbs powerfully; and your circulation is excellent.

11. Your hands and feet are always warm; your pulse is slow, strong, and regular; and you are not liable to any disease of the heart. Your heart, from its large size, resembles that of the unbeaten Eclipse, a famous race horse of England. His heart was found after his death to weigh fourteen pounds.

12. The systole and diastole of your heart resemble the strokes of a steam-engine they are so powerful. The muscular fibres and fibrous rings of your heart are remarkable in their power. The mitral, tricuspid, and semilunar valves are strong and faithful guards, performing well their duty. Such is almost an exact description of the action and physical

power of the heart of the Herculean author of the "Nootes Ambrosianæ," and Editor of the vigorous "Blackwood's Magazine." He was the greatest athlete, poet, philosopher, wit, and satirist of his day.

A. To CULTIVATE THE HEALTHY ACTION OF THE HEART:—Exercise all your system can endure without wearying yourself; change the extremities from heat to cold alternately, by plunging them into water as warm as can be borne and then into cold momentarily. Afterwards rub briskly with a crash towel, and avoid ever eating and excess of labour.

B. To RESTRAIN THE ACTION OF THE HEART:—A healthy and regular circulation needs no restraint; but if you are too excitable work one-third of your time steadily; be calm; keep cool; and carefully avoid all excitement.

THE LUNGS.

The office of THE LUNGS *is to receive the component elements of the air, and to expel the disintegrated and excrementitious materials from the body.*

1. Your blood requires more aëration; there is a general closing up of the air cells of your lungs; the elastic fibre of the subserous areolar tissue have lost their elasticity to a great extent; the columnar ciliated epithelium is very nearly dead; hence your lungs are extremely weak.

2. As you prize life and its pleasures, so strive to cultivate the lungs; yours are sadly diseased; your complexion is too sallow for good health; and you are rapidly approaching the grave.

3. You are liable to sigh and yawn thus indicating a tendency to pulmonary affections; even at morn you often feel wearied and inclined to lassitude. Your lungs do not enspirit your blood with new life.

4. Did you possess larger lungs the azotic corpuscles of your blood, as well as the corpuscles of oxygen would become more abundant and better rounded.

5. Your inspirations are not deep; you do not possess a tough enduring constitution; you are liable to a cough and hence you should never neglect a cold.

6. Bear in mind that your lungs are not very strong, yet you may never be afflicted with consumption.

7. You are neither ardent nor passive; you are not burning too much of the carbon of your system nor yet too little.

8. The oxygen of the atmosphere you use well. Nothing would prove more injurious to you than impure air.

9. You largely appropriate the vital gases of the air; you are well developed either by nature or by culture in lung-capacity; usually you feel buoyant and full of animation.

10. Your lungs are excellent and when they inhale pure air you feel sprightly, vigorous, and elastic. You demand the most *pure* air, your blood cannot long remain charged with surplus carbon.

11. You have a full, deep, copious manner of breathing and throw off a large amount of carbonic acid gas. Your inspirations and expirations are slow and powerful; the whole lung is used; hence you can run a race with extraordinary strength and cast off colds readily.

12. You are burning out your system. Great care has been taken in the cultivation of your lungs, or, your inherent lung-power was unusual in strength.

A. To CULTIVATE THE HEALTHY ACTION OF THE LUNGS:—When in open air, draw in all the air you possibly can—several successive inspirations—following up the experiment several times per day, the year through, and continue the practice yearly; wear all apparel loosely upon the body, walk erect; throw the shoulders back, draw in a full breath, then holding in the inspired air, drum and pat upon the chest; use the axe, be much of your time in open air; use the spirometer; climb the mountains; ride on horse-back; row a boat if you feel able, if not feeling to possess sufficient strength, try as well as your strength will permit; cultivate assiduously, in pure air, the lungs, remembering that "Old Boreas" can do more for you than your best friend.

B. To RESTRAIN THE POWER OF THE LUNGS, is unnecessary unless they are burning away too much material, when you should sit more and live in a flat low country. To Restrain the Action of the Lungs:—Avoid carbonaceous food; sit within doors much of your time and your lungs will decrease in their action and size; live on low flat land bend over hard and consecutive study; tighten your waist and only breathe a little in the upper portion of your lungs and rest assured that they will rapidly become weaker.

THE COLOUR.

THE COLOUR *is an important indication of character.*

1. Black. By nature you are well adapted to endure the intense heat of a torrid climate.

2. Dark Brown. Your skin absorbs the rays of sunlight and performs perspiration in a vigorous degree.

3. Your colour is quite similar to a quadroon or dark yellow. Light Brown. The warm days of summer agree with your organization; but the cold frosts of winter impair your circulation and disagree with your general health.

4. Dark Copper Colour. Exposure to the chilling blasts or the scorching sun's rays are endured by you without a murmur.

5. Light Copper Colour. The miasmatic influences of low lands rarely affect you very seriously.

6. Dark Yellow. There is such strength in the action of your portal and hepatic systems that the material for bile is readily taken from your blood and toughness marks every fibre of your being.

7. Being Octochromo in Shade you possess a Light Yellow complexion. The soft mellow expression of your skin bespeaks an excellent share of physical stamina.

8. Sallow. Cool climates and pure water are the only means whereby you can prolong life right here.

9. Light Skin and Dark Hair. Your vitals are poor and you cannot expect to live to 100 years' yet you are a high type of humanity.

10. Commonly Fair. Overwork dissipations or improper food readily clog your vital flow and impair your health.

11. Quite White. The tenderness of your constitution subjects you to many little ills and will eventually abbreviate your days.

12. Very White. Clearness and the freedom from red in your skin denote a tender constitution and pure desires, but, alas! you are one of few days and of limited usefulness.

A. To Strengthen or Darken your Colour:—Live in a hot climate, eat carbonaceous food, exercise much, and engage in heavy labour.

B. To Weaken or make your Complexion Lighter in Shade:—Bathe much in warm water, live in a cold or temperate climate, abstain from the use of sweet or greasy food; exercise properly. yet avoid the heavy drudgeries of laborious life; read much and keep good hours; use not coffee or tea and in due time you may bleach out somewhat, if not as much as you desire.

CORPOREAL OR BODILY TEXTURE.

Tall, slim people are like tall, slim trees—in texture coarse; whereas the short and broad man and tree are fine grained and compactly knit together.

1. Being formed of the coarsest material and your entire structure being gross you are totally devoid of refinement and elegance.

2. In you the rough and coarse grained abounds; in organic quality you have a coarseness which cannot withstand the wearing and sinuosities of active business.

3. Unsubstantial and flimsy is the intertexture which enters into your bodily mould, as you are naturally gross and coarse of texture.

4. Being a good, solid, and practical soul, there is much of the genuine native homespun in your constitution.

5. Not much of the angelic about you, you were evidently born for the wear and tear of life.

6. The textural quality of your substance cannot be considered very fine; yet should you have the good fortune to form good moral associations you will probably even likely lead an exemplary life.

7. Wonderfully you stand the wear and tear of life, though your tissues are neither the coarsest nor the finest.

8. Though of good wearable material, your texture is not of the finest quality. Should your spiritual nature be well treasured and cultivated, your life may be very useful.

9. Being subtile in material and high wrought, every fibre in your frame is of fine quality.

10. Such refined and elegant persons as you are, will often have to meet with those who are rough-grained and repulsive.

11. From the soft and silky texture of your anatomy, your delicacy of mind springs: no rugosity enters into your framework.

12. The pure fine material of which your organization is composed renders you very compact. This reflecting through your mind will give you a dislike to the cold vulgar world as you generally denominate your surroundings; your feelings and emotions will find few sympathisers; hence you must feel almost alone in the world.

A. To Cultivate and Improve the Quality of your Bodily Structure:—Associate with the higher and purer spirits; devote your spare cash to a library; spend your life in a city and live on the finest kind of food; be patient in cultivation and recollect that the world was not formed in one day

B. To Restrain and Coarsify the Fine Quality of your Bodily Structure:—First conclude that your *eau-de-cologne* and rose-water temperament has none or very few sympathisers; engage in rough sports and recreations; brave the tempest with an iron will; search out the jewels in rough characters; and give your sqeamishness to the dogs.

HEALTH:—PRESENT STATE.

HEALTH *is the normal action of all the physical and mental powers. Disease is an abnormal condition of one or more parts of the body or mind.*

Perfect Health.

Mr T. Glover, a dry goods merchant of Quebec, who is 52 years of age has crossed the Atlantic Ocean upwards of 70 times; never took five shillings worth of medicine, and never lost a day's work by sickness.

1. Your blood being tainted and your body vitiated, the immedicable condition of your structure has made it a mass of corruption and must soon complete your mortal span.

2. The present state of your system is very low.

3. You are in poor trim and your life-force is at a low ebb. While remaining in this condition you can do very little.

4. You are indisposed and affected with disease; still there is no symptom in your body that may not with proper remedies be restored or renovated.

5. With care you may still retain slender health; yet overwork will likely prostrate you.

6. Should you have delusions about sickness use all available means to cast them away and never argue about them; but remember that your life is of value to the world.

7. You need a little toning up; be regular in your habits.

8. There is a wholesomeness about your system which you should guard with strength, as the Spartans of old trained their youth to defend their cities and country.

9. While your present healthy condition lasts, push on in the enterprise of the world, for the sun of vigour may not always shine upon your pathway.

10. Healthfulness has breathed her flowery aroma along your course of life. Appreciate and care for your good health, that when the shades of time rest heavily around you, the retrospect may bring joy and peace rather than pain and sorrow.

11. There is a heartiness and vigour in your system which enables you to surmount difficulties and enjoy the world. You are well fitted for great effort.

12. You are as fresh as a May-morning as sound as a bell—entirely healthy.

A. To Cultivate the Health of Body and Mind:—Court a calm, quiet, joyous frame of mind; enjoy everything; exercise properly; exercise aright your faculties in pure air. Use your will against disease, but never, never, no, never yield! Remember the terse old maxim, "Keep the head cool; the feet warm; and the bowels open," and as Galen says, you may almost defy disease.

B. To Restrain the Health of Body and Mind:—This is never necessary: but should you have so unnatural a desire as to restrain your good health, you can lace tightly, wear thin shoes, live in impure air, indulge sensual desires, eat largely of rich food, &c.

MIND—ACTIVITY OF.

Great MENTAL ACTIVITY *manifests itself over all the facial muscles whose rapidity of motion corresponds with that of the mind; also it may be marked in the lively and elastic step; sudden motions of the body; quick speech, &c., which are all general, bodily indications of great mental activity.*

1. Inactivity, sluggishness, slackness and latency are apparent in your character.

2. Your natural love of torpor and inertion woo inactivity of mind not endurable among energetic people.

3. You are passive, slack, flat, tame, dormant, and unexcitable.

4. There may be much latent power in you, but you are sluggish and heavy minded; in society, uninfluencible and without influence.

5. You may be adapted to the heavy enterprises of life but quite unfitted by nature to a light active business.

6. Ever interesting yourself in thoughts and fancies from the mint of your own mind.

7. Inaction of mind is not keenly relished by you. Thousands of thoughts dart through your mind like fish through the sea, leaving no trace behind.

8. Each emotion of your mind is fairly vivid and keen, and the corresponding feelings are equally intense.

9. The interworking of your mind affords you much mental excitation.

10. Your voluntary energy is capable of performing untold labour.

11. You are always equal to the occasion in pungency and vigour and your mental energy is sufficient to give you standing in any society

12. The keenness, acuteness and intensity of your mind are prominent traits; and so also is your mental elasticity. Such minds are seldom known yet we may venture to mention Plato, Socrates. Solon, Solomon, Talleyrand, Richlieu and Bismark as prominent examples in ancient and modern times.

A. To Accelerate Mental Activity:—Never allow yourself to doze and drowse away an hour; live life in earnest. Cherish fondly in thy breast the following beautifully expressed lines which were selected from Longfellow's "Psalm of Life."

> "Lives of great men all remind us
> We can make our lives sublime,
> And, departing, leave behind us
> Footprints on the sands of time;
>
> Footprints, that perhaps another,
> Sailing o'er life's solemn main,
> A forlorn and shipwrecked brother,
> Seeing, shall take heart again.
>
> Let us, then, be up and doing,
> With a heart for any fate,
> Still achieving, still pursuing,
> Learn to labour and to wait."

Be energetic in mind; allow no inertness to steal your wakeful hours; stir, be brisk, look alive and keep your mind in operation. Let assiduity characterise your life.

B. To Retard Mental Activity:—Be remiss, sleep, hybernate, take your ease; relax and palter away time; be unemployed and live at your leisure; be exanimate and soporific; refrain from business affairs; avoid active people and busy enterprises. In a word. go to sleep and don't trouble yourself to awake, as no one needs your presence.

CLASS I.

SUPPLYANT POWERS.

WHERE THE POWERS OF THIS CLASS ARE LARGE, THE ABDOMINAL FORM PREDOMINATES IN THAT ORGANIZATION.

CONTENTMENT, OR ACQUIESCIVENESS.

THE DISPOSITION TO BE SATISFIED IN A QUIET MANNER.

Acquiesciveness small. Acquiesciveness large.
Mrs Bachus, of California. Welsh Woman.

Full cheeks and placidity of countenance indicate acquiesciveness, or contentment generally, especially if the aspect is cheerful.

1. Yourself and those around you are rendered miserable by your incessant grumbling and regretting.

2. Ever dissatisfied, always wishing for something you have not, your life-pathway is strewn with disappointments.

3. The following stanza is most strikingly apposite to your character:—

> "Still falling out with this and this,
> And finding something still amiss;
> More peevish, cross, and splenitic
> Than dog distraught or monkey sick."

4. Being apt to repine, you may grumble and lament at your lot, discontent and inquietude will acidify your happiness.

5. Few there are that enjoy perfect tranquillity of mind, and you are one whose tide of life is rippled by the winds of regret.

6. Though you would not willingly ride far on the car of discontent, some things there are that may displease you.

7. The rust of uneasiness may tarnish your soul, but you will scour it away again and again, and as often apply the unction of complacent satisfaction.

8. Being rather comfortably satisfied and serene, you are exempt from longing and entire dissatisfaction.

9. Being devoid of envy, you can heedlessly view frowns and favours as well as the magnificent robes and profuse dresses of the rich, or listen to the censorious remarks of the crowd without experiencing the least discontent.

10. An unrepining character, you discard all strife from your motives and intentions; and to you, time seems not to drag too slowly, nor to fly too swiftly.

11. To your circumstances you are completely reconciled, and ready to rest with complacency in your surroundings while you are perfectly resigned to your fate.

12. Being perfectly at ease ; no one is more fully satisfied with his lot in life than yourself.

A. To Encourage Contentment :—Learn of the ox that a contented disposition ever enhances your own happiness as well as that of those with whom you are associated. Allow no discontent to enter your mind; choose your company from those who are conciliatory; and ever be resigned.

B. To Repress Contentment :—Always desire something you have not ; constantly find fault ; invite and cherish heart-griefs ; at everything pine and regret ; and never cease quarrelling with your circumstances.

ANIMAL IMITATION, OR ANIMALIMITATIONALITY.

THE POWER OF IMITATING THE MOTIONS, POSTURES, AND ACTIONS OF ANIMAL FORMS.

A wide mouth, in a narrow face, may safely be defined as indicative of ANIMAL IMITATION.

1. Your walk, laugh and general deportment, are like yourself more than like any other person; you are odd peculiar and eccentric in every act you perform; and you are not at all up to the fashions of the day.

2. Your oddities and peculiarities of manner give certain assurance that very little of the physical in imitation enters into your composition. The cultivation of a lifetime would not suffice to make you a Garrick, Mathews, Clara Fisher, Malibran, Coriolanus, Edwin Forest, Booth, Charlotte Cushman, Ristori, Mrs Siddons, or Lotta.

3. Powers of mimicry, you have none, hence your attempts to personate the peculiarities and characters of others are not life-like.

4 The facial expression which some individuals give when conver-

sing or speaking you omit in your speech, lacking the automatic perfection of imitation.

5. The walk or gesture of another you cannot assume, hence you would never become distinguished as an actor.

6. That of a mean, servile, animal imitator is not the character that befits you.

Animalimitationality large.
A Fort Rupert Indian. At one time this tribe existed as Cannibals.

Animalimitationality small.
Horace Greely.

7. You can to a certain extent conform to your surroundings· Though not an adept in it yourself, you can thoroughly enjoy the mimic personations and gestures of others

8. With practice you could become a fair mimic, yet you are not largely inclined to devote much time to imitation, and would not be apt in mimicry unless you take special pains in cultivating this faculty.

9. Being rather dramatically inclined, you can readily assume the character adapted to the associations among which you move.

10. With telling accuracy you can mimic the follies, fashions, and practices of the masses, and you are capable of rising to eminence in scenic representations. You enjoy the burlesque, and with study and practice you would become a capital buffoon.

11. In mimicry you delight; you can imitate, bug, bird, beast, railway engine, or whistle, as well as every sound, animal or artificial, with wonderful exactness. The tones, gestures, and gaits of persons, you can to the life portray. With study and practice you could excel in dramatic art.

12. In doing as others do you are a perfect ape; imitation is your forte. rather than origination. To be and do as others do is in you a strong characteristic. Travesty would be your strong point if you cultivated the propensity of your nature. Voltaire says, "A good imitation is the most perfect originality."

A. TO IMPROVE THE POWER OF ANIMAL IMITATION:—Assume the manners of those around you and follow the fashions; attend dramatic performances; imitate all that is worthy of imitation; associate with those who are servile imitators; mock, personate, and burlesque the shoddy aristocracy; make good and intellectual people your antitypes and patterns rather than being theirs; tread in the footsteps of your friends and parody everything.

Animalimitationality large.
Chimpanzee, taken from life in the Zoological Gardens in London.

B. TO WEAKEN OR MINIFY THE ANIMAL-IMITATIVE FACULTY:—Be odd and unique in dress, ways, habits, and manners; set yourself up as a prototype to the world; be yourself a pattern rather than a counterfeit; nine-tenths of the world are counterfeits of good and original characters. Then try to be the tenth one and be unmatched and inimitable in the noble enterprise of the world.

LOVE OF LIQUIDS, OR AQUASORBITIVENESS.
APPRECIATION AND LOVE OF WATER-DRINKING, WATER SCENERY, BATHING, ETC.

A rounding or puffy fulness of the cheeks, from one-half to three-fourths of an inch outwards, backwards, and slightly upwards from the mouth is that part of the face where the love of liquid first manifests itself.

AQUASORBITIVENESS.

1. You have a great dread of water-bathing, and abhor the very sight of water nearly as much as the dog afflicted with hydrophobia.

Aquasorbitiveness large.
George Morland, a talented painter, who died as he had lived, a great drunkard.

Aquasorbitiveness small.
Nicholas Copernicus, who drank very sparingly of water and was exemplarily temperate.

2. Naturally you consume very little liquid and will likely be temperate so far as intoxication by liquors is concerned.

Aquasorbitiveness small.
Peter the Great, when young.

3. To be a teetotaler would accord well with your nature; and you are as naturally averse to bathing as to imbibing.

4. Instinctively you are, in every sense, moderate in the use of water, so that you will imbibe little of this element, and though water scenery may afford you some pleasure, yet you instinctively shrink from putting yourself in dangerous proximity to the fickle element or entrusting yourself to the hazardous and questionable pleasure of a sail in a small boat or canoe.

5. Though you have no great thirst for water, still you have not much aversion to this element.

6. Not being very partial to water you partake of it only in moderate quantities.

7. Normal in your desire for water in any of its applications, internally or externally, a parched tongue gives you no foretaste of impending misery when the burning sun lances

down his scorching rays and treacherously exhales the dews from mountain, and dries up the rills and their springing fountains.

8. Water, you can pretty freely imbibe, and enjoy in an ordinary degree scenery in which it is one of the principal features.

9. Having a thorough natural relish for water, you can imbibe it copiously, and delight in viewing the broad expanse of ocean, the rapid resistless torrent, and the thundering cataract.

10. The aqueous element enters largely into your organization, often pleading with your better reason for a larger supply; hence you drink frequently.

11. Were we to form a judgment from appearances, it would seem that your mouth was made for bibulous purposes. Far too often, for the health of your system you imbibe liquids; still your abnormal appetite for liquor is hard to control as you too generally accede to its craving cry of "give, give."

12. "Grog-bag" is your proper designation. Once you had some common sense and self-control, but these have been drowned in tipple. Hence you may aptly be described as a winebibber, bacchanalian, drunkard, or sot or all of these. Still you seem somehow to indicate that reformation is not yet totally impossible; but this can only be achieved by your adhering to the advice given in the following paragraph marked B.

A. To ENLARGE AND RENDER MORE ACTIVE THE TENDENCY OF BIBACITY:—Imbibe small quantities of water frequently; constantly let earth's virtuous juice flow inward; if healthy and vigorous, bathe daily; luxuriate in the bath, sporting in it like a fish,—health, strength and leisure permitting; visit every kind of water scenery: springs and torrents at the sources of mighty rivers; lakes; rivers; rapids, waterfalls, and cataracts; stand on the rocky ocean-shore during a tempest and allow the blinding spray from the exhausted wave as it shatters itself on the beetling cliffs to drench you. In such a sublime moment of aqueous delight when you almost feel as part of the element, let your spirit luxuriate in contemplation of the majesty and grandeur of the everlasting sea. Then fall down on the top of a projecting cliff and read Byron's address to the ocean,—one of the most sublime pieces of poetry ever penned,—beginning with the words: "Roll on thou deep and dark blue ocean roll!" Follow the example of Peter the Great (of Russia) who subdued his aversion to water. So strong was his constitutional fear and antipathy to water that cold perspirations and even convulsions would seize him when compelled to pass near water; yet he thoroughly overcame his natural aversion by throwing himself every morning into a cold bath, and continuing this practice until the horror of the element was abated.

B. To REPRESS THE PROPENSITY OF BIBACITY:—Take your food dry and avoid gravy; keep from drinking saloons and associates who tipple and guzzle down the fashionable poisons of the day; make no new years or any other calls where ladies tempt you to drink; let your mouth become parched before you take a glass of beer, ale, porter, or any kind of liquid which consumes your rational faculties as fire devours dry stubble. Never go sailing or swimming; use neither tea nor coffee as they pamper and cultivate appetite for more stimulating beverages, and are auxiliaries to intemperance as springs and small streams are to rivers —the feeders and main support. The wonderful influence that mothers can exert in suppressing intemperance and guiding aright the young by kind words and judicious upbringing is well illustrated in the case of the Hon. Thomas H. Benton who worked thirty years in the Senate of the United States as one of America's ablest statesmen. His own words are —"My mother asked me never to use tobacco; I have never touched it from that time to the present day. She asked me never to gamble, and I have never gambled; I cannot tell who is losing in the games that are being played She admonished me, too, against hard drinking; and whatever capacity for endurance I have at present, and whatever usefulness I have, I attribute to having complied with her pious and correct wishes. When I was seven years of age she asked me not to drink, and then I made a resolution of total abstinence; and that I have adhered to it through all time I owe to my mother."

PHYSICAL HOPE, OR PHYSICŒLPIDICITY.

THE FACULTY OF HOPE RELATING TO THE PHYSICAL WORLD AND MATERIAL THINGS.

Full, moist eyes, plump cheeks, large neck, and an elastic, springy step, can be safely relied upon as signs of physical hope. The sunken, dull eye, hollow cheek, and drooping corners of the mouth are physiognomical indications of a gloomy nature.

1. Your heavy sodden, melancholy nature dispirits every one and discourages every enterprise. Alas! a confirmed hypochondriac, you are a perfect personification of dejection.

2. Your listless day-musings on the future put no silver lining into your despondent nature. The dark and gloomy side of the affairs of life are alone visible to your grumbling disposition. Such demure and sedate gravity as yours belongs, properly, only to the years that have been reckoned to fourscore.

3. The great depression of spirit which constantly weighs you down will ultimately impair your own health as well as that of those around you. As rain clouds pass over the earth, scudding across the sky, so do solemn thoughts and light fancies bespeak their presence in the changeful expressions ever observable on your countenance.

4. Though grave and of a solemn visage, your winsome and playful ways evidently show that genuine modesty casts the retiring expression over your countenance. More vivacity would make your body more healthy and your life much happier. Should circumstances lure you on by prospects of great advantage you will not attempt more than your hope will allow you to accomplish.

5. Being a little too sedate and placid you have acquired a heaviness of spirit. Had you a little more fun and jocularity in your composition, your friends and acquaintances would increase. The intense sadness and depression of your spirits will occasionally make you miserable but you will again spring up to a new and more cheerful state. You know, however, that "Hope is a flatterer, but the most upright of all parasites; for she frequents the poor man's hut, as well as the palace of his superior."
—*Shenstone.*

6. Inclining at times to be demure and serious you have acquired much solemnity of manner. As are clouds to the sky so are the dismal

and melancholy to you; but when they depart all is sunshine and cheerfulness.

Physicœlpidicity small.
Dante, the Author of Paradise, Purgatory and Hell.

7. Being happily free from the extremes of gaiety or dejection your moments of disconsolateness soon vanish. Steady cheerfulness and an even tenor, you thoroughly admire in all persons, and yet you, yourself, are liable to elation and dejection of spirit.

8. Being naturally of a cheerful turn of mind, you will imagine your future prospects to be fair and favourable. In good health, you are generally devoid of melancholy and oft-times even vivacious.

9. The most of your time, you are in good and often in high spirits; hence you are merry and playful in all your winning ways. If you are young, fairy prospects are flitting before your imagination; if elderly or aged, your mature judgment sensibly regulates your thoughts.

10. Joy prevails over sadness in your inner life The bright side, on reflection, always turns up and becomes manifest in your look and deportment. Being happily so constituted that you have sufficient vivacity and sprightliness in your nature to illumine your path and gladden it

with joy through life you are apt to be exuberant and frolicsome, and are able to bear up amid severe troubles and suffering.

> "A merry heart goes all the day,
> A sad tires in a mile,"
> —*Shakspeare.*

11. Elatement of feelings and thoughts lend a charming good humour to your deportment. Your sprightly form points you out as vivacious and debonair, which must contribute largely to your happiness ; yet should disease that thief of cheer, enter your portals it may pilfer all earthly desires and leave in their stead only despondency.

Physiœlpidicity large
James Fisk, jun.

12. Your elastic and lively spirit is never depressed by circumstances; ever gay and giddy, as you appear, and ever and anon that sparkling vivacity beaming in your countenance puts to flight all the sadness that others endeavour to cast around you. The brilliant diamond is no more sparkling than are those hopes of yours which bewilder while they delude. Full of air-castle notions, you are as joyous as the warbling birds of a summer morning.

A. To Foster Physical Hope:—Cultivate a perfect state of health; cheerfully recollect that the bright and glorious sun is above the darkest clouds and severest storm and besides that he has hitherto outshone all storms; b'ot out of your vocabulary the word despair, and speak and think of the future as bright and hopeful Take, as your choice companions and associates, the healthy, temperate, light-hearted, merry, gleeful joy-loving wherever you find them. Live in a light, sunny, airy, and cheerful situation; keep singing birds, prating parrots, squirrels and kittens (but not in your sleeping-room), dogs and colts, and join in their playful pastimes. Never despair ; by hilarity and sportiveness banish dejection; associate with those of a buoyant and happy disposition, and remember that no desert, however dreary and howling, is without its oasis. Sometimes think over what Jeremy Collier says: "Hope is a vigorous principle; it is furnished with light and heat to advise and execute; it sets the head and heart to work and animates a man to do his utmost. And thus by perpetual pushing and assurance, it puts a difficulty out of countenance, and makes a seeming impossibility give way."

B. TO CURB AND RESTRAIN PHYSICAL HOPE:—Never venture further than your cooler judgment approves, or your friends advise; avoid all kinds of speculations, gambling, horse-racing, &c.; let only your industry and prudent forethought of to-day insure the success of to-morrow. Discard all high-flown theories; cultivate a calm and quiet life; avoid the genial and enlivening rays of the sun; sit in dark apartments and gorge yourself with rich and indigestible food. Let your associates be the aged and down-hearted; recollect that though you are flushed with pleasure to-day, and jubilant thoughts course through your mind, yet the shades of to-morrow may darken your soul almost to despair; and also, that there is no day so radiant with cheering sunlight that is not succeeded by the dreary, depressing darkness of night.

RAPACITY, OR GRASPATIVENESS.

THE PROPENSITY TO GAIN BY EXTORTION, OR ADDICTION TO GAIN BY PLUNDER OR OPPRESSION.

Heavy jaws, large neck, and heavy chest are signs of large rapacity.

1. Utterly incapable of appreciating the difference between *meum* and *tuum* (*mine* and *thine*), the marked trait in your character is an utter indifference as to whether or not you appropriate what is not lawfully your own.

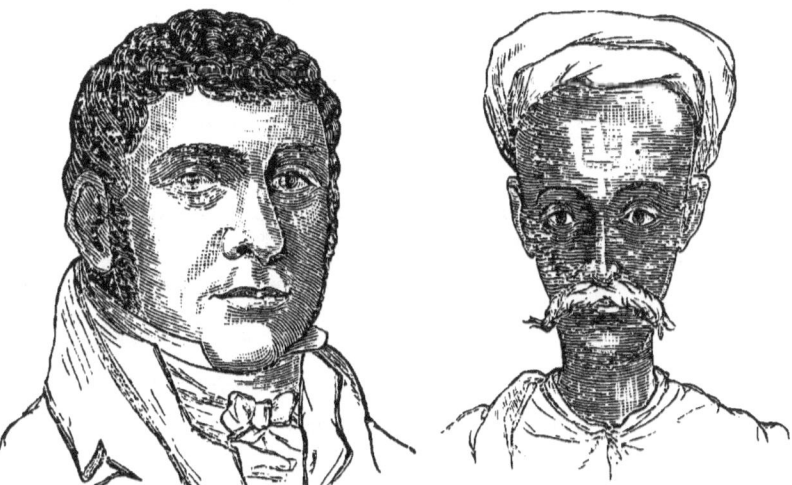

Graspativeness large.
Robert Gregson, a Notorious English Pugilist.

Graspativeness small.
Nana Narian, an East Indiaman.

2. Not being covetous, but placidly listless, and unsolicitous about the property of others, you would not wish to take anything by force for which you did not make proper remuneration.

3. Being inclined rather to relinquish your own than trespass on the rights and property of others, you would not appropriate by force or violence, not being rapacious either lands, money, or chattels, much less would you deprive others of personal or constitutional liberties.

4. The brutal eagerness and stealthy rapacity that characterises the feline species is only a minor element in your constitution, and under favourable circumstances may remain in abeyance to your better judgment.

5. Inclined rather to share with others what is your own, than to grasp, by force, the most trifling thing belonging to them, you cannot be tempted to overstep the limits of equity.

6. Though strong temptations may present themselves to you, yet you will endeavour to allow others their equitable rights.

7. Being happily balanced in this respect, you can have few occasions for repentance for having forcibly intruded upon the possessions of others.

8 Anxiety, in her dismal forebodings will sometimes lure you into rapaciousness; but such is your nature that, as soon as you have obtained your coveted objects through rapaciousness and plunder, you will neither relinquish nor compensate, unless the potent hand of the law is laid upon you.

9. Though much removed from being a fit subject upon whom to commit depredations, yet seizures or violent robbery will not be among your tendencies or acts of rapaciousness.

10. Of the vulture tribe, a voracious bird, you delight in plunder, and in extortion from a conquered foe.

11. How fortunate you are not an irresponsible despot, as it is almost c rtain that the records of your rule would prove replete with memorials of unlawful greed of gain and injustice oppressive.

12. Your predilection to seize by force and violence has had in all ages some notorious, representative, and unfortunately irresponsibly despotic character, such as Sennacherib, Alexander the Great, Xerxes, Peter the Great, and Napoleon I. The propensity of these could not exceed yours!

A. To CULTIVATE PREDACIOUS RAPACITY :—Join a band of American-Indian Hunters; live principally upon animal food, but especially upon the flesh of some of the *carnivora;* allow no conscientious scruples to deter you from entering an enemy's country, and living on the stores of the land. Wherever you can obtain a handsome bonus or "haul," by foreclosing a mortgage don't procrastinate or scruple for a moment; allow your inextinguishable desire of seizing by force to satiate its appetence at every opportunity; encourage the faint grasping and rapacious fancies that spring up in your mind, and ever promote the propensity to vaulting impetuosity.

B. To CHECK AND RESTRAIN THE PROPENSITY TO RAPACITY :—Love mankind and put on the rein of reason adorned by the bit of equity; live and work according to the golden rule—" Do to others as you would that they should do to you;" never seize or grasp at what is not your own; do not prey on the animals or property seized from another;

endeavour to curb and smother your voracious greed of gain; when by force or law you obtain the property of another, do not take the advantage by oppression; never hold slaves or dwell in a country where such contaminating practices exist; crush all feelings of undue greediness which ever tend to extort by injustice; avoid animal food, spices, wine, and all fermented liquors; allow your spirit to go out in laudable and sympathetic aspirations towards the meritorious and seraphic enterprises of the world, and with patience and the correct use of reason you may eventually attain self-conquest, which is of far greater value than material wealth—lands, money, or princely power.

APPETITE FOR FOOD, OR APPETITIVENESS.
THE FACULTY OR QUALITY OF APPETITE.

Width and general fulness of the cheeks opposite the molar teeth and a large mouth are never failing testimonials of good sustentative propensities.

Appetentiveness large.
Vitellius, the sensuous gourmand Emperor of Rome.

1. So dainty is your appetite, it is almost impossible to please you at table; still this is easily accounted for by your delicate constitution; often for days, you scarcely eat anything, and never on any occasion take a surfeit.

2. You are peculiarly indifferent about food, and often, for several days, your inappetency for food is almost alarming; your thoughts are never absorbed in the things you eat or drink; hence you need not fear that you shall ever become a glutton. Still you should try to overcome your squeamish, fastidious fancies at table, as they often place your host in a very uncomfortable position, not knowing what is the trouble with you.

Appetentiveness small.
John Wickliffe, a celebrated English Divine who was remarkably abstemious.

3. Mincingly and very daintily you feed, not manifesting sufficient vigour and healthiness of appetite; more appetite would be very desirable in your case, but to have it in a safe and healthy condition you must be more actively employed in the light and heat of the sun.

4. Being dainty and at times eating rather sparingly the most trifling thing disgusts you at meals. If a fine hair be discovered in mashed potatoes, or swinging with one end embedded in the bread, or flies crop up among the meat which have sacrificed their lives in their ambition for hot grease, you are annoyed and your appetite is gone.

5. Though far from becoming an epicure still you desire your meals, as did King Alfred at regular hours.

6. Imperfectly appreciating gustatory pleasures during the time of participating of refreshments; and hence you have no desire to eat five

times a day as did the Romans in the most luxurious periods of the empire, and as do the Londoners at the present day.

7. Though you may not consume a large quantity of food still you fairly enjoy the luxuries of the table. The example of Marcus Antonius, whose breakfast was only a hard biscuit, you would not care to follow.

8. Have tolerable or moderate enjoyment of a good dinner. This soul finds other pleasures more congenial than simply the repletion o its clay tenement. Have no fellowship with Vitellius or other voracious eaters. Are no gourmandizer.

9. Have fair taste in the selection of food. Capable of restraining this appetite when necessary. Find pleasure in dining with a few good friends; yet your notions of good living and gastronomy will not likely lead to unreasonable excesses at table.

10. This desire for food is generally good, especially if in good health, yet you have the strength of will to control it. Are usually reasonable in your demands for food, and yet this faculty needs no appetizers with which to whet the appetite.

11. Possess a better appetite than power to digest the viands consumed. You desire plenty of food and like that of wholesome quality, and if you can have what suits your taste you eat heartily and enjoy it quite highly.

12. An insatiable appetite for food absorbs almost your every thought; you are voracious and a perfect animal gormandiser; hence the throne at which you worship is your stomach; or as old Paul put it: "Your god is your belly." We forbear to complete the quotation, as it is in nearly every cookery-book.

A. To CULTIVATE THE PROPENSITY FOR SUSTENTATION:—Let the quantities of food be proportioned to the exercise you take and the climate in which you live; live on mixed diet of farinaceous and animal food; keep a good cook; never over-eat; exercise much and engage in out-door amusement; and "take a little wine for thy stomach's sake;" but of all things be regular in your meals as to time and quantity; eat with social jolly companions; and be careful to avoid excessive thinking as it will destroy the animal appetite.

B. To RESTRAIN THE PROPENSITY AND CRAVING FOR SUSTENANCE: —Starve out like John Hales who fasted every week from dinner on Thursday until Saturday at breakfast; touch not rich food; drink not beer, porter, stout, nor any fermented or spirituous liquor; eat slowly and limit the quantity of every meal; partake of only one or two dishes at a meal; and take the advice of Epicurus: "Leave off with an appetite." An instance in favour of temperate living is recorded in the life of Galen, who was one of the most successful and celebrated physicians of ancient times. When young he was delicate, but at the age of twenty-eight he began to live temperately, thereby gaining strength which carried him on to the rare old age of 90 years. Apply yourself continuously every day to scientific or systematic reading, writing or thinking. Read the works on health by Hippocrates, Galen's great model, Celsus, Plutarch, Galen, *Sanctorius* Porphyry. Actuarius, Lessius, &c., and attend to their advice as regards temperance in diet. An instance could be mentioned where intemperance in eating swayed monarchies and kingdoms. It was the following of Charles VI. Emperor of West Austria, who died of indigestion caused by excessive eating of mushrooms, "and thus a plate of mushrooms changed the destinies of Europe" remarked Voltaire, which was the truth. But if you like the sententious, take the advice of the late Dr Edgar, the apostle of temperance in Ireland. When he was sending his son to college he said at parting: "Now my boy, you'll always be safe if you only fear God and keep your bowels open."

REVENGEFULNESS, OR RETALIATIVENESS.

THE DISPOSITION OF RETURNING LIKE FOR LIKE—"TIT FOR TAT."

This disposition being stronger in the dark races and animals than in the light, we conclude that persons are retaliative relatively in proportion to the depth of their colour. Another sign of revenge is a hollow in the centre of the forehead. The elephant is an example of a revengeful character; and the hippopotamus and rhinoceros are exceedingly retaliative. Horses with this deep indent in the forehead should never be trusted

Retaliativeness large.

1. Being ever ready to pardon any offence against your feelings, and overflowing with forgiveness towards the erring. you are ever indulgent and conciliatory.

2. Being of an unresenting nature, you can make allowances for the wayward while you can as easily forgive and exonerate others for real or supposed injury.

3 The differences between your friends and yourself you can compromise. In your constitution there is very little of the American-Indian character—of revenge.

4. You will be able to overlook many insults from others, and can find cause for the acquittal of those who have incurred your displeasure.

5. The eternal gnawing worm of revenge is nowhere found in your soul.

6 Your meditative hours of judgment are not soured by revengeful impulses.

7. Being slightly revengeful, you should remember these words of Lord Bacon:—"He that studieth revenge keepeth his own wounds green."

8. It is difficult for you to overlook an intentional wrong. Though you may not actually revenge an injury yet you feel sometimes more than half inclined to do so.

9. Having a thorough aversion to forgive, and possessed of vengeful nature your constant determination is to avenge an injury.

10. Rigorous, implacable, and unforgiving you scarcely ever relent.

11. Always able and ready to retort in a vindictive manner you naturally seek revenge for imaginary or real injuries.

12. Revenge to you is sweet. The following couplet well expresses the normal state of your feelings:—

"Oh! that the slave had forty thousand lives!
One is too poor too weak for my revenge!"

A. How to Strengthen the Feeling of Retaliation, though this is Rarely Necessary:—When another strikes you return the blow; hold in your hand, ever ready for use, the spear of vengeance; retribute every imagined wrong; be vindictive and unrelenting; cultivate that feeling which says "an eye for an eye, a tooth for a tooth."

B. How to Retard and Diminish the Feeling of Retaliation: — Overlook, pardon, and forgive injuries inflicted by others, whether they ask it or not; allow your heart to go out in noble reprieve; heed not the faults of the wayward; be just and ever exculpative.

SOCIAL DISPOSITION, OR ASSOCIATIVENESS.

THE DESIRE TO CONVERSE WITH OTHERS AND BE IN THEIR COMPANY.

Open, protruding, red lips, full cheeks and large abdomen are signs of sociality.

Sociativeness large.
Samuel R. Ward, a Negro remarkable for his strong social disposition.

Sociativeness small
David Duncan, a hermit of Michigan.

1. Like a deserted and abandoned city, you are devoid of social life. Secluded and sequestered privacy are yours.

2. Being unsocial and cynical, you may be considered a recluse, anchoret, or cenobite.

3. Seclusion and retirement you enjoy, and liking to keep aloof, you will shut yourself out of society.

4. Though you may not be fond of exclusion, yet you will care little for festivity.

5. At times you can remain alone; but much company would weary you.

6. You like company tolerably well and are likely to enjoy the society of others better than would appear by your manner.

7. While you are neighbourly and convivial yet your propensities in this direction are not extreme.

8. Being full of social companionship, you delight in merry-making at an entertainment.

9. By your companionableness, aquaintances are a long time retained by your powers of conversation and love social visiting.

10. Your life is rendered quite happy by your associations and society, since you so much enjoy fraternising with many.

11. Being one of the most companionable persons, your fellowship and heartiness are truly eminent and make you entertaining.

12. In the busy world of society you are ever delighted to be absorbed; but when alone a terrible discontent creeps over you, for you detest and abhor solitude.

A. To ENCOURAGE SOCIALITY:—Keep company with many; club with others; make acquaintance and have numerous places and people to visit; often interchange visits and cards; call often upon friends and neighbours and make advances to strangers; entertain travellers and keep open house; be sociable and avoid the sneering and cynical.

B. To COUNTERACT SOCIALITY:—Retire from society and live more solitary, remembering that "unbidden guests are often most welcome when they are gone," as Shakspeare wrote it. Avoid flourishing towns and cities by living in the country; seek the pathless woods and there invoke revery.

CLASS II.

PROTECTIVE ABILITIES.

IN PERSONS WHERE THIS CLASS OF ABILITIES IS RELATIVELY LARGE THERE IS AN ASCENDANCY OF THE THORACIC FORM.

DESIRE TO BE SENTINELLED, OR SENTINELITIVENESS.

THE PRECAUTIOUS DISPOSITION THAT SETS ONE OR MORE ON THE WATCH, TO KEEP A SHARP LOOK-OUT, AND GIVE WARNING OF APPROACHING DANGER.

Great fulness of the forehead, immediately above and close to the junction of a long nose with the forehead evinces a desire to be guarded and sentinelled against danger.

1. By your unwatchful nature, you often imperil yourself and others, thinking it worse than useless to keep sentinels. Hence you are insecure and often surprised.

2. By nature you are quite too rash and daring, and imperil your safety by neglect of precautions, not even a watch-dog is considered necessary to raise an alarm should danger threaten while you are asleep.

3. Though always preparing to meet danger yet you are seldom ready on its approach. Should you be camping out, you would be careless in placing guards or pickets.

4. Less guarded you are than the wolf or fox, or a flock of geese, that station one of their number on the watch to give timely warning on the approach of an enemy.

5. Being rather lax in preprotection, you would be liable to surprises were you in command of troops

6. Being well balanced in this faculty, and inclined to heed the warnings of others, you do, however, occasionally feel insecure

7. Though on the alert you will not manifest uneasiness if things appear safe.

8. Whatever you possess or have for safe-keeping, you will dutifully and faithfully guard.

9. Nothing pleases you more than to find a sentinel at his post and dutiful. As a general or commanding-officer, you would manifest good judgment in posting your sentries and occupying such watch-towers as seem essential to your safety

10. The watchman and patrol are considered by you as essential to the safety of the city as the sentinel and picket are to the safety of an army. You possess this quality which is essential to a police inspector.

11. Being careful to render everything safe and secure, you are ever ready to protect, guard, and warn against approaching danger. Men of your qualities and habits should always be selected as railway managers and station masters, captains of vessels and their officers.

12. You are eminently protective in your nature and as sleeplessly alive to the necessity of guarding against the slightest approach of danger as a watch-dog. Such a constitution as yours is pre-eminently that for the command of an army; your sentries, sentinels and scouts would, by imbibing your own enthusiasm, be ever on the alert and in sympathy with yourself. Such was the very essence of the character of the great Napoleon, showing that watchfulness and precaution are concomitant with dauntless courage and fearlessness.

A. TO STRENGTHEN THE FACULTY OF SENTINELITIVENESS: – Fail not to station sentinels when dangers are lurking; in your house keep a good watch-dog; use all imaginable precautions against surprises; when in an enemy's territory, send out your most alert scouts to give you timely notice of danger or attack; give attentive heed to every low warning note or voice.

B. TO RETARD THE SENTINEL INSTINCT OR FACULTY:—Let your powder be wet or dry, throw aside your arms and trust all to Providence or luck; do the best you can in time of danger; take no precaution against dangers or surprises, and just let what may come—time enough to look out when the enemy is scaling the wall or the burglar in the plate-closet. Place no alarm bells on doors or windows, and heed not signals of distress or the warnings of friends.

MORAL COURAGE, OR MORIVALOROSITY.

THE ENDOWMENT THAT PROMPTS ITS POSSESSOR TO BE COURAGEOUS WHEN THOUGHTS REQUIRE MORAL SUPPORT.

A long prominent nose which rises high from the face in its upper part is the very best evidence of large moral courage.

1. When moral subjects only interest, you become a coward.

2. When judgment and sentiment wage war against animal passions, you become timid and flinching.

3. Your early education must have been sadly neglected, or your associates have not been of a high grade; and hence you prove a coward when moral topics and questions are under consideration.

4. Corporeal punishment you may perhaps be courageous enough to inflict, but you would shrink from engaging in public debate.

5. Forensic disputes are so distasteful to you that you would suffer wrong to overturn right rather than become conspicuous in giving oral evidence in defence.

6. In the maintenance of truth, if there is no danger of bloodshed, you are possessed of quite a sufficiency of moral courageousness.

7. The right, you will staunchly defend, and *that*, without danger of giving offence. Not being disputatious, unless aroused in support of some just cause, you naturally abhor fighting and quarrels.

8. Whenever you discover that wrong is triumphing over right, you manifest your natural stamina and staunchness in defence of the right,

even if it were necessary to encounter the popular storm of opposition and stem its surging tide.

9. Having the elements within you to combat erroneous notions and advocate new ideas, your moral courage would admirably fit you to become an able and successful reformer.

10. As soon as you are once imbued with their spirit and tendency you enjoy debates, and you w ll ably and warmly defend the cause of a friend in his absence, and manifest therein great intrepidity and fortitude.

11. While, no doubt, you would courageously fight physically in a just cause, still your powers are better adapted for the forum or legislative halls than for the field of battle.

12. Having a keen sense of moral obligations, both to God and mankind, you will, when duty calls, sacrifice home, pleasures, and even life itself.

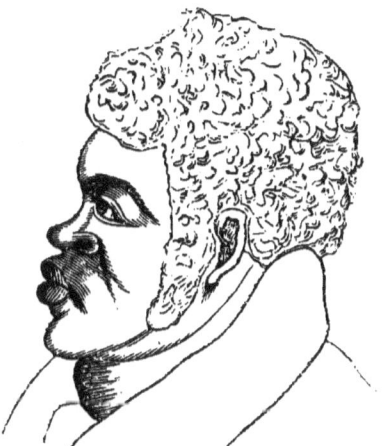 

Morivalorosity small.
Thomas Molineaux, a brutal English Pugilist.

Morivalorosity large.
Thomas Becon, Professor of Divinity at Oxford, who first wrote against bowing at the name of Jesus.

A. To CULTIVATE AND INVIGORATE MORAL COURAGE:—Engage in argument; join debating societies; write for the press advancing new, correct, and startling ideas; and when they are assailed (as new and valuable discoveries always are) stand forth nobly in their defence with heart, mind, pen, and tongue. Read the biography of Mrs Fry and try to emulate her noble example. She undertook the reforming of Newgate, the great central criminal prison of London, and she was successful.

B. To RESTRAIN MORAL COURAGE:—Give ready assent to the opinions of others without troubling yourself to put them into your scale of justice; pay less attention to high moral monitions, and never argue or debate with any one; the lofty sense of moral protection which you throw around what pleases you is often repulsive to others and gives you the appearance of a stickler. Remember that "he who ruleth his spirit is greater than he who taketh a city."

TENDENCY FOR ELEVATION OF MIND OR BODY, OR ELEVATIVENESS.

THAT QUALITY OF MIND THAT TENDS TO ELEVATE CHARACTER AS WELL AS BODY.

The nose that stands well out and up at the point accompanies the elevative disposition in men and animals

1. Low thoughts harbour in your mind. You would rather live in a low flat country than on an elevated region or mountain.

2. You prefer to sit rather than stand; to climb a mountain you are not inclined.

3. The lowering of your body and detrusion of your mind, are the natural tendencies of your disposition.

Elevativeness small
Flat Head Indian of Puget Sound.

Elevativeness large
Lavater, who had an inordinate desire to ascend every tower, cupola, steeple, monument, or mountain.

4. To dive, plunge, and go down are more agreeable acts to your nature than to leap, spring, vault, dance or caper.

5. It is less pleasurable to you to upheave or upbear a body than to lower or cast down material.

6. Neither do you care to rise or fall; are able to remain fixed as to altitude, or change it as occasion may require.

7. Elevation of body and preferment of mind afford you much pleasure.

8. The flowing tide you prefer to that of ebb; you rather assist others up to reparation than to bring them down to caducity.

9. There is real enjoyment for you in ascending towers, climbing mounds, hills, or mountains.

10. Progression, betterment, and amelioration accord well with your nature; whereas debasement, degenerateness and deterioration are exceedingly distasteful to you.

11. Nobleness, loftiness, and exaltation of mind will ever carry you from baseness and the mercenary up towards the elevated and magnanimous.

12. You ever desire to raise your body, mount a horse, climb trees,

ascend church steeples, rise in a balloon and hope to go up when done with this earthly form.

Elevativeness small.
Hare, that rather live in a swamp or burrow in the ground, than ascend and dwell on elevated lands.

Elevativeness large.
Red Deer, that desires to occupy elevated situations and scale the mountain tops.

A. To Increase the Desire for Elevation:—Live among the mountains, exercise daily in running up steep acclivities, climb the trees, ascend to the highest accessible point of every church monument, or tower your opportunities permit you to do; study subjects of an ennobling nature, such as astronomy, geology, physiognomy and anthropology; dance, jump, play at ball, ever breathe the pure air and enthrone your thoughts, feelings, and acts pre-eminently above anything unbecoming or dishonourable.

B. To Check the Tendency of Elevativeness:—Settle and live on low lands; crouch and slouch down anywhere; occupy the basement instead of the chamber of the house; prostrate yourself; go down into the cellar or wells whenever it is practicable, instead of up in a balloon; be less lofty in your bearing; seek self interests, eat heartily and be contented and time the monarch of improvement will modify your excessive elevativeness.

SENSE OF SMELL, OR OLFACTIVENESS.

OLFACTIVENESS IS THE SENSE OR FACULTY BY WHICH WE PERCEIVE THE QUALITIES OF SUBSTANCES BY THEIR EFFLUVIA OR EMANATIONS.

Long sharp noses invariably accompany great smelling or olfactory abilities.

1. Disagreeable odours never incommode you; hence, you may frequent sewers, gas furnaces, chemical laboratories, and manufactures, without the least unpleasant sensation or inconvenience.

2. Fetor, stench, rancidity, or putrescence cause you little or no unpleasantness. Cesspools, slaughter houses, and decaying materials will never deter you from entering the occupation of a scavenger, or sewerman.

Olfactiveness large.

Olfactiveness large.

3. Offensive odours, putrescent emanations, and mephitic exhalations, you may be able to detect, though they occasion you little unpleasantness.

4. Rancidity and mustiness, you may readily detect, yet sweet aromas and delicious redolence are seldom perceived and more rarely appreciated by you.

5. Being almost wholly indifferent to delicate perfumes and sublimated scents, you care little about visiting gardens to inhale the perfumes arising from the fragrant flowers, or frequenting meadows of new mown hay to inhale and feast upon the sweet fragrance wafted upon the gentle zephyrs. Hence, your surplus funds are rarely or never expended in purchasing, musk bergamot, brilliantine, or eau-de-cologne.

6. Being moderate in your use and appreciation of perfumes, though you are endowed with a fair capacity for perceiving and discerning fumes, and putridity, yet you are not likely to impregnate the air with the perfume of musk or any other offensive odour, when you draw your handkerchief from your pocket.

7. Your investments in perfumery will not be sufficiently large to cause you to become bankrupt. The odours arising from the savoury viands of a rich dinner, the aroma of steaming coffee, the delicate perfume of sweetmeats, fruits. and redolent nectar, may delight your olfactory sensations, yet their effect upon you will never drive you into foolish or extravagant expenditure, in the indulgence of your sensory appetites.

8. Unpleasant odours possess no charms for you; but the scent of the rose, violet, or locust, you fully appreciate.

9. Delightful sensations pleasantly thrill through your nature when breezes waft aromas from flowery fields and blossoming copse and forests.

10. Noble thoughts and beautiful images fill your mind, when you inhale the aromatic and infinitesimal particles which are the gifts of nature to calm and expand the mind while they purify and elevate the soul.

11. Rank noisome, and offensive effluvia sicken your body, irritate your disposition blast your pleasures, and cast shades of repugnance upon your mind. You abhor sewers reeking with stench, and the whole world where foulness and frowzy substances abound.

12. So intensely exquisite in the delicate perception of smell, is your olfactory nerve, that keenness and intensity characterise your nature when the balm of Gilead and the scent-bag lend their enchanting powers towards the elevation and enrapturing of your subtle and psychic attributes.

A. To CULTIVATE THE PERCEPTION OF ODOURS:—Live upon the purest food; drink only of that which flows from the natural crystal fount; breathe uncontaminated air; frequent flowery gardens, and blossoming fields; ascend the mountains while you inhale the perfumed air that ascends with you from the sweet scented valleys; cultivate flowers, fruits, and vegetables; and be careful to shun a hogsty, or a foulsome pool, as you would a cougar's den or a Bengal tiger's lair.

B. To RESTRAIN THE SENSE OF SMELL:—Abolish your old maid, squeamish proclivities of scenting your handkerchief; throw away your camphor bottle and smelling basket; be less fidgety about a slight stench; in a word, use your judgment more and your nose less. The practice of the sewermen of London, who go down the gratings to examine the underground filthy passages of that vast city, is to take an allowance of half-a-pint of gin, for each man, or a gill and a half of whisky, or two glasses of brandy, before descending into the noisome regions, to prevent them from fainting under the effects of the poisonous effluvia that they must inhale. I would rather faint, or endure the stench of a sewer, than that of whisky or brandy, or than take the poisonous drinks which the low Irish swallow, who do such unnatural and dirty work as sewer cleaning.

RESISTANCE, OR RESISTATIVENESS.

THE QUALITY AND INCLINATION TO RESIST THE IMPULSE, PRESSURE, AND ENCROACHMENTS OF OTHERS.

The elevated nose, short neck, and scowling brow are sure indications of the faculty of resistativeness.

1. Should it be necessary for you to engage in battle, you would prefer open-field fighting to that behind parapets, walls, breastworks, entrenchments, towers, dykes, abattises, or portcullises.

2. It requires strong provocation to arouse you to self-defence, or the sacrifice of a cherished principle to call you to arms even in defence of your country.

3. Being liable to be surprised, you would make a poor hand at arming or defending yourself.

4. In self-protection and defence you evince a poor degree of aptitude; it would be doubtful whether you would even draw down the window blinds or lift your arm to ward off the thrust of a murderer.

5. Your fearless nature could not brook being shut up in a walled city or a land walled in like China—such life would be imprisonment to you.

6. Though you are not remarkable in this respect yet you will exhibit fair spirit and pluck as defendant when others assail or encroach upon your rights.

7. You can defend the character of a friend and repel indignantly the advances of those who are, to you, distasteful

8. Having a natural love of being protected from unwelcome intrusion, you keep the enemy at bay and maintain well your position.

9. In battle, you prefer entrenchments and fortifications, and fully appreciate the advantage of being well-armed.

10. Though willing to maintain your ground when attacked you would not venture to lead a sortie to attack the enemy. Are likely to evince the spirit of self-defense; possess excellent inherent power, whether exerted or not.

11. As soon as encroachments are made upon your rights you assume the defensive and can guard and ward off all intrusions and aggressions. Have an innate desire to live in a house of strong construction.

12. Having an instinctive desire for something to fall back upon as a shield, you would be dissatisfied without a wall or breastwork to protect you against an enemy. Have a desire to supply yourself with abundance of clothing.

A. To IMPROVE YOUR POWER OF DEFENCE:—Learn fencing and bayonet exercise; parry and repel every thrust; bear the brunt of an attack upon friends or yourself; build high fences; curtain your windows and bar both them and the doors.

B. To Curb your Propensity for Defending Yourself :—Don't: but you may, if you think fit, overlook your friend's faults; sit unconcernedly by and hear your friends defamed; run any risk; incur and encounter dangers; be unguarded; and never carry arms or refuse to be shot at.

DISPOSITION TO ATTACK, OR ASSAULTATIVENESS.

THE DISPOSITION TO ATTACK THE RIGHTS OR PERSON OF ANOTHER.

The nose that stands out far from the face, in the region of the bridge or its centre, can safely be regarded as a certain sign of an AGGRESSIVE NATURE.

1. Being pacific and easily snubbed, you very naturally shun all contentions, broils, debates, and conflicts.
2. Even were you in battle you would not desire to charge an enemy.
3. Defend, ward off, and shield, you might, but would not be aggressive; nor would you invade or beleaguer the country of others unless impelled by duty.
4. You are not inclined to press others to contest unless they have contravened the law.
5. Having an instinctive aversion to see any one commence a quarrel, you will always act on the defensive rather than the aggressive.

Assaultativeness small.
Chinese Girl.

6. Unless certain that your cause is one of justice or rather a just cause, you are not hasty in words or blows.
7. Wherever error is trampling down right, you would volunteer to assail the former in defence of the latter.
8. In war, you would give a whole broadside or a raking fire, nor would you wait long, if you could do good by assailing persons or principles.
9. To invade the country of others would be inspiriting to your nature; and if necessary you would storm a castle.
10. Freely you will attack opinions or assault persons, if uneducated.
11. By your aggressiveness you are ready to assail and impugn character and make yourself offensive to others.
12. Being inclined to pinch, strike, and kick others, you are detested and hated by many and called mean.

A. To Cultivate the Propensity to Aggression:—Enter into debates, battles, and combats; march on to meet the foe; pinch the cat's tail; kick the dog; thump the children; attack every one who may unfortunately come in your way; accuse others of wrong and return blows for words.

B To Restrain the Inclination to Attack or Aggression:
—Never charge any one with offence; guard against onsets or sieges; avoid

Assaultativeness large.
Egbert, first monarch of all England.

pelting or beating any one; do not advance against foreign countries, persons, or principles. Remember to beset, besiege, or invade is unprincipled, except in defence of the right.

WAKEFULNESS, OR VIGILANCE, OR WATCHFULNESS.

THE STATE OR QUALITY OF BEING WAKEFUL.

Anxious expression, uneasy manner, with full eyes and a rather long nose strongly indicate this idiosyncrasy.

1. Drowsy, somniferous, and always somnolescent, you seem to aim at emulating the "sleeping beauty," by attracting the attention of every one by your sleepy inanition.

2. A mental log, you are unfit for any responsible situation in the arduous enterprises of active life.

3. Never more than semi-conscious about half of the day, a stupor steals over you and will lull you to sleep, even while you take temporary rest in your chair.

4. Not naturally eager, but aimless, and without intent of any kind, you can sleep soundly in the morning.

5 Though you are not very solicitous, yet you will not allow murkiness or dreamy fogginess to envelope your mind

6. Your quiet moods during the day and your dreams by night will not be harassed by watchfulness and anxiety.

7. Not very listless, and mindful of your duty, you may have inconsiderate moments as you go not to extremes in either giddiness or thoughtfulness.

Watchfulness large.
A very kind and trusty Newfoundland watch dog.

8. Keenly alert and argus-eyed, you are wide-awake and solicitous.

9. Being very wary and as watchful as an American Indian, you rarely sleep soundly except profound quiet reigns.

10. Wakefulness is one of your strong traits of character; hence you keep a sharp look-out and are keenly alive to the affairs that demand your attention.

11. Requiring less sleep than most people you resemble Napoleon the Great in being ever on the alert.

12. From your extreme vigilance there are those who think you are always awake as you are like the watch-dog or weasel, never caught sleeping.

A. To CULTIVATE WATCHFULNESS :—Rise early; be active and always alert and on the move; engage in out-door risky business ; eat freely of meat ; assume responsibilities; be ever ready and zealous ; and remember that "Eternal vigilance is the price of *liberty*."

B. To REPRESS WATCHFULNESS :—Take no thought for the future ; consider everything as perfectly secure ; cultivate inaction ; relax, loiter, and trifle in the affairs of life ; adopt hybernation and oscitation ; don't take pains with anything ; be listless and inattentive ; live a vegetarian, and let everything take care of itself.

SUSPICIOUS DISPOSITION, OR SUSPICIOUSNESS.

THE DISPOSITION TO IMAGINE AND SUSPECT THE EXISTENCE OF SOMETHING WITHOUT PROOF.

The visible evidence of suspicion is the length from the face directly forward to the point of the nose. The crow is one of the best examples of suspicion.

Suspiciousness small.
Owl.

Suspiciousness large.
Crow.

Suspiciousness large.
Red Fox.

1. You confide in every one and are an unsuspecting dupe.
2. The busy, heartless, selfish world hurries along in all its hollow

SUSPICIOUSNESS. 59

pretences while still you are simple enough to believe that all things are as they seem.

3. Being too unsuspecting you are often surprised by the sad mistakes you make in simply confiding in others.

4. Trust and confidence, however injudicious on your part, will render you liable to be greatly chagrined on finding your reliance in some persons sadly misplaced.

Suspiciousness small.
Ox

5. Your pure nature, void of suspicion, is fostered and cherished by your confiding reliance in others.

6. So beautifully balanced are you in this respect that you prove yourself worthy of the approval of others.

7. Though generally actuated by good faith and confidence in others, yet, at times, you are a little distrustful.

8. Although a strange or unusual appearance of persons or things may arouse suspicion in your mind, still you are wary enough not to mention it or even allow your countenance to betray you, until you make further observations.

9. When others act strangely and matters seem not quite right, you are liable to mistrust and quietly set on foot secret inquiry.

10. Suspicion may cause you to become hostile and render you uncertain towards those who were your friends.

11. Shyness and hesitation are poisoning your social happiness and decimating your friends.

12. A paradoxical character, you are as suspicious as a crow; married or single you will render your partner or intended as miserable as need be by your incessant jealousies.

A. TO EXCITE AND CULTURE SUSPICION :—Neither trust nor confide in any one; keep an eye in the back of your head; watch everybody and suspect your best friends of wrong-doing; and remember that you are too confiding and liable to become the dupe of sharpers by your extreme confidence; and that undue suspicion is more abject baseness even than the guilt suspected.

B. TO RESTRAIN SUSPICION :—Hand your purse and valuables to another to keep for you; take everything to be what it seems; doubt no one and imagine no more wrong things of friends or acquaintances. Bacon says: "Suspicions are to be suppressed or at least well guarded, for they cloud the mind." "He that dares to doubt, when there is no ground, is neither to himself nor others sound."

PROPENSITY FOR LOCOMOTION, OR LOCOMOTIVITY.

THE DESIRE OF ACTION AND ABILITY OF CHANGING PLACE WHILE PRESERVING IDENTITY.

The faculty of locomotion manifests itself physiognomically by a long and thin nose. The grey-hound and stag-hound are fine examples of locomotive construction, while the sloth's nose indicates the opposite extreme and the fact is verified by its motion being only a few feet each day.

Locomotivity small. The Sloth.

1. At the moment of your creation the motional principle was forgotten, hence you are the most dull, inactive, and sluggish composition that makes an effort to move from place to place.

2. Your compeer in sluggishness, the sloth, you resemble strongly; necessity alone, being her own law, has the power to rouse your motion, and she may often be heard complaining of her weary task. Your heaven is the paradise of immobility. Gœthe the German poet had no

sympathy with you when he wrote: "Nature knows no pause in progress and development, and attaches her curse to all inaction."

Locomotivity large.   The Greyhound.

3. Few can bear rest better than you; the aversion to physical labour grows upon you apace; lazy indeed you are, physically all through and ever.

4. In utter inaction you luxuriate; let storms howl, and thunders roll and lightnings flash, but only let you feel that you can remain at rest and be happy.

5. How you rest and sympathize with the sultry hot days of July when even the mighty forces of nature are quiescent. Only let me be still and luxuriate in perfect repose, you exclaim, or rather, peevishly entreat. Attilus, the Hun, must be considered your most inveterate enemy since he exclaimed: "Better to have nothing to do than to be doing nothing."

6. Your muscular system being neither active nor sensitively excitable, you care little for exercise unless impelled by circumstances demanding action.

7. Necessity alone will impel you to energetic exertion; and though not still and impassive any length of time, yet sometimes you are as peaceful and reposing as the lake without a ripple or Diana in a midnight cloudless sky.

Locomotivity large.
Captain James Cook.

8. As repose and activity are almost equally congenial to your nature, being neither transitional nor stagnant, you can alike enjoy the peripatetic and the quiescent state of existence.

9. Restlessness being the distinguishing characteristic of your nature, you take delight in all the active and athletic pastimes of life, such as, walking, skating, sliding, swimming, driving, riding; ever on the move, you are always athirst for fresh scenes and excitements.

10. Your poetic designation is "a bird of passage." As there is scarcely any friction in your muscles, their action is easy and natural and thoroughly efficient so that your motion resembles most the even flow of the rapid river.

11. The rapidity and frequency of your motions are ample evidence that you possess in an extraordinary degree the impelling power of locomotion.

12. Nothing in animal-character-life you resemble so much as a bounding flea ; rest or stillness is to you abhorrent and unnatural; your pace is fleet as the deer and bounding like the antelope.

A. To ACCELERATE LOCOMOTIVE POWER:—Sit and lie less ; be more upon your feet; climb heights, hills, and mountains; dance, romp, run, play, swing, work, keep acting and operating. From these pleasures will spring a corresponding increase in your power of locomotion ; never allow quiescence or stagnation to steal away the valuable jewel from your crown of motion; ramble, stroll, journey, emigrate; migrate and circumambulate; be astir early and late with a cheerful spirit and good will to all mankind.

B. To RETARD LOCOMOTION :—Find an anchoring place and come to anchor, a resting place and settle down; by all means keep perfectly still; let the winds whirple about the leaves and dust, the waters toss and tumble their light burthens, the fires disintegrate the vast strata of rocks and make the globe tremble from centre to circumference, but do you remain still and unmoved as the everlasting hills. In a word avoid motion of any kind, and repress all your desires, inclinations or predilections to activity.

INQUISITIVENESS.

THE ABILITY TO FIND OR OBTAIN INFORMATION—THE QUALITY OF A DETECTIVE.

A long prominent nose and thin cheeks are evidences of an inquiring disposition.

1. You will never peer into key-holes or take much interest in flying rumours, or be detected opening the letters of others.

2. Being quite uninquisitive you pass trifles by without many questions.

3. Being almost devoid of curiosity you take little interest in the affairs of others.

4. Though not too obtrusive, you can both ask questions and candidly reply when necessary, being somewhat like a sponge both absorbing and exsorbing.

5. You are not too zealous about unknown things of which you have an inkling, nor do you care to pry into the arcana of nature.

6. Though ever thirsting for new truths you are nevertheless courteous in your quest for information.

7. Having a natural love for probing and scrutinizing, you have talent and tact for following up a law case or any unknown subject.

8. You would stare and wonder in your eager desire for knowledge or information, your mind being Socratic in constitution.

9. Being naturally an investigator, and having curiosity and inquisitiveness in full strength, you are always inclined to question others closely and keenly.

10. Apt and adroit in asking questions and delighting to dip into and fathom your subject, you would make an excellent spy or detective, or be well fitted to act on a reconnoitring expedition.

11. Being always curious and ever prying into matters around you, looking over and through subjects of interest will delight you, and make you an excellent investigator.

12. Prying curiosity renders you an inveterate quiz, disagreeable and detestable to others.

Inquisitiveness large.
Niclas August Wilhelm.

Inquisitiveness small.
A Kyast Baniau man of Surat in India.

A. TO IMPROVE YOUR TALENT FOR INQUIRY:—Search, trace out, and examine every trifle of gossip and news you hear; live in Quizland; visit chemical laboratories, watching narrowly the experiments, and then earnestly inquire of your friends all the information they can afford on the facts you notice; be pryingly inquisitive, inductive, Baconian in your method of research and investigation. "Prove all things, hold fast that which is good."

B. TO RESTRAIN THE TALENT FOR INQUIRY:— Ask no questions; pass by as of no interest all rumours; never lay aside a book or leave your business to see Punch and Judy or a dog-fight; and always bear in mind that no one likes to be closely quizzed or poked after about their own business.

AMBITIOUSNESS.
THE DESIRE OF DISTINCTION, OR PRE-EMINENCE.

Thoroughly defined and well marked features are nature's evidences of a keen aim in life, and wide, grasping, and far reaching AMBITION.

Ambitiousness large.
Julius Cæsar.

1. Always, like Dickens' Mr Micawber, you are waiting for something to turn up. Like a rudderless boat or ship drifting down the stream, you are carried down life's eddying current with almost perfect certainty of being a total wreck on the desert shore of life.

2. Your lukewarmness almost amounting to disdain of position, power, or influence, gives complete indifference in you to the attainment of any worthy achievement.

3. Not having within you the germs of success, your designless efforts cannot succeed in garnering a harvest of rich promise. Over-anxiety will not likely ever destroy your rest by night or aimless peace by day. You mildly console yourself with La Bruyère's decision: "The slave has but one master; the ambitious man, as many as are necessary to contribute to his advancement."

4. Being unsolicitous about the great enterprises of life or position in the world, you trust in God for the common necessaries, and dream on, an aimless believer in chance. How little you can sympathise with Oliver Cromwell whose advice was: "Fear God and keep your powder dry."

5. Like the poor timid recruit, who could never venture to open his eyes when he fired, many a random shot you make, and yet remain destitute of forecasting thought, or have very little ambition. With Jeremy Taylor, you feel that "Ambition is the most troublesome and vexatious passion that can afflict the sons of men."

6. Though you would not decline emolument or preferment when they are pressed upon you, still you have no carking or consuming longing for office or honour. Raleigh said of such as you:

"Fain would I climb but that I fear to fall."

But Queen Bess answered in her own vein,

"If thy mind fail thee, do not climb at all."

7. Quietly you value honour and preferment, and yet somehow you are unsolicitous of votes or the suffrages of the multitude, being your-

self of reliant and self-conscious nature. Your "chaste strong mind's by chaste ambition nursed."

8 The attainment of superiority and distinction you highly prize: this is plainly indicated by your style. "Within your breast as in a palace lies wakeful ambition."—*Fletcher*.

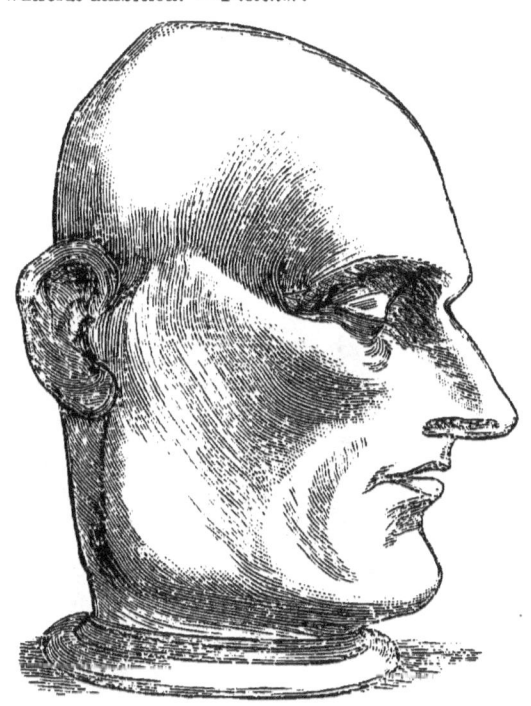

Ambitiousness large.
Napoleon I.

9 While you are strongly desirous of office and honours, yet nothing would induce you to sacrifice your reputation or happiness to that end. "The brave and honest thirst of fame your bosom warms."

10. The inordinate thirst for power and renown which is inbred in your very nature, and gnaws your vitals, may some day raise you to distinction. Yours is the ambition pointed at by Byron when he says:

"There is a fire and motion of the soul,
But, once kindled, quenchless evermore!"

11. Though generally you delight in true honour and highly prize noble fame, still there is great danger that your keen ambition will ruin your happiness by defeating the noble efforts of your life. Penn said quaintly: "The tallest trees are most in the power of the winds, and ambitious men of the blasts of fortune," and then Shakspeare:

"Fling away ambition:
By that sin fell the angels: how can man then,
The image of his Maker, hope to win by't?"

12. Ambitious in the fullest and widest sense of the term, like the Great Napoleon, the little Corporal of Corsican origin, and aspirant to universal dominion, you have an inordinate love of power and superiority. Your intuitive aspiration and innate sense of the power to overawe and

Ambitiousness large.
A jealous dog.

Ambitiousness large.
Horse.

govern by despotic dictation would rouse the mind of every free-man to chain you to a rock and watch you gnaw the strong-linked chain you yourself had forged. Your personal ambition renders you the unique foe of liberty, and co-laborateur with the Devil.

"O cursed ambition - thou devouring bird,
How dost thou from the field of honesty
Pick every grain of profit or delight,
And mock the reaper's toil."—*Havard.*

Ambition, "Proud crested fiend, the world's worst foe."—*Bloomfield.*

A. TO FOSTER, FEED, AND CULTIVATE AMBITIOUSNESS:—Read the biographies of Nimrod, Alexander the Great, not forgetting his father Philip of Macedon; of Julius Cæsar; of Peter the Great of Russia; of Timur the Tartar; of Napoleon I.; and of his reputed nephew, Napoleon III. Then strive to become renowned in some good cause, circumambulate the city for votes; shake off your listless inappetency as an encumbering garment, and feel that your character is just the very model for the office to which you aspire; contest earnestly all claims to positions of influence; aspire to the high stations in the gift of a nation or people; allow the fire of ambition to kindle within you, and let its warming influence kindle and intensify your aspirations and utterly consume any listlessness that may still lurk within your spirit.

B. To Curb and Restrain Ambitiousness:—Shakspeare says:

> "Ambition's like a circle on the water,
> Which never ceases to enlarge itself,
> Till by broad spreading it disperse to naught."

Bear in mind that your covetousness of power, position or wealth may drag you to an untimely and dishonourable grave; suppress every longing desire for office or position; let the sun of detestation scatter the dew of ambition which often gathers around your ardent spirit; be moderate in your aims and you may become more happy. Still remember what Hume says: "Where ambition can be so happy as to cover its enterprises, even to the person himself. under the appearance of principle, it is the most incurable and inflexible of all human passions."

SELF-ESTIMATION, OR AUTOHEGEMONY.

THE FACULTY WHICH GIVES A HIGH ESTIMATE OF ONE'S OWN ACTIONS OR CAPACITIES.

Carrying the head well back, and relatively great length from the point of the nose to the lower part of the chin are indications which belong only to those who fully appreciate their own merits, and in many instances overrate themselves. Beau Brummel, the fop in the reign of George IV. of England, was intensely egotistical. Hence we have given his likeness as an illustration of large or exaggerated self-appreciation. Emanuel Kant, the eminent German philosopher, was very deficient in self-appreciation.

Autohegemony large.
Beau Brummel, a noted fop and courtier of George IV.

1. Constantly sensible and sensitive on the point of your own abasement and humility, you are never guilty of sounding a trumpet before you to attract attention.

2. In the stormy shadow of the lofty rocks of your modesty, your sterling worth and real merits lie unobserved, while other more self-confident individuals shove you aside and stalk on in the highway of life.

3. Moderately estimating your own abilities and merits, and being devoid of self-assurance, you are too ready to concede to others more than their due.

4. Being naturally more retiring than disposed to push yourself forward, your humility and bashfulness free you from all arrogance and presumption.

5. Coming into contact with others you experience abasement and agitation, which often renders you ill at ease, and yet no one but yourself may perceive that you experience this feeling.

6. Being yourself neither egotistical nor pretentious, though not too modest in the presence of others, you very much dislike to observe conceit in those you encounter.

7. Without much dignity and not very censorious you nevertheless possess self-confidence enough to keep you from looking sheepish.

8. Not easily abashed and quite self-reliant if an attempt should be made to impose upon you, victory may inflate you a little; still, should you suffer defeat you will not be crestfallen.

9. Possessed of a noble pride and feeling quite self-reliant and independent, the world cannot detrude you.

10. The implicit confidence you repose in your own opinions is quite sufficient to support you in any emergency or controversy.

11. Your strong self-centration united with your self-charity affords you a high estimate of your own abilities.

Autohegemony small.
Emanuel Kant, a German Metaphysician and Philosopher.

12 Naturally egotistical and excessively arrogant, you imagine that every one is staring at you; hence you feel the utmost self-satisfaction, and become disgustingly self-opinionated, aping the character of Beau Brummel.

A. TO CULTIVATE SELF-APPRECIATION:—Rely implicitly on your own will; yield not so readily to the wishes of others; be always perfectly self-satisfied; give due consideration to every special desire that springs up within you; feel and act with more importance; bear yourself in an abundantly dignified manner during your daily intercourse, so that you may command respect; be bold; hold up your head and look like a man; and remember that humility is a virtue only when it does not cause you to be trodden under-foot.

B. TO RESTRAIN SELF-APPRECIATION:—Be humble; avoid pomposity and egotism; study to correct your own deficiencies; pride yourself on what you can do instead of what you are; cultivate suavity and humility; and never look down upon those you consider inferiors.

CLASS III.

PROPAGATIVE INCLINATIONS.

THIS CLASS OF INCLINATIONS WILL BE FOUND LARGE WHEN THE MUSCULAR AND FIBROUS FORM PREDOMINATES.

APPRECIATION OF NATURAL MOTION, OR TEMPORINATURALITIVENESS.

THE POWER OF JUDGING OR COMPREHENDING THE TIME OF THE YEAR, THE SEASONS, OR THE REVOLUTIONS OF THE PLANETS.

The round form of the face and physique bespeak for the individual the ability to comprehend and produce natural time.

Temporinaturalitiveness large.
Bach.

Temporinaturalitiveness small.
Callam Bay Indian.

1. To you days and years pass like dreams—once here now gone.
2. Irregular in the time of your movements, you are always belated, and then go hop, skip, and jump. You are as Lord Wilmington said of the Duke of Newcastle when he was prime minister: "He loses half an hour every morning and runs after it during all the day without being able to overtake it."

3. From your organization arise tardiness and unpunctuality. You "take no note of time but from its loss."

4. Hours being of little moment to you Time becomes your master, and from neglecting his rapid but stealthy movement you are liable to encroach upon others' time. Take to heart what Mrs Sigourney has said of such constitutions as yours: "Who ever looked upon his vanished hours—recalled his slighted years—stamped them with wisdom—or effaced from Heaven's record the fearful blot of wasted time?"

5. Prochronism and procrastination are failings of yours; hence, being unable to tell the day of the week, the month, or the year, you are almost certain to misdate your letters. Lavater says of such characters as yours: "You prorogue the honesty of to-day till to-morrow, and will probably prorogue your to-morrows to eternity."

6. Though you are fairly accurate as to time, you are not very skilful in chronometry. Seasons, and circumstances which occur in connection with particular epochs or great natural phenomena, you are fairly accurate in, though not an expert. You sometimes must feel the truth that Longfellow has so beautifully expressed:—

"The leaves of memory seem to make
A mournful rustling in the dark."

7. Though others may differ from you in opinion, yet it seems to yourself "much of a muchness," whether you rise at ten or eleven in the morning. With Sterne you say: "Rest unto my soul! 'tis all I want—the end of all my wishes and pursuits."

8. With fair expertness you can determine solar or astronomical time; still, when hurried, you are quick and unnatural.

9. You are one of the rare specimens of mental power who appreciate absolute and relative time without training or education.

10 To be able to keep correct time, you need no teaching, naturally possessing this faculty in an eminent degree.

11. Often you make happy hits in judging when events will happen, being quite an expert in estimating natural time.

12. No one is a better judge of the time of day than you; and you can remember accurately the year and day on which an event occurred and yet you can scarcely remember the hour.

A. TO CULTIVATE THE APTITUDE FOR APPRECIATING NATURAL TIME: — Watch the glittering stars, mild moon, and peerless sun, and try to estimate their motions, distances, and duration; make a note of the time you saw comets in the sky, meteors shooting, aurora borealis, and every other display of the endless and wonderful phenomena in the mighty, eloquent, and majestic drama of nature.

B. TO RESTRAIN THE TENDENCY TO APPRECIATE NATURAL TIME:— Never engage in a vocation in which you will have regular recurrence of duty; trust to chance and uncertainty as to when incidents may transpire; don't heed the quarters of the moon; notice not the beating of your pulse; antedate one letter and postdate the next; be aoristic as to the time of events of natural occurrence. Try to appreciate Seneca when he says: "The greatest loss of time is delay and expectation which depends upon the future. Let go the present which is in our power and look forward to the future which depends upon chance—let go certainty for uncertainty."

PHYSICAL COURAGE, OR PHYSIOVALOROSITY.

MATERIAL AND CORPOREAL COURAGE; RESISTANCE TO EVERY SPECIES OF PHYSICAL FORCE.

The wide nostril, short neck, large thorax, and eyes set directly in front, instead of outside of the head, are indubitable indications of physical courage; while timidity is physiognomically recogniseable by a long slim neck; large eyes set on the sides of the head rather than in front; and narrow long ears. The rabbit and giraffe are fine examples of timidity.

Physiovalorosity large.
John Broughton, a base pugilist of England.

Physiovalorosity small.
Joseph Justus Scalliger, who filled the chair of Belles Lettres in the University of Leyden.

1. Scarcely knowing whether your soul is your own or the ghost of some one else, the most trivial noise. the falling of a leaf, or breaking of a twig as you pass through a forest will startle you. Cowardice and inefficiency sum up your physical characteristics.

2. Having an innate love of peace you prefer being stigmatized as a coward to lowering yourself by pugilistic encounters. Apprehensive even of shadows, and fearfully full of misgivings, you would quake and tremble at a sudden noise or unexpected form.

3. Full of trepidation, consternation. and dismay, your nervousness and inquietude make you miserable. To you it seems foolish for human beings to adjust their disputes and differences on a low plane like the lower animals.

4. Being of a gentle, mild, and inoffensive disposition, and not very courageous when brute force is required, you would be ill-adapted for the exigencies of the tented field or onset of battle. So timorous you are that you become a false alarmist, being easily terrified by goblin stories and scarecrows.

5. Being easily alarmed, you are naturally chicken-hearted and unwarlike, and would scarcely lift a hand to defend yourself. Much rather would you cry for your big brother to help you. Although you are not likely to assault another, being naturally gentle and conciliatory, nevertheless if provoked or insulted you would be cross and nervous.

Physiovalorosity large.
Lion.

Physiovalorosity small.
Giraffe.

6. Neither excessive cowardice nor great courage belong to your character; the medium entitles you, however, to neither the charge of effeminacy, nor fearlessness of startling adventures. Naturally you love to be at peace, yet you will battle your way manfully, and struggle with life's circumstances when it is necessary.

7. Though you may shrink and quail when under severe trials, yet you entertain slight ideas of courage. Not believing it sufficiently dignified to put yourself on a level with the brute creation, it is rare for you to a have a difficulty that leads to blows. This arises, however, from no lack of courage.

8. Fortitude seems to be instilled into your character by a fair amount of fearlessness. If necessary, you are sufficiently gallant to attack, or

act in defence, but still you do not deem it requisite to maintain a high sense of honour by physical strength.

9 Having a natural aversion to shrink from personal difficulties, you will readily rebuff all indignities if you are in the mood. One of the last to shiver at your own shadow you could be brave, gallant, and daring should circumstances demand your prowess.

10. Not being easily terrified by trifles, you could confront dangers and be audacious in defence or attack. Hardy and venturous by nature, your valour would not fail you in war, nor your bravery in single combat.

11. More of the lion than of the hare being in your constitution, you will naturally delight in fortitude as much as you detest timidity. Even the insinuation that you would shun or avoid physical encounters would be a disgrace put upon you. In riots and town brawls, you would be well calculated to be a leader and abettor but your fine physical powers are capable of figuring in nobler performances than these.

12. In nature and physical constitution you most resemble the bulldog; hence you are a brutal pugilist, and revel in accounts of war, personal combats, and rows of all kinds. Brimful of courage, you instinctively abhor the timorous and skittish soul that locks its closet door with itself inside when the burglar enters the house, or ensconces itself in the cellar when the enemy is at the gate.

A. To CULTIVATE PHYSICAL COURAGE:—Put on the bearing of fearlessness and intrepidity; meet trouble unflinchingly; eat meat, and bear up against fear; never show the white feather, but turn and face danger and assume the defiant. Associate with the roughs of large cities; attend bull and cock-fights, and every row you can come within reach of; read the biographies of Joan of Arc and Lady Verulana Gracilia, and try to follow their examples; peruse the stories of personal encounter among the ancients; be present at athletic games and pugilistic arenas; enter the army and show yourself valorous; eat largely of pork, drink ardent spirits, and in due time you will feel as courageous as a hen in defence of her brood, a bull-dog or a bear robbed of her whelps or an hungered tiger, but with this human result, that your features, as a consequence of this course of training, will likely become hideous.

B. To RESTRAIN PHYSICAL COURAGE:—Flee from war and opposition of every kind; woo the peaceful; avoid pork and all other kinds of gross food as well as every species of ardent spirits, shun all the associations of the quarrelsome; discard the absurd and erroneous notion that it is honourable to fight; and remember that persons of high culture avoid physical combat as they would a mad dog or the plague. Hearing a strange noise, run and never wait to learn the cause; associate with cowards and old women and listen to their tales repeated, until cowards become in your estimation more famous and worthy of renown than courageous men; eat no meat and avoid the places where courage is requisite, specially keeping at a respectful distance from the brave and undaunted.

SOPHISTICALNESS.

THE INCLINATION TO BE FALLACIOUSLY SUBTLE AND UNSOUND.

Sophistry shadows itself forth on the facial lineaments by giving them a smooth and round expression.

1. Long since, no doubt, you have learned it is an easy thing to be mistaken; hence you never use satire or boasting, and most likely you will avoid invective.

2. Heartily detesting false colourings and artful dodging, you will neither wince the truth nor meddle in the affairs of others.

3. When completely beaten in argument, you are willing to submit.

4. Being averse to evasion, and liking straightforwardness, you naturally scout sophistry and chicanery when resorted to for a mean purpose. Vile practices cannot be traced to you.

5. You dislike the common shifts and resorts to which many have recourse while occupying positions of trust or when the lowering storms of adversity test them.

6. Knowing and caring very little about the shifting undercurrents of character, you may employ artifice to escape censure or the aims of argument, yet, according to your own manner of thinking, you would not do this unless you felt it to be honourable.

7. The gabble of the goose will not betray your tongue into garrulousness though you are inclined to be sarcastic and ready for most exigencies; still you court not that which tries the soul of man.

8. You have an instinctive aversion to self-condemnatory acknowledgments; still you will not bemean yourself by fox cunning for the purpose of accomplishing a mean trick.

9. A useful member of society if in the proper position; hard to corner, and instinctively disliking to acknowledge a mistake, you would make a good detective to bring rogues from their lurking places.

10. Never fearing emergencies, feeling confident of being able to meet them, you manage to keep your head above water, and are capable of making many shifts to avoid failure. Your ironical capacity gets you through many difficulties, by keeping sharp customers in awe.

11. Extremely cute, it is hard for you to be honest, as you are brimful of intrigue; hence your life is poorly regulated.

12. Abundant in your resources, you are prolific in ways and means for accomplishing your projects and designs; hence you are liable to make mischief. As a village attorney you would set all the inhabitants by the ears.

A. TO CULTIVATE SOPHISTRY:—Never allow yourself to be thwarted in your designs; make an effort to be more self-sufficient by placing yourself in unfavourable situations and then meeting them boldly, shifting, foxing, and dodging about until your object is accomplished. Don't give up the pursuit of your game because you have lost the scent; cross the stream and like the blood-hound, keep trying until you come upon the scent again, and set the world at defiance. "Never say die."

B. TO RESTRAIN THE SOPHISTICAL PROPENSITY:—Hold your tongue, if it makes mischief; say and feel you are beaten; never undermine the character of another; and bridle your tongue knowing that it is an unruly beast

PLAYFULNESS.

THE ABILITY THAT GIVES, APPRECIATES AND ENJOYS LIVELY RECREATIONS AND EXERCISES FOR THE SAKE OF AMUSEMENT.

Fulness in the centre of the forehead, face, and every bone of the whole frame, indicates a playful nature.

Playfulness large

1. Having a horror and detestation of being tantalised, you will never tease or pester another, nor can you tolerate those who harass others.

2. Glumness and cold dignified reserve so largely characterise your demure nature, that you can neither enjoy nor appreciate the playfulness of youthful beings.

3. Soberness and solemnity pervade your disposition to such an extent that they have smothered all sprightliness, and rendered your days of frolic and fun almost nothing.

4. Occasionally, you are somewhat sportive and frisky, but your sportive and jubilant moods are brief, and seem to leave you in an uneasy state.

5. The gambols of lambs, playfulness of kittens, and sportiveness of children you delight to see, though you cannot participate in their diversions.

6 Troublesome and teasing children may not harass you, yet you are fond of seeing their recreations and knowing that they are happy in their pastimes.

7. Though you will never allow your deportment to descend to tantalization, yet you are quite playful and frolicksome.

8. Should circumstances prove favourable you might engage much of your attention and spend some of your time in games and sportive amusements.

9. Occasionally you may feel inclined to run, hop, jump, and dance,

but age will impair these inclinations and cause demureness to occupy their place.

10. Jocularity and animation will exhilarate your character and give you a relish for levity and recreation.

11. To torment and irritate others seems to afford you much pleasure; and you are fraught with playfulness and pranks to such a degree that you are become a distressing tease.

12 A perfect tantaliser, you use every means to vex and mortify your most intimate friends. You closely resemble those who condemned Tantalus, the Phrygian King, to stand up to the chin in water with a tree of fair fruit over his head, both of which, as he attempted to satiate his hunger and allay his thirst, fled from his approach.—*Fabulous History*.

A. To CULTIVATE PLAYFULNESS :—Tease, tickle, pester, push and pull others; catch the cat by its caudal appendage; stir up the monkeys with a sharp stick; put hot coals on the turtle's back; rub the dog's ears; join in the children's sport, and become as nimble and playful as a kitten or a squirrel; jump, run, joke, laugh, and bear in mind that you are too dignified and stiff and need limbering into mellow playfulness.

B. To RESTRAIN PLAYFULNESS:—Be glum, sedate and dignified; forbear to join in the gleeful romps and amusements of children; keep no kittens, dogs, squirrels, lambs, or colts; live every hour of life as if in earnest; no longer poke sticks at others; keep your fingers to yourself; remember that your teasing nature is in excess and needs to be restrained.

LOCATIVE HABITS, OR ATTACHMENT TO PLACE, OR PHILOMONOTOPICALNESS.

THE AFFECTION FOR ONE PLACE, OR, HABIT OF BECOMING ATTACHED TO ONE SITUATION OR LOCALITY.

Vertical wrinkles in the forehead above the nose, and no oblique curved wrinkles starting near the top of the nose, or in the above wrinkles and curving outwards and upwards over each eye, with full round cheeks, indicate that you may feel assured that such individuals are inclined to have a home, with the desire to remain in it, if possible.

1. The intense desire for change renders you unable to locate yourself; hence you are fond of rambling and become cosmopolitan in your habits and feelings. At last you say and feel with Lord Byron :

"To the mind
Which is itself, no changes bring surprise."

2. To tarry in one place long and remain quiescent would prove distasteful to you, but you so thoroughly enjoy roaming that you feel at home in any latitude, zone, or country. You "run after felicity like an absent-minded man hunting for his hat while it is on his head or in his hand," as Steele words it. Your facility of disposition needs but little aid from philosophy.

3. Your life thus far having been very changeable you may have become, through association, attached to things and friends, though not to place or home.

4. Of an itinerant disposition you manifest restlessness at the home-

stead; and it is almost impossible for you to stand any length of time in one position. You agree with Wynne that,—

> "The same stale viands served up o'er and o'er
> The stomach nauseates."

5. You have a fair desire to become permanent in a fixed situation or residence, yet you can leave the old domicile without regret, and remain away a long time if necessary.

6. Harmoniously developed and evenly balanced in this habit, you can ramble or remain with equal ease whenever it becomes necessary.

7. Entitled fairly to the name of settler, denizen or inhabitant, you can well enjoy a place of resort which might be considered your home-stall.

8. When returning to the fatherland after long absence the very essence of your soul seems to leap afresh into a new era of life reinvigorated.

9. The dearest land on earth to you is the land of your nativity. Your desire is for a local habitation and to be resident in cot, house, castle, or tabernacle. As Washington Irving beautifully expresses it:—
"Home to you is the paternal hearth, that rallying place of the affections."

10. You can readily become located and settled in any new situation, and having once had a settled abode it is hard to commence travelling again. "To be happy at home is the ultimate result of all ambition; the end to which every enterprise and labour tends, and of which every desire prompts the prosecution." Thus writes Samuel Johnson, and thus you feel.

11. The intense warmth you manifest in your love of home would indicate in you a strong aversion to migration.

12. Such is your intense love of home that your desire would be never to leave it for a day. Heartily you can say with Montgomery:

> "There is a land of every land the pride,
> Beloved by heaven o'er all the earth beside.
> Where shall that land, that spot of earth be found?
> Art thou a man? a patriot? look around
> Oh, thou shalt find, howe'er thy footsteps roam,
> That land thy country, and that spot thy home!"

A. To CULTIVATE LOCATIVE HABITS:—Avoid rambling; make your home, however humble or exalted, as comfortable and attractive as possible. In short, make it your world. In this respect imitate the Greenlanders, who never leave their native land unless compelled to do so. Cowper has it thus:—

> "This fond attachment to the well-known place
> Whence first we started into life's long race,
> Maintains its hold with such unfailing sway,
> We feel it e'en in age and at our latest day."

B. To RESTRAIN LOCATIVE PROPENSITIES:—Avoid the selfish feeling of thinking your hermitage so much superior to the abode of others. If possible, travel, become a cosmopolite, notice critically the faults of your own country, and try to appreciate more the beauties of other lands. "Be thine own palace, or the world's thy jail," says DONNE, when comparing the rambler with his knapsack on his back to the *snail* with its house (or shell) on its back.

SUBSTITUTION, OR INTERMUTATIVENESS.
THE CAPACITY OF CHANGING OR PLACING ONE THING IN LIEU OF ANOTHER.

INTERMUTATIVENESS, *which is the ability to put one thing or person in the place of another, may be discovered by a general fulness in the centre of the face, from the hair to the centre of the chin inclusive.*

1. Fixed, stagnant, inconvertible, self-confirmed, stereotyped, you cannot transpose or adapt yourself in the smallest trifle.
2. So strongly you enjoy intransmutability that you cannot tolerate swapping or exchanging.
3. Though your nature is to have things settled and stationary, yet you can with reluctance vary and modify.
4. Being substantially disinclined, you have an aversion to substitute or be substituted.
5. Though generally averse to putting one thing in lieu of another, yet you can supersede or take the place of another.
6. Though capable of substituting bank notes for gold or silver, or putting one clerk or official in the place of another, yet you feel little interest in so doing. Your mind is well balanced in this respect.
7. You love to supersede or supplant by the intermutation of things.
8. Able to make shifts, you have the power of representation and can find substitutes for whatever you need.
9. Having a natural love of enallăgĕ, you are capable of substituting in the mental or material world.
10. Having an aptitude for metaphorical representation, you would often yield your place to others. You could conveniently use a pencil if you break your pen.
11. Having the power of exchanging one thing for another widely different. without difficulty, you are ready to barter and commute.
12. Means and appliances for doing what you wish are ever at your command; hence you are full of proxy, plastic and variable.

A. HOW TO INCREASE THE FACULTY OF SUBSTITUTION:—Bar out all invariableness; frequently change; study and use metaphor; let metonomy and synecdoche play a part in the acts of your life; if you have not a match at hand to light the gas, take a roll of paper or a splinter and obtain fire wherever it is most convenient; look over your manuscript, crossing out and interlining; be willing to improve by accepting a more reasonable doctrine in place of your former belief or opinions.

B. HOW TO MINIFY THE FACULTY OF SUBSTITUTION:—Cast aside all reciprocation; never give place to another or supersede him; avoid interchange and the subditions; wear your old clothes as long as possible; never swap or exchange horses; love one and that one only; retain your servants and employés as long as they are dutiful and command your confidence.

RECEPTION OF TONE, OR TONIRECEPTIONALITY.
THE ABILITY OF RECEIVING AND APPRECIATING TONE, OR SOUND.

The round ear which stands well forward and outward from the head is well adapted to catch the fine or coarse sounds and convey the wave motions to the tympanum of the ear, and especially musical sounds. An ear lying flat on the side of the head, or angular or pointed in form is not adapted to receive and judge musical tones.

Tonireceptionality large. Tonireceptionality small.
Tamberlik, the highest tenor singer in the world. J. H. Newman, D.D.

1. Almost a musical idiot, no melodious sounds bask softly on the sunny side of your spirit; no tinkling of cymbals or plaintive airs of the flute afford glory and delight to your unmusical nature.

2. "God save the Queen" and "Yankee Doodle" are about the same tune to you.

3. It is very difficult for you to comprehend the fine bearing of one tone upon another, and hence you are quite incapable of entering into the musical world with intelligence.

4. Your capacity for discerning fine musical tones is deficient, and you must feel that your ear was never formed for music. Perhaps you can more fully appreciate the bustle and buzz of business, the hammering, thumping and hum of mechanical industries. Your ear may appreciate "The Harmonious Blacksmith."

5. Lacking in the soul for music and hence in the joys arising from harmony, those fine and tender modulations and waftings of air heard in melodies are too etherial to stir your heavy nature or cause your heart to beat responsively.

6. You enjoy melody but appreciate heavy music better than light. The soft low mellow tones of the human voice steal through your ears and bury themselves in your heart, yet you give them little heed.

7. Rhythm you appreciate well and detect the slightest discord. Intonations of voice, the rustling of the aspen and poplar, the hushing murmuring of wind-shaken reeds, the sighing of the zephyr through the forest, and the splashing of the ocean waves when no wind moves them, your ear catches, and your spirit drinks deep of their music.

8. You may recognize and learn tunes well by note, but your ability to perform on an instrument will depend entirely upon practice.

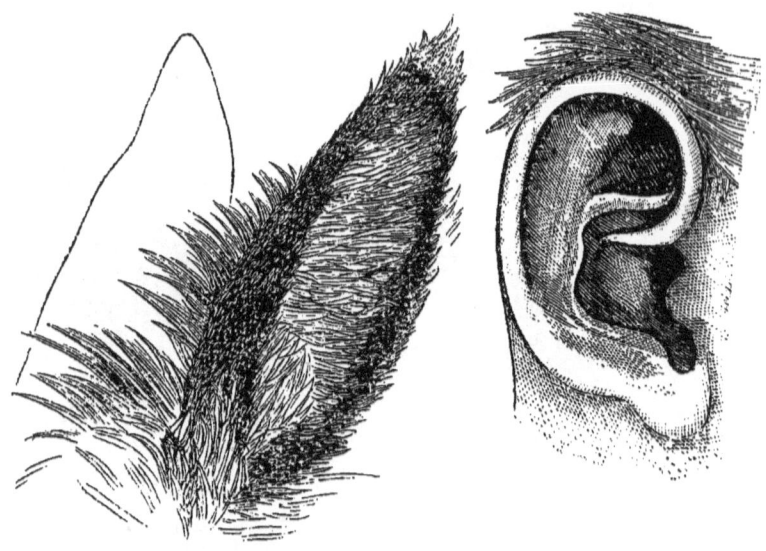

Tonireceptionality small.
The unmusical ear of the ass.

Tonireceptionality large.
The ear of Adeline Patti, formed to receive tones of a round and musical nature.

9. Naturally you love concord and can readily appreciate tone. The least dissonance or jar grates upon your ear. Good music you thoroughly appreciate.

10. The melodies of song-birds have power to arouse your feelings and elevate your aspirations. Hence you are attentive to the voices of animals, as they most wonderfully accentuate and modulate them to express their feelings; and also every tone of the human voice catches your ear and indicates an immense amount of character though you may not see the speaker.

11. In spite of your controlling reason, music quiets or rouses your passions; hence you would like to set your laws, prayers, and lofty aspirations to music as did the ancients.

12. You have the very best musical judgment, hence your criticisms must prove invaluable to the aspiring composer or performer.

A. TO CULTIVATE AND IMPROVE THE POWER OF RECEPTION OF TONE:— Listen most attentively to the soft airy notes of the violin, and allow your soul to enjoy and feast upon good music at least once a day. If favoured with an opportunity listen to the best musicians of the day, such as Jenny Lind, Miss Russell, Tamberlik, Sims Reeves Parepa Rosa, Santley, Cummings, Karl, Canissa, Adeline Patti, and other living and soul-stirring celebrities in the musical world. Attend good musical concerts and there allow your soul to feast to satiety on ineffable sounds until pleasing reveries waft you away to spiritual recollections which charm while they ennoble.

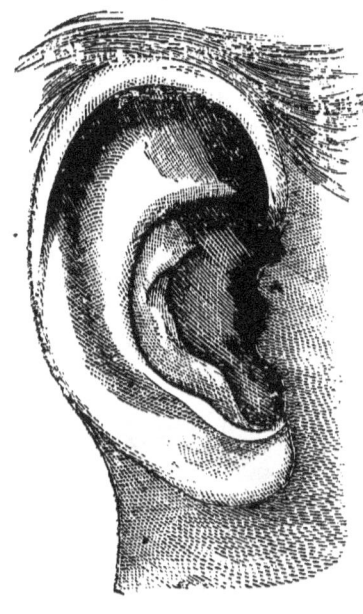
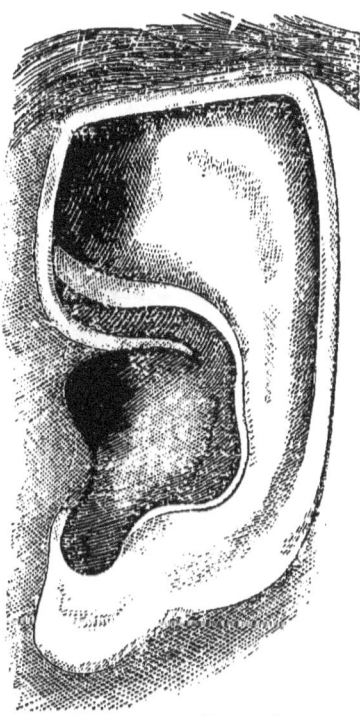

Tonireceptionality large
The ear of Miss Flora S. Johnson, who at the age of five years could learn difficult tunes by once hearing them.

Tonireceptionality small
The ear of a man who was unable to distinguish tunes.

B. To Restrain Receptivity of Tone:—Avoid the soul-stirring strains of Pagannini, Ole Bull, and Jenny Lind; don't sing, but direct your mind into channels of usefulness rather than pleasure; remember that music has become an injurious passion in your nature, and will probably draw you down and debase your passional mind, while it entices you to misbehave.

SECRECY, OR CONCEALATIVENESS.

THE INCLINATION TO HIDE OR WITHHOLD THE KNOWLEDGE OF THINGS OR THOUGHTS—THE INSTINCT NOT TO TELL THE MOUSE THAT THE CAT IS WATCHING UNTIL THE MOUSE IS CAUGHT.

Secretiveness may be known by thin closely compressed lips, hollowed and flexed hands, arched or cat-shaped foot, closing of the eyes, &c. The principle of this faculty is to hold on, its action affects all the flexor muscles of the organization. It may be seen largely developed in the feline species with the round face, and small in the goose or ox-foot. Flat feet are indicative of small secretiveness. Other signs of this faculty there are—such as archness of look, and a peculiar shy and side-long glance of the eyes.

For the principles of secretiveness and those of other faculties, have the goodness to consult my large work on "NATURE'S REVELATIONS OF CHARACTER."

Concealativeness small.
E F. Simms, father of the author of this book.

Concealativeness very large.
Miss Stuart, of Portland, Oregon.

1. Relaxed and communicative, and noisy when excited, you are open-mouthed, and divulge all that you know, and too often appending or interlarding something that nobody knows.

2. Incapable of assuming a fictitious character, being naturally plain, sincere, and straightforward, your distinguishing traits are sincerity, innocence and want of restraint.

3. Naturally a gossip and a quid-nunc, you take delight in hearing and retailing every item of news, and keep nothing in reserve. Wishing

to give full and immediate account of whatever you come to know, yours is the character to make a good reporter or penny-a-liner for the press.

4. Being sincere, plain, and straightforward, and like a Moor; caring little for a secret, you can never successfully aspire to the tact and character of Hannibal, Maximus, or Napoleon.

Concealativeness small.   Concealativeness large.

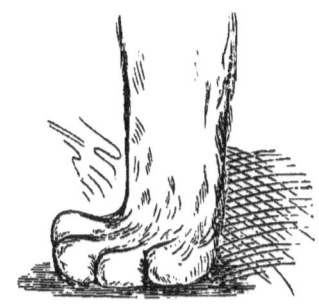   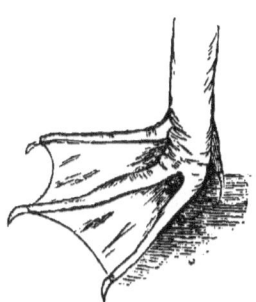

Foot of the Cat.   Foot of the Goose.
Secretiveness large.   Secretiveness small.

5. Your unvarnished and transparent nature is easily penetrated by those of keen perception, as your entire physique and physiognomy are pregnant with meaning.

6. Having a natural love of transparency of character and frankness of deportment, you cannot appreciate those who are secretive and ambiguous.

7. Sometimes you are quite communicative, then rather dark and impenetrable, but evidently full of meaning.

8. The happy balance of this faculty in you will screen many blunders and furnish a bar to close the door of virtue against vice.

9. The principle embodied in the following lines from Shakspeare apply to you:—

> "She never told her love;
> But let concealment like a worm i' th' bud
> Feed on her damask cheek.
> She pined in thought,
> And sat like patience on a monument
> Smiling at grief."

10 Your power of keeping a secret is so well known to your friends that no one doubts it; and they well know also that you have a good share of policy, but dislike to betray a friend.

11. Possessing a strong power of concealment, it is difficult to fathom you, as you would not commit yourself, while you like to look into the hearts of those you meet, but still prevent them from peering into yours. You need not be astonished if some fear to trust you because they cannot understand you.

12. Your ruling passion being deceit, you try to disguise your real sentiments and purposes by dissimulation; you have abundance of tact and sly, stealthy, deceitful intriguing; crooked in policy, you are disposed to mislead; in these respects you strongly resemble, in character of mind, Louis XI. of France; Henry VII. of England; Ferdinand V. of Spain; and Cardinal Talleyrand.

A. To Cultivate Secretiveness:—Don't carry your heart in your hand; talk and laugh low; keep your thoughts to yourself; be politic; take heed to the words of the poet: "How little do they know what is, who frame their hasty judgment upon that which seems;" hear attentively what Lavater says: "Trust not him with your secrets who, when left alone in your room, turns over your papers;" and finally when you lock a secret in your own breast, be sure you conceal the key from every one.

B. To Restrain Secretiveness:—Appear only what you are; never equivocate; constantly blab out what you know; never mislead others; and in whatever you say or do, be sincere. Lay to heart Lavater's words: "The more honesty a man has the less he affects the air of a saint. The affectation of sanctity is a blotch on the face of piety."

ECONOMY, OR ECONOMOSITY.
THE FACULTY OF ECONOMICAL MANAGEMENT.

The broad, square, full face, like Franklin's, is the physiognomical premonstration of economy.

1. Being open-hearted and generous to a fault, your purse is ever open, and as you handle it unsparingly its supply is liable to be exhausted.

2. Disposed to spend your means freely, princely and munificent company and bounteous living would accord well with your tastes. Prodigality and profuseness mark your course of life.

3. Being quite too free and unsparing of the substance of this world, you are compelled to live from hand to mouth, and are negligent with regard to future needs.

4. Without avariciousness or parsimony you are nevertheless fairly careful of your means.

5. You may try to retain what you get, yet you are not specially marked in this respect.

6. Prodigality or stinginess seem to you alike unnecessary, as you neither covet nor squander; nor will you waste foolishly or grudge your necessary outlay.

7. Being saving but not miserly, you will evince fair ability in planning, scheming, or forecasting in regard to business, money, or the necessaries of life; and you will endeavour to store up sufficient to meet your coming wants.

8. Chary of your money, you try to retain what you get, but can use it in some necessary or thrifty investment.

9. Being frugal and economical with your income retrenchment will likely protect you from want.

10. Naturally you dislike to see things going to waste, and it is long since you practically learned the maxim: "A penny saved is worth two earned."

11. Saving and careful in your expenses, you keep quite well, gather up the fragments, and you don't forget to take care of the scraps.

12. You are a valuable member in a family as nothing can escape your notice as to every scrap of anything useable being carefully put to the most economic purpose, besides being keenly aware as to what things can be used to the best advantage.

A. To CULTIVATE ECONOMY:—Become more "close-fisted;" save the driblets; practise systematic frugality; and never allow your generosity or magnanimity to run away with your purse.

B. To RESTRAIN FRUGAL PROPENSITIES:—Learn that liberality in doing good has made many a one reputable and while so doing has raised that soul to sublime greatness; only think that by holding a sixpence sufficiently near the eye you can hide a shilling a little further away, and perchance the pound; share with others; be generous as well as just; and imitate Shakspeare's character:—

> "For his bounty
> There was no winter in't; an autumn 'twas
> That grew the more by reaping."

JUDGMENT OF CURVATURE, OR CURVATIVENESS.

THE CAPACITY OF BEING ABLE TO APPRECIATE AND JUDGE OF THE BEAUTIES AND QUALITIES OF CURVES.

Relative width between the eyes, rounding face, limbs, ears nose and head, are indications of the faculty of curvature.

Curvativeness large.
Miss Harriet C. Hosmer, the famous sculptress.

Curvativeness small.
Ji n, a Piute Indian of Utah Ter.

Curvativeness large.

Curvativeness small.

1. Being extremely deficient in your appreciation of the line of beauty, you have much difficulty in remembering in detail the aspects and picturesque appearances of the beautiful and ever-changing views, vistas, and elevations of shrubs, trees, rocks, hillocks, bogs, and lakes ; they fail to leave upon you any due impression of their wavy outline and general undulating peace-inspiring beauty.

2. As a guide you should scarcely be trusted as you are apt to forget the animals you once petted, and look into the face of old acquaintances as if you had never seen them before

3. Your memory of faces is not retentive; and it is quite possible that old acquaintances and even friends may pass you without your recognition.

4. Scarcely noticing outlines for any practical purpose, you need not attempt drawing, and it is scarcely probable that you can even spell.

5. Having a slight weakness in appreciating the beauty of curves makes you rather incline to admire objects with straight outlines and smooth flat sides

6 Though beautiful and well defined outlines afford you much pleasure, you would, nevertheless, fail in representing them, not being strong in curvature.

7. You are well adjusted in the degree in which you possess this faculty.

8. In recollecting faces, you possess ordinary ability, and in viewing a landscape the objects of interest are well impressed upon your mind.

9. Discerning and recollecting the outlines of objects with ordinary ability, you can find your course without difficulty after having once explored the route.

10. Such is your talent for recollecting forms that you will scarcely ever forget the face you have once seen. In this respect, you resemble George III. of England, Lafayette, and old Hayes, a New York detective, who were all celebrated for their inability to forget the face or form

11. Having a wonderful eye for a curve or circle, you can, from memory even, draw them accurately, and can recollect all the bends, curves, and irregular lines of paths, rivers, and roads you have found in your rambles or travels.

12. You would pre-eminently excel as an artist since you can never forget a feature, route, object, or face you have once seen. The features and physique of any one on whom your eye rests for a moment are fixed in your mind with the accuracy of the photographer's camera.

A. To CULTIVATE AND INTENSIFY THE APPRECIATION OF CURVATURE:—Accurately and carefully observe the outline of every object that comes within your notice; outline in pencil or etch any object or face you consider remarkable; and practice stenographic writing. This organ was very large in Cuvier, and Thomas Allen, and is usually large in portrait and landscape painters, such as Sir Joshua Reynolds, Sir Wm. Allen, Belisario Corenzio, Angelico, Peter de Laer, Louis Lagurrie, Theodore van Thulden, Leonardo da Vinci, Francisco Zurbaran, Allesandro Allori, Bernadetto Lutti, George Morland, Michael Angelo, Raphael, Titian, Hudson, and Van Dyck. The last was the most eminent of all portrait painters in modern times "His pencil speaks the tongue of every land."—*Dryden.*

B. To Restrain the Love and Appreciation of Curvature :—
Refrain from drawing, sculpturing, or modelling, and from tracing patterns; do not visit galleries or study animals in which the curve of beauty abounds; study inorganic matter more and organic bodies less; work at some mechanical trade and thus free yourself from an inordinate passion for the plastic arts.

DESIRE OF POSSESSION, OR ACCUMULATIVENESS.

THE INTUITIVE TENDENCY OR DISPOSITION TO ACQUIRE.

Whenever the face is rather broad in the centre and rather long with a prominent nose, the individual will have the capacity, if well used, to accumulate.

Accumulativeness large.
Commodore Vanderbilt.

Accumulativeness small.
A squanderer.

1. Lacking enterprise, industry, and thrift, you possess a poor and weak capacity for business.
2. Caring little for money and being a very indifferent financier, you need not expect ever to become wealthy, as you possess very poor abilities for business
3. So easily are you thwarted in your efforts to accumulate, that it seems to you to require an immense amount of labour to gain riches, yet you may gather much information and valuable ideas.
4 Wanting in readiness to perceive opportunities for speculation and good investment, you are not very prudent in collecting riches; hence

naturally enough you often wonder how it is that such men as the Rothschilds, Astor, Peabody, Dillon. Morrison, and Stewart have been able to amass such enormous fortunes.

5. Being rather of an easy-going nature, worldly desires neither prey upon your vitals nor conquer them; hence the strivings of your life will neither disturb your neighbours nor much discommode yourself.

6. Not being excessively anxious about anything, you manifest no great anxiety about what you have, and still less about what you may possess.

7. Though you are not the best at acquiring or procuring, yet you closely calculate the chances as to whether your speculations shall prove a losing or a winning game.

8. Though you are liberal in expenditure, you have a desire to accumulate more than you spend, so that you may have a good balance on the right side at the end of the year.

9. Because you accumulate property easily you have a disposition to spend it freely, if not lavishly, still you have a laudable desire of gain and generally have abundance.

10. The fundamental idea with you in devising all your plans, is, will they prove profitable and advantageous; hence profits and credit are always resulting from your speculations.

11. Your anxiety to acquire wealth renders you keen and acute in all your dealings and transactions; and your motto is: Let me make money, honestly.

12. Mammon is your god, and you can worship the 'golden calf.' Had you an eligible offer, you would not hesitate to barter your soul for filthy lucre, but so worthless is it that the purchaser, if you obtain one, must be a dupe or too flush of cash.

A. To CULTIVATE THE PROPENSITY TO ACCUMULATE:—Hold fast what you have got; invest your means where it will while safe return the best interest; be industrious and frugal; garner the littles and earn all you can, remembering the Scotch proverb: "Many littles make a muckle;" never let the grand idea slip—determine to get rich; launch boldly into well-planned speculations; take counsel of those only who have made financial life a success; engage in any active industry for which you are adapted after having ascertained this by a scientific examination of your abilities Industry and perseverance will accomplish almost anything. Ben Johnson's plan was not amiss: "When I take the humour of a thing once, I am like your tailor's needle, I go through."

B. To RESTRAIN THE DESIRE FOR ACCUMULATING:—Do not allow your whole soul to become enclosed within the circumference of a penny; live for a high and noble purpose; and reflect that your riches cannot be carried into another state of existence; consider that gold is to the soul what sand is to the balloon—the less of either in each case, respectively, the more speedily will each ascend.

MONOGAMOUS LOVE, OR MONOEROTICITY.

THE DISPOSITION TO LOVE ONE ONLY.

The dove or round shape of the eye openings is the most unexceptionable evidence of large mating love.

Monoeroticity large.
Mrs Margaret Fuller Osoli, whose connubial love was so strong that she preferred to drown rather than to leave her husband.

Monoeroticity small.
Brigham Young, the noted polygamist,

Monoeroticity small.
Hog.

Monoeroticity large.
Turtle Dove.

1. Being thoroughly averse to marriage and loving and living with one for life, you can love one person as well and yet no better than another.

Had you a perfectly pure angelic mate, so far as faithfulness is concerned, it would be impossible for you to remain true as a conjugal partner.

2. Nearly quite destitute of conjugal affection, you prize little the tokens and pledges of early years; and you are not likely to prove faithful to a companion for life.

3. Marriage would prove to you a species of pseudo-slavery; but single blessedness would well accord with your weak connubial love.

4. Unique regard and esteem is weaker in your constitution than promiscuous affection, and hence you fail to appreciate monogamic relations.

5. Though hesitating and tardy about entering the state of wedlock, you would, if married, endeavour to be conservative, and try to live in harmony.

6. Not being strongly characterised in this respect education and circumstances will best denote your affectional path rather than natural organization.

7. The tender fancies of your love-passion will picture many fair forms with angelic charms in fleshly bodies.

8. Feeling that wedded life is the natural and normal condition of mature men and women. you have a high esteem for the charming selected object of your affections.

9. Naturally considering marriage as something heavenly, to love and be loved in return would afford your devoted character unalloyed happiness.

10. Naturally you evince devoted attachment to one of the opposite sex but it may be feared, that, in so ardent and affectionate a nature as yours, the love-visions of childhood, so beautifully wrought up in your fancy, may fail of realization in years of maturity, unless you mate with a spirit perfectly congenial.

11. Naturally constituted like Heloise in her unity of personal affection for Abelard, the entire and exclusive devotion of one, who would live faithful in wedlock, would confer lasting happiness on your heart.

12. A disappointment in love would prove to you worse than death; so wonderfully faithful is your love that it would cause you to treat a nuptial partner with pre eminent kindness and devotion,—so thoroughly monogamic is your manifestation of love.

A. To CULTIVATE AND FOSTER MATING LOVE:—Cherish earnestly all those tender, warm, and loving emotions that are generated in early life; forget not a single vow; trust and feel trusted; live faithfully; never turn coldly away from those who love you tenderly; reflect that their hearts bleed as yours may also some day; but of all things, let your love be *inviolable* Never forget that wedlock is the key to progressive civilization the fundamental support of morality, the safeguard against disease, and the only safe and sole course to social happiness.

B. To RESTRAIN MATING LOVE:—Don't imagine that all nature speaks to you of the *one you love;* speak out unreservedly all your sympathetic loving feelings; never pardon any infidelity, however small; dispel loving memories of the past; instead of novels, read books of science, study the imperfections of those you love; be cautious about entering into marriage relations, and bear in mind the following lines, the truthfulness of which many worthy people have learned to their disadvantage:—"Hasty *marriages* cannot be expected to produce happiness; young people who are eager for *matrimony* before they are fully aware of its consequences will purchase their experience at the expense of their peace."—*Crabb.* Visit amusements and fashionable places of resort and learn from experience what Dr Johnson long ago observed: "The men who would make good husbands if they visit public places, are frighted at wedlock, and resolve to live single."

WILL, OR VOLUNTATIVENESS.
HAVING STRENGTH OF WILL AND POWER TO EXECUTE IT.

The ability of exercising the will or of forming a purpose may be known by the fulness of the posterior part of the neck, near the point of junction with the head. The neck of George III. of England indicated the strength of will for which he became notorious, and was the primary cause of the freedom of North America.

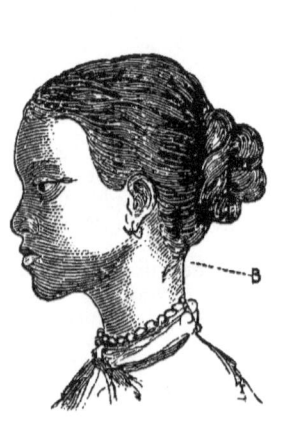

Voluntativeness small. Chinese woman, who is subjected to the will of her purchaser.

Voluntativeness large. Geo. III.

1. Vacillating and unreliable, shrinking from responsible positions, knowing your inability to fulfil the duties, you are as unsteady as the wind.

2. Like the vane on the spire you veer and turn with every whiff.

3. The principle or project you propound or entertain to-day you abjure and abandon to-morrow.

4. If severely tried you flinch and swerve, skipping from one side to another, being in every circumstance of life changeable and versatile.

5. Ofttimes you imagine things are fated, and that mankind are controlled by the necessities of life.

6. Though you cannot be denominated an extremist in doing as you please, your intentions are well founded.

7. To whatever is irrevocable, you will submit, though you dislike to be under the necessity of acting contrary to your wishes.

8. The spontaneousness of your mind is remarkable, and you would overcome strenuous opposition if it stood in your pathway.

9. Whether pleasing to others or not, you try to accomplish what you choose, feeling a real pleasure in exercising your own discretion.

10. Your volition is very strong; others cannot easily control you, so much do you dislike to bend to circumstances.

11. Will do as you like if it is possible.

12 Your will has never been conquered by any one, hence your intensely wilful and extremely disagreeable manners and overbearing disposition.

A. TO CULTIVATE AND ACCELERATE THE POWER OF THE WILL:— Never change your political opinions without a reason worthy of the change; be positive and self-opinionated; believe in free agency and advocate it strenuously, cease to counsel others, and be yourself in every act and thought.

B. TO RETARD OR RESTRAIN THE WILL:—Cast off your fanaticism; be less zealous and dogmatic; become more tractable and facile; should you be in error, your wilfulness becomes ridiculous. This faculty when excessive, though the most god-like in our nature, causes the possessor to be disagreeable to others. Hence try to become pliant and yielding, and avoid being stigmatised as a stickler.

MERRINESS.
THE QUALITY OF BEING GAY AND LAUGHING.

Wrinkles obliquely outwards and downwards from the eyes, open lips, and a round large forehead are evidences of large merriness. Mirth also gives an expression of half-smile and funny look and an arch and knowing expression of countenance.

1. Admirable counterpart of your antetypes—Charles I. of England and Blackhawk, who never laughed in the latter part of their lives—you are mirthless and you seem to think it almost a sin to laugh. You renitent mirthful emotions.

2. Utterlessly careless of amusement, and seemingly devoid of social merriment, not to mention mirth you seem to have lost your intended, or at least your best friend, so rueful is your visage and loose your gait.

3. As flat and dull you seem, as if the last sentence of the law was pronounced against you, and you were hopeless of reprieve.

4. Powerless in exciting or arousing sportive glee, rather slow in catching the point of a joke, you are sober and earnest, awfully fond of plain assertion.

5. Being more able to appreciate than to originate a jolly association, you are simply jocose and sympathize heartily with merry-makers. You vote "The cheerful man's a king," with Bickerstaff, and admire him.

6. Though not exceedingly jocular yourself, still, "when merry feelings abound, and the laugh goes round," you will then heartily join in the fun.

7. The company in which the high excitement of pleasurable feeling abounds you really enjoy occasionally. With Judge Haliburton, you quite coincide :—as "God has made sunny spots in the heart, why should we exclude the light from them?"

8. Possessing the power to be perfectly sober and restrained, yet you are rather fond of jollity at times. You like Milton's idea of

> "Jest and youthful jollity,
> Quips and cranks and wanton wiles,
> Nods and becks and wreathed smiles.

9. Nature, the good old dame, has considered you one of her pets by placing in your composition so large a share of the ability to relish hilarity, mirth, and gladness. Lord Byron's opinion was that yours was the greatest talent when he said that "the greatest talent was that of appreciation."

Merriness large.
Thomas C. Haliburton, "Sam Slick," humorous writer of Nova Scotia.

Merriness small.
Charles I, who never laughed after he became king. Beheaded 1649.

10. Your jolly and gleesome face would evince an unusual love of festivity and a mirthful nature. Perhaps you sympathize with Byron when he sings :—

> "O mirth and innocence! O milk and water!
> Ye happy mixtures of more happy days!
> In these sad centuries of sin and slaughter,
> Abominable man no more allays
> His thirst with such pure beverage No matter,
> I love you both, and both shall have my praise."

11. The mirthful element largely abounds in your character. Rare Ben Johnson and you should have made acquaintance. You know he says :—

> "When many a merry tale and many a song
> Cheered the rough road, we wished the rough road long.
> The rough road then, returning in a round,
> Blocked our enchanted steps, for all was fairy ground."

12. Almost incessantly laughing, you are noisy and overflowing with gaiety and jollity. Fun and frolic you enjoy to the utmost extent. Dryden has photographed you well when he said :—

> "Our mirth should be the quintessence of pleasure,
> And our delight flow with that harmony,
> Th' ambitious spheres shall to the centre shrink,
> To hear our music; such ravishing accents
> As are from poets in their fury hurled,
> When their outrageous raptures filled the world."

Also think of what the comic Garrick says :—"Fun gives you a forcible hug and shakes laughter out of you, whether you will or no." But the immortal Shakspeare has caught you best when he says:—"From the crown of his head to the sole of his foot he is all mirth; he hath twice or thrice cut Cupid's bowstring, and the little hangman dare not shoot at him: he hath a heart as sound as a bell, and his tongue is the clapper; for, what his heart thinks his tongue speaks."

A. To Cultivate the Talent and Appreciation of Mirth:—Cast off your dignity and haughty manner; read books from laughing authors; at all you hear and read that is witty or funny, laugh; let your long melancholy face extend in breadth by your hearty grin, even if you cannot laugh; but of all things call to mind that you are the only animal that can laugh, then cultivate the hilarious faculty as one of the highest qualities of human nature. But remember what Lavater says :— "He who always prefaces his tale with laughter, is poisoned between impertinence and folly." Also the same penetrating author says:—"The horse-laugh indicates brutality of character." "Smiles from reason flow, to brutes denied, and are of love the food."—*Milton.* Then again Carlyle says: -"How much lies in laughter; the cipher-key, wherewith we decipher the whole man! Some men wear an everlasting barren simper; in the smile of others lies the cold glitter as of ice; the fewest are able to laugh what can be called laughing, but only sniff and titter and snuggle from the throat outwards, or at least produce some whiffy, husky cachinnation, as if they were laughing through wool: of none such comes good."

B. To Restrain the Talent and Appreciation of Mirth:—Cease from that perpetual giggling and laughing at every trifle, especially as it often lowers you in the estimation of more grave characters; read metaphysical works and especially those of earnest reasoners, and enter fully into their spirit; choose sober, staid, and dignified companions; avoid places of amusement and rather visit houses of mourning; be serious and sedate, and pass your life in an honest and earnest manner. Carlyle says:—"Earnestness alone makes life eternity." And Dickens puts it thus:—"There is no substitute for thorough-going, ardent, and sincere earnestness."

PROVIDENTNESS.

THE DISPOSITION TO FORESEE WANTS AND MAKE PROVISION TO SUPPLY THEM.

Wide hips and full muscles are the distinctive signs of a provident person. When this characteristic is excessively large it is accompanied with protrusion of the lower part of the face.

Providentness large.
Miss Margaret Clephne, of Edinburgh, who is said to be very miserly.

1. Utterly improvident in your nature, you evince no timely readiness to provide for yourself or friends; and equally defective are you in pre-

paring for future exigencies. Hence you must always lead a hand-to-mouth existence. Reference was made to your character when one of old wrote: "He who will not provide for his household is worse than an infidel."

2. No wise precaution in preparing for the future will ever break in upon your meditations.

3. No measures of a precautionary nature are ever taken by you to counteract an evil, not even to provide against the inclemency of the weather.

4. Such is your nature that you always feel disposed to take things easy. Like Dickens's Mr Micawber, you quietly "wait for something to turn up." When an emergency occurs, then comes the hurry-scurry — nothing ready.

5. If you do provide yourself with more than one coat or dress, it arises from your education, not your nature.

6. Though you are not neglectful of the due needs of humanity, your time will not be largely occupied in superintendence and guidance of the matters and concerns of life.

7. Your wisdom duly guides you in husbanding and directing your forces and resources in suchwise as to insure a happy result.

8. Every act of yours indicates a provident nature which prompts you to anticipate and provide for the needs as well as the pleasures of humanity.

9. An instinctive quality of your nature prompts you to anticipate and provide against emergencies. Were you a builder or an educator you would bestow special care in the laying a good solid foundation of either the material or the mental structure.

10. Your provident disposition will be manifest under all circumstances in the ability with which you manage and control every varied event in the drama of your life.

11. The prudence you display on all occasions is worthy of the consideration of a knight or the smiles of a lord or a lady fair.

12. The wonderful foresight and forethought evinced, in all your preparations being so perfect, renders it apparent that sound judgment presides over and directs all the transactions of your life.

A. To Strengthen Providentness:—Bend every power to its utmost to use precaution in preparing necessary supplies; forecast everything; furnish food, clothing and thought necessary for yourself and others dependent upon your endeavours; choose your associates from among the provident; shun the company of those who live from hand to mouth; put no trust in that fickle dame, "Luck;" but give prudent attention to the management of all your concerns, and be attentively provident. Lay well to heart what *Johnson* so well says:—"The great end of providence is to give cheerfulness to those hours which splendour cannot gild, and acclamation cannot exhilarate." Nothing in life will supply the want of this virtue; negligence and irregularity, long continued, will make knowledge useless, wit ridiculous, and genius contemptible.

B. To Restrain Providentness:—Jump at conclusions; trust to Mrs Fortune for food, clothing and home; this will enable you to become intimately acquainted with her charming daughter, Misfortune; laugh when it rains; be solemn during prosperity, but indifferent when showers of trouble come and drench every shred of your tattered affections; learn and maintain identity of character, unshaken by circumstances; never lay by means, or calculate for future wants; fall into the arms of ease, and with indifference float down life's stream in the frail barque of chance, whethersoever it drifteth thee; sleep much, eat freely, and live only for to day; and in time the desired end will be accomplished just as you and your rudderless craft are hopelessly stranded on the shores of desolation.

CONTRARINESS, OR CONTRATIVENESS.

THIS QUALITY, OR FACULTY, IN HUMAN BEINGS. IS THAT WHICH GIVES THE DISPOSITION TO ASSUME THE OPPOSITE, AND IN ANIMALS, TO ACT CONTRARY TO THE WISHES OF INDIVIDUALS, EITHER MEN OR ANIMALS.

The capacity of CONTRATIVENESS *exhibits its indices by width through the face, at the angle of the jaws. It is large in the hog and the Hottentot.*

Contrativeness very large
Napoleon I., copied from a mask taken from his head after death.

1. Being almost totally destitute of this faculty, you will fail to manifest the action of its influence, and will consequently be swept along by the will of others.

2. To be of the same mind, and to act in concert with others, is far more pleasurable and congenial to your concurrent nature than to counteract, contravene, or engage in retroaction.

3. The secret inclination of your mind is to oblige by doing what will please others; hence, you are often ancillary and coadjutant to the aims and enterprises of others.

4. Naturally delighting in promoting the will and wishes of others, you will never be found contradictory or denyant in your character.

5. Being neither oppugnant nor antagonistic in your natural inclinations, you will not be disposed to act contrariwise to the wishes of others.

6. Though you might take some pleasure in inverse ratio, if accustomed to practise in that rule, yet you would never become contrary or contradictory, unless irritatingly provoked to oppugnation.

7. Being very well balanced in this faculty, you are pleased with the medium between the extremes of concurrence and antagonism.

8. At times you are liable to become antagonistic, contrary, and cohibitive, though you do not intend to interfere with, or run counter to any good or moral enterprise

9. Interclusion and interception give you some delight; but, it is more pleasing to one of your disposition to give than receive, being strongly inclined to contravention

10. So large a degree of contrativeness do you possess, that you feel it to be a delightful task to disconcert and interclude the designs of others.

11. Such antithesity and contradictoriness is so congenial to your inmost nature, that you are inclined to go the contrary and opposite way to that desired by others, or which they wish you to go. You even take pleasure in hindering and incommoding others; but, to drive you, it is impossible.

12. Hog-like, you are ever endeavouring to turn aside and contravene the endeavours which others may put forth to urge you along the various paths and channels of customary life. You will feel real pleasure in doing the very opposite of what others desire.

A. To CULTIVATE ANTITHETICALITY OR CONTRATIVENESS:—Study what would be opposed to every wish of others; and bend every power to do that which you know is most opposite to the desires or designs of others; be cross grained, contrary, and antagonistic to the whole world in every project; eat pork, and associate with those who are contradictory towards others; read the life of Napoleon I. and imitate him in the possible peculiarities of his character; never accept the advice of any one, except he be a captious or capricious person. In a word: Choose that which is diametrically opposite to what others wish you to have or accomplish, on every occasion; and, at last, you may need only the quills to bear, with becoming appropriateness, the name of the porcupine, or belong to the genus *sus*.

B. To RESTRAIN CONTRATIVENESS OR ANTITHETICALITY:—On all occasions, do as others wish you to do; coalesce with others in their thoughts and the manner of exerting your will; allow no discordant, adverse or perverse thoughts to allure you into being contrary to others. Avoid pork, whisky, and the company of those who are always opposing you; live to a high and noble purpose, and ever be coalescent.

POLYGAMOUS LOVE, OR POLYEROTICITY.

THE DISPOSITION TO LOVE MANY.

The amount of love for the opposite sex may be known by the fulness of the eyes, and its quality by the shape of the commissures or opening between the lids of the eyes. When the opening is quite almond shaped, promiscuous love prevails in that form; if the commissure has great vertical measurement, the love is connubial.

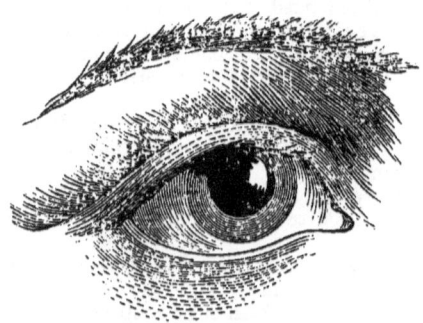

Polyeroticity small.
Eye of Mrs Margaret F. Osoli.

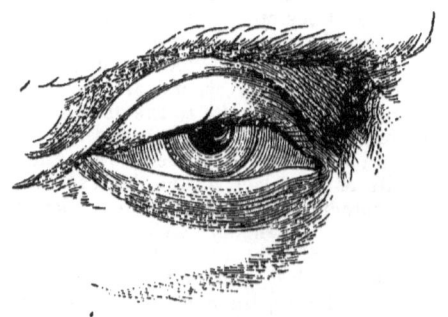

Polyerot'city large.
Eye of Brigham Young, taken from life at Salt Lake.

1. The feebleness of your organism would cause disrelish for matrimony

2. Your devotion towards the opposite sex is not very ardent.

3 Your indifference towards the opposite sex will fail of winning for you many ardent lovers.

4. So small is the amount of the erotic and uxorious in your constitution that it will never draw you beyond the promptings of your prudent judgment.

5. Though naturally fond of being caressed by one you admire, you may lead a chaste life as long as no undue temptation is thrown in your way.

6. While free from extremes in this respect, you possess in a happy degree the genial share of attraction which Plato defines as "An interposition of the gods, in behalf of young people."

7. Though you are rather fascinating, yet you have well under control your love-nature.

8. Those full, moist, and liquid-moving eyes, in you, bespeak an excellent degree of desire to love and to feel it reciprocated.

9. The strong passion in you to love and be loved is consuming your vital stamina

10. Your feelings are intensely active, and none know so well as yourself your temptations.

11. Your natural propensities would subject you to strong temptation, against which nothing can so safely guard you as a sound judgment.

12. Many and varied will be the amours of your intensely ardent life. Such is your indiscriminating propensities that you can love any one of the opposite sex as well as another, your amatorial passion being almost uncontrollable. In this respect you resemble Brigham Young. Your love-nature tends to render you thoroughly polygamous. Were your full round form, with its immense powers of generation, and having such an abundant surplus of life, subdued by being directed into intellectual channels by close study, writing, and speaking, it would astonish the world by rendering immeasurable service to humanity.

A. To CULTIVATE PROMISCUOUS LOVE:—Study the excellences of the opposite sex and ignore their faults; feel, say and play the agreeable by studied complimentary politeness; try to charm; return love for hatred; live on generous diet; associate much with those of the opposite sex who are warm, ardent and voluptuous.

B. To RESTRAIN PROMISCUOUS LOVE:—Fortunately for the continuance of our species, the world in general needs more restraint in this propensity than culture: hence the following suggestions should be carefully conned over. Love and admire mind more than body; shun vulgarity as you would the Bohun Upas; avoid familiarities; partake not of heating food or drink; cultivate the intellect rather than the affections; associate with those of high moral and intellectual character and tastes; spend your time in study and writing; never associate with questionable characters of the opposite sex, but should unforeseen circumstances throw you into the society of such persons make an excuse to be rid of them at the earliest moment; avoid the reading of novels and other books that tend to excite the passions and appeal to the propensities rather than the intellect. Bathe every morning in cold water; live on fruit and vegetables; and finally avoid and shun every temptation to animal gratification. Treat every person of the opposite sex with that delicacy and respect that Alexander the Great manifested towards Statira the queen of Darius the Third, King of Persia, when she was a prisoner of war in the camp of the Macedonian King.

MEMORY OF NAMES, OR MNEMONICNOMINALITY.

THE MNEMONIC POWER OF RECOLLECTING NAMES.

Memory of names manifests itself by a forehead full in the centre, from the nose to the hair, and a pair of lips full and flexible.

Mnemonicnominality small.
A Kyast Banian woman of Surat, in India.

Mnemonicnominality large.
John Reinhold Foster, the eminent naturalist, botanist, linguist, and traveller who accompanied Capt. Cook round the world.

1. Your memory of names is very faulty. Almost the moment you hear them, they are forgotten, whether personal or geographical; even common names can hardly be retained by you.

2 It may often be matter of surprise, even to yourself, that you have not forgotten your own name.

3. From a great vacuity of mind, you are almost always at a loss when you attempt to mention names and it requires a few moments of meditative and associative thought to relieve your painful and awkward embarrassment in your desire to recall the name; then still worse, when the name won't come, you have likely forgot the connection in which you were about to use it. At last, in sheer despair and annoyance, you say well, well, I'll remember it by-and by. Then in the midst of some totally different subject, you suddenly burst in with, "Oh, I have it now."

4. Names readily vanish from your memory, and you are painfully and inconveniently forgetful of unusual or, as they are sometimes called, hard words, or Latinised and foreign words or phrases. Hence being very deficient in verbal memory you can never be depended upon for a verbatim repetition, either of what you learn or have heard.

5. Being rather forgetful of names, words, sentences, phrases as general names are of little moment to you, since you think more of the subject or object than its designative appellation.

6. Being contented by obtaining an idea of a subject or object, even should the name not be mentioned; you will sometimes apply a wrong name to a person or object without perceiving the mistake.

7. As your tendency is to refer to persons, places, scenes, and things rather by description than by name, you may often think as Shakspeare expresses himself in the succeeding couplet :—

> "What's in a name? That which we call a rose,
> By any other name would smell as sweet."

8. You like a beautiful phrase or a smooth sounding name, and your retention of words and set phrases is in excellent proportion but not extreme.

9. Your memory of names being fair, you may by cultivation render it good. On seeing anything you have much ease in applying to it the proper designation.

10. Association most readily reminds you of the name of any thing or person.

11. With definite accuracy the names of persons and objects are remembered by you. In this respect your talent is remarkable. The mention of some names affect you as portrayed in the following lines :—

> "Yet who has not felt the strong power of a word
> The magic that thrills us when some names are heard."

12. Unsurpassed in your ability and readiness in recalling names of all kinds, when a name is once accurately heard and understood, it becomes so indelibly stamped on your mind that it springs forth at the instant it is needed.

A. To CULTIVATE AND STRENGTHEN NOMINAL MEMORY:—Write every name you hear and when you hear it; repeat frequently every name just after hearing it; tax yourself with several Latin nouns and search out their meaning ; refresh your memory by a mental recapitulation of all the names, difficult words, and terms you can recall; associate a name as soon as heard with a similar name which is more familiar to you; study the Dictionary and Thesaurus of words and phrases by Roget, when writing, study a supervapid and unlaboured style of expression ; read authors distinguished for their easy flowing language and freedom from parenthesis and circumlocution, such are the writings of Irving, Macaulay, and Ruskin. Among poets may be mentioned Pope, Scott, Byron, and Longfellow.

B. TO RESTRAIN OR WEAKEN MEMORY OF NAMES :—This is unnecessary in any one, except an insane person. In this sad exception it may be mentioned that sleep, quietude, and plain living would afford assistance as a curative remedy.

PERCEPTION OF COLORS, OR CHROMATICALNESS.

THE INNATE QUALITY THAT CLEARLY PERCEIVES AND JUDGES TINTS, HUES, AND COLOURS.

A pale or milk colour of eyes and a livid white hue to the skin indicate a poor judge of colour. When we find all the bones of the nose and lower part of the forehead very prominent relatively, as compared with the other portions of the face, the person with such features can readily judge COLOUR. *But, should the centre of the eyebrows be narrow and sunken backwards, the person will be partially, if not entirely, colour-blind. Chromato-p eudopts are quite common, as the late Dr George Wilson of Edinburgh, while investigating the subject, discovered. Out of 1154 persons, whom he examined, he found that there were over five per cent., who were idiopts, or colour-blind.*

Chromaticalness small.
Wm. Ross, emp'oyed in Chambers's Publishing House in Edinburgh. He is a Chromo-pseudop, or colour-blind.

Chromaticalness large
Antonio Allegri, or Corregio, the most distinguished colourist among Italian artists.

1. Being colour-blind, black and scarlet are to you alike, so also is blue and pink; the sky, violet, and indigo, seem to you as colours identical.

2. At times you mistake blue for green; pink for dark blue; and as to stains, you have no eye to see them unless they are strongly contrasted with the ground colour on which they appear.

3. Being exceedingly weak in the recognition of colours you scarcely notice their shades and blendings sufficiently to remember them; hence you manifest no interest in shades of colour, paintings, and flowers. The statuesque beauty is as fascinating to you as the loveliest fresh blushing belle or flower of the season.

4. The primitive colours you perhaps can discern and appreciate, but you cannot perceive the nicer and more delicate harmonies of shade, hue, and intensity that thrill the artist, and give vividness to his " work immortal."

5. Incapable of appreciating the beauteous work of the mighty and potent artist, Nature, you can unconsciously pass over the country without observing the delicate hues and shadows and ever changing beauties passing over the outspread landscape.

6. Being moderate in your appreciation of bright colours, and not particularly enamoured of the "loud" and brilliant shades, you nevertheless like to let your eye rest on the soft, subdued, and delicate tints that soothe and soften the feelings of the beholder.

7. Being naturally indifferent as to nicety of hues, and scarcely observant of them when haziness affects the atmosphere, still you seem aroused to feel much interest in them when the brilliant light of the sun intensifies your appreciation.

8. Though not a Raphael, still, by persevering practice, you may become a proficient in your judgment of colouring, and in the delicate management of the commingling of shades.

9. Having the rare faculty of being able to distinguish the prismatic colours of the rainbow, you delight to see and thoroughly enjoy fine paintings; the complexion of every one you meet produces its effect upon you; in fact you intensely enjoy the beautiful shading and colouring in every coloured object that presents itself to you.

10. You might have been, or might become, a modern Corregio, so much ability you have for the science of chromatics. The irridescent blush of everything in nature or art you closely scrutinise; and clashing contrasts of two opposite colours offend your eye.

11. With true appreciation you observe all the hues attending the rising and setting of the sun; you appreciate the magnificently blending colours; as a painter you would delight in soft delicate tints Autumn brown, half-lights, and long yellow lancing rays, which spread their blended mantle over ravine and mountain, your fine artistic instinct realizes with a zest seldom felt by mortals.

12. Being almost a monomaniac on hues, the very finest and most delicate tints and shades pain you if they are not harmoniously blended.

A. To CULTIVATE THE APPRECIATION OF COLOUR:—Closely observe the finest tints in paintings as well as the beauteous blendings of colour throughout nature's vast flower-garden; closely attend to the golden and silver pencilling of light in the rich and glorious sunrise and sunset; visit the wondrous treasures of fine paintings in the European galleries and America; study their shades, and try to appreciate their harmonic and elevating effects on your supersensuous affections. Try to paint but not your face, unless you transfer it to canvass; endeavour to count the seven prismatic colours of the rainbow; contemplate and try to conceive all the little harmonies or discords produced by blending various hues.

B. To MISTIFY AND SUPPRESS YOUR SENSE OF COLOUR:—Say to your tailor, never mind the colour; let any one choose for you as to colour; doff every gaudy garment and lay aside your livery; ask brother Jonathan, the quaker to select the tints of your raiment; and most carefully shun art galleries and flower gardens, as there, you see the loveliest flowers *botanical*, as well as the choicest and most fascinating specimens of *human loveliness*, as Gothe has beautifully put it, ' *The living visible ga·ment of God.*"

INCLINATION TO DESTROY, OR DEMOLITIOUSNESS.
THE PROPENSITY TO MAR, DEFACE, OR DESTROY.

The low flat nose, which is particularly wide where the wings of the nostrils join the face; the wide short ear, broad foot, deep chest, large neck, heavy jaw, and low forehead, are the signs which point out large destructiveness as unerringly as the shadow on the dial indicates the direction of the sun.

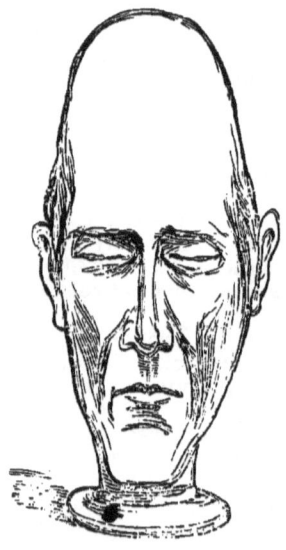

Demolitiousness small.
B. Gosse, Esq., of London, who gave indiscriminately to every object irregardless of its worthiness and could not bear to destroy anything

Demolitiousness large.
John R. Webster, a murderer and natural thief; confined for life in the Penitentiary in Jackson, Michigan, since 1854

Demolitiousness small. Hare.

Demolitiousness large. Tiger.

DEMOLITIOUSNESS

Demolitiousness large.   Striped rattlesnake.

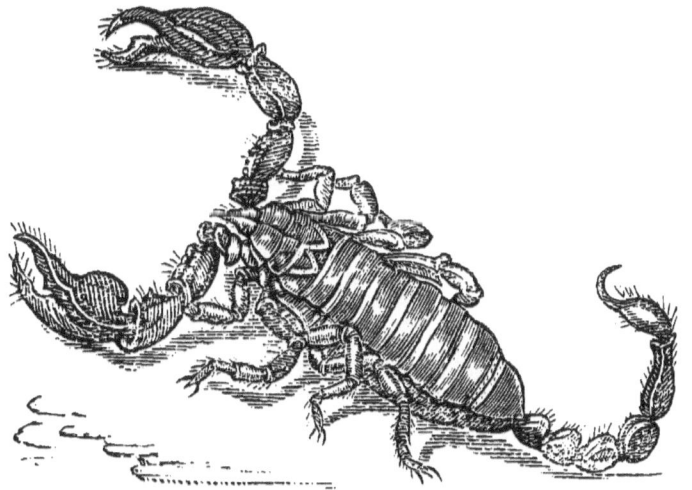

Demolitiousness large.   The European scorpion

1 You are so good that you are good for nothing, and so perfectly harmless and full of tenderest sympathies that the very sight of blood makes you faint.

2. Such is your gentle and kindly nature that you would shrink from harming the most defenceless person or animal; as void of destructiveness as a Hindoo, you prefer sustaining to demolishing a worthy object; and you thoroughly dislike maltreating or abusing any one.

3. Others are likely to take advantage of your good nature and impose upon you; your natural mildness, forgiving disposition, and amiability will win you many friends, and none will fear you, as you retail in plentiful measure the milk of human kindness.

4. Malice finds no sympathy in your tender nature; you are averse to inflicting pain, hence you will threaten more than you execute; you need more force and stamina to infuse "push" into your constitution.

5. Though not inclined to be vindictive or malignant you can say sharp and cutting things when enraged; but regret soon tries to make amends for the injuries inflicted upon the feelings of others.

6. A Nero, Bruce, Henry VIII. of England, Cromwell, or Napoleon I., you have too little of the destructive in your nature to imitate; you dislike even to harm or injure any, and would shrink from persecuting an enemy.

7. The happy balance and equipoise of this faculty in your organization will enable you to accomplish much good if you but strive for that end.

8. Although you are by no means savage in your nature, yet you sting by your words though you inflict no blows.

9. If your education has been rightly conducted, you would endeavour to subvert whatever you deem wrong; besides, you have sufficient executive force for the ordinary affairs of life.

10. Being of destructive nature, you like to demolish old structures and obsolete notions; hence you rarely forgive and never forget an intentional injury.

11. Of its kind, you carry much weight of character. Being naturally harsh and severe, and full of virulence, you are admirably constituted for the carrying out of executive justice. Your delight when you do read is to pore over the accounts of murders, suicides, riots, fires with loss of life, &c.

12. As if the demon of destruction had presided at your birth, your consummate delight is in destruction, torture and death with violence. You would enjoy shooting birds, deer, and all kinds of game, and watching the death-agony; you would delight in attending such sports as old Rome provided in the days of its physical and moral declension—when hundreds of human beings were compelled to enter the arena with wild beasts and fight them to the death. Possessing much of what the French call the *penchant au meurtre*, or propensity to kill; did opportunity occur, you would equal in cruelty Caligula, Gracilia, Nero, Bloody Mary, Catherine dè Medici, Robespiere or the Nana Sahib, if your moral sentiments were as weak as theirs and you had similar surroundings.

A. TO ENHANCE THE POWER OF DEMOLITIOUSNESS:—Eat meat; attend executions of criminals; engage in field sports, gunning and fishing; visit slaughter houses and handle the meat; go into battle and assist in burying the dead; be severe and sarcastic; read descriptions of murders, assaults, pugilistic and arenal encounters; endeavour to live more like Nero, Caligula, and other monsters of cruelty, and at length you may partially overcome your too kind and too tender disposition.

B. TO SUBDUE YOUR EXCESSIVE TENDENCY TO DESTROY:—Avoid carnivorous diet; if any one injure you, be merciful to, and forgive them; never allow your thoughts to dwell a moment upon revenge; cultivate sympathy, charity, and a spirit of brotherly kindness towards all mankind.

LOVE OF THE YOUNG, OR PHILONEPIONALITY.

THE CHARACTERISTIC OF FEELING PLEASURE IN THE YOUNG.

Watery or moist eyes, and lips thick in the centre are indicative of the love of children.

Philonepionality large.
A loving Italian mother. Costume della donna di Mariennella.

1. Utterly destitute of sympathy with the young or the least interest in them, you consider the babe a pest and a nuisance. Children are in general your detestation.
2. As a parent you are almost perfectly indifferent about your offspring, and in this respect resemble Catherine II. of Russia.
3. Cold and distant towards children, you are liable to neglect your own; and, when you do take cognizance of them, it is only as a tyrant to rule them with a rod of iron.
4. The young and helpless are to you a burden instead of a blessing. The sweet smile and innocent prattle of the lovely child you turn from

you with a growl; hence you only see tears and terror when you might enjoy one of the sweetest solaces of life—the pure loving gratitude of childhood.

5. Though you would with a grave unsympathising aspect supply the mere wants of the young, you would not feel admiringly devoted to those in their nonage or minority.

6. It is quite refreshing to observe the perfect equipoise of this faculty in your organization; hence you can govern the young if you wish to do so, especially the children of others.

7. While free from a tendency to pet and spoil children, and loving those who are young and dependent, those in their teens are very dear to you, and still you cannot be said to dislike the aged.

8. So much does the warm and earnest love you feel for your little dependants and offspring thrill through your frame, that, were you to lose a child it would almost break your heart.

9. Your heart and soul delight in the welfare of youth, and infantile sports are so attractive to you that you seem to live anew your happy juvenescent years, in joining in their gleeful pastimes.

10. Your peace and pleasure largely depend upon children if you have them; but if you are so unfortunate as to have none you will need pets upon which to bestow your paternal affection.

11. You have intense delight in caressing and petting those who are in the morning of life; and the warm tears of parental affection often moisten thine eyes when your love reverts to the lost and withered loved blossoms of humanity, or those children whose memory clings twiningly around your spirit.

12. Such is your intense love of children that you almost deify them and leave them to govern themselves; and not children alone but tender plants, you carefully guard and esteem as your most precious treasures. Hence budding spring in fresh beauty is your favourite season

A. To Cultivate Love of Children:—Make children your playmates; associate with them; overlook their faults and interest yourself in their sports and foibles; and if you wish to descend to lower natures make pets of cats, dogs, ponies, and try to like them; but nothing will so much promote your love for the young of your own species as being among children, taking them in your arms, talking to them, trying to answer their wonderfully difficult questions, and thus allowing your tender and confiding sympathies to become enlisted in their behalf. How beautifully sings the poet Lloyd of children:—

> "In a child's voice is there not melody?
> In a child's eye is there not rapture seen?
> And rapture not of passion's revelry;
> Calm though impassioned; durable though keen!
> It is all fresh like the young Spring's first green!
> Children seem spirits from above descended,
> To whom still cleaves heaven's atmosphere serene;
> Their very wildnesses with truth are blended;
> Fresh from their skyey mould, they cannot be amended."

B. To Restrain Love of Children:—Though this is the last virtue that ought to be lessened, yet we may say, if you are too ardent in admiration of these redeeming features of our race—"born from perfect harmony of power and will"—remember that you are liable to spoil children as well as less natural pets by over-indulgence; let cool judgment govern your affections; avoid children and cease to talk of their good qualities; never refer in fond remembrance to those children you so tenderly loved; do with those children you are spoiling by excess of petting what Catherine II. of Russia did with her's—send them from you and never ask to see them again !

SPOKEN LANGUAGE, OR LINGUISTIVENESS.

THE ABILITY TO UTTER ARTICULATE SOUNDS SUCCESSIVELY IN SUCH A MANNER AS TO CONVEY INTELLIGENCE.

Protruding and flexible lips, capacious mouth and jaws with a full throat, are determining evidences of large spoken language.

Linguistiveness large.
Mr John B. Gough, the eminent temperance lecturer.

Linguistiveness small.
Beautiful and intelligent deaf and dumb girl of Illinois.

1. Silent as the moon, your mouth was not formed for the utterance of ideas.

2. Seldom more than a monosyllable escapes your lips in reply to a question.

3. Painfully without words to express your ideas and feelings in a satisfactory manner, you are naturally much annoyed by your difficulties of utterance.

4. Though sometimes you may be able to speak rapidly, yet it is often with difficulty you express yourself. Fitful in utterance but not copious, still you may become a critical linguist.

5. Being fluent in utterance, only when excited, you will not excel in entertaining a company, yet, with practice you may become a passable talker.

112 LINGUASTIVENESS.

Parrot, the only thing except man that can talk.

Linguastiveness large.
An Irish woman, a babbler.

6. Not being much of a speaker, you will feel incompetent to make long, flowery, elegantly turned periods; and while the power to think may be good, the ability to give easy expression to your ideas is hardly satisfactory.

7. Though you may think many excellent things, yet you cannot enunciate them in an elegant manner. This arises very much from the natural diffidence which steals over you when you attempt public speaking, but which also springs in part from your conscious inability to command an audience

8. As a conversationist you could become fair had you sufficient practice, but your tongue does not keep up an eternal clatter, neither are you as " grum " as a post.

9. You may never have been accustomed to public speaking though your gifts of utterance are very good. Hence knowledge and practice are what you require in order to excel.

10. Never at a loss for words you delight in conversation; and articulate language is more within your capacity than symbolic

11. When speaking you would never hesitate for something good to say, and your flow of language is naturally good and well chosen.

12. Your natural gifts of utterance are very great. Your words flow like the pellucid stream, become resistless as the impetuous flood, and in the rolling harmony and music of your impassioned appeals and perorations, you sweep along with you in irresistible sympathy, the thousands who hang breathless on your tongue. The famous lecturer, John B. Gough, could not surpass you in rolling forth his harmonious periods. Like the great Demosthenes, Calistratus, or the modern Kossuth, your fluency and command of language is pre-eminently of the highest style.

A. TO CULTIVATE SPOKEN LANGUAGE:—Be wordy and, if possible, talk more; relate anecdotes, tell stories, repeat conversations. But never become so listless as to say eh! humph! Ah! indeed! dear me! and other insipid, stupid interjections. Don't grunt and drawl out your words, but enunciate them in a clear, distinct, earnest tone, and talk often; converse often with those who excel as ready, easy, fluent talkers. Let your thoughts flow out well if you can; but poorly if you must; keep the stream of conversation rolling and flowing, and it will wash its own channel and keep it clear and ready for the outflow of the most copious floods of eloquence.

B. TO CURB OR RESTRAIN FLUENCY OF LANGUAGE:—Let your tongue have now and then a moment's rest while you are awake; avoid tittle-tattle, chat, and the retailing of scandal; try to feel your own boorishness, and be careful to understand that it may be that your tongue has some affinity to the hiss of the goose or serpent, or the croak of the raven, or melodious scream of the peacock.

PHYSICAL PLEASURE, OR PHYSIODELECTATIOUSNESS.

THE DISPOSITION AND INCLINATION FOR SENSUAL DELIGHTS.

Those who prize most highly sexual pleasures, and devote most time to their enjoyment will have a thick under eyelid which crowds up upon the eyes, except in those given to indulge in intoxicating beverages, whose lower eyelids in age will fall away from the eyeball as if tired of their situation, or weary in assisting the eyes to such low desires; they turn away in disgust from screening the drunken stare of their degraded owner.

Physiodelectatiousness small. Marchioness of Hertford, a pure minded woman.

Physiodelectatiousness large. Henry VIII., who never spared man in his anger nor woman in his lusts; beheaded several of his six wives.

1. Your miserable existence will always be tortured by most intense pain and affliction.

2 Pangs and mental anguish will visit you oftener than pleasing emotions.

3 Instead of bodily enjoyment, yours will be the pains and sufferings of life.

4. Though you can endure pain and suffering quite well, you would willingly and lovingly give and receive pleasure.

5. Not being an extremist in this respect, yet you can tolerably well endure pain or even misery.

6. No burrowing animal desire lurks about your happiness to usurp your higher nature.

7 Appreciating both physical and spiritual comforts, you are admirably equipoised in this respect

8. Though you may enjoy animal gratification, yet you do not entirely ignore the more elevated and noble delight of the spirit.

9. In your estimation, the joys of the mind and soul are not so much esteemed as corporeal pleasures.

10. Very gratifying to you are the pleasures of a fleshly nature, and they are calculated to lead you into bad habits.

11. Sweet smells, beautiful sights, melodious sounds, all that tastes sweet, all that is soft to the touch and agreeable, of whatever nature, you enjoy.

12. Having an intense desire for animal gratification, there are no pleasures you prize more highly than those connected with the flesh.

A. To Increase and Accelerate Physical Pleasure:—Try to give and receive all the bodily pleasure compatible with your physical good health; revel, riot and bask in pleasures of the most voluptuous nature; court the society of those given to animal gratification. But as this propensity is generally too large, it will be unnecessary to prescribe further for its cultivation. For the cold-blooded and stony natures only the above hints are necessary.

B. To Repress and Diminish the Propensity for Physical Enjoyment:—Allow no moral, mental or corporeal felicity to escape you; cast out all voluptuousness and rise to your higher nature to experience profitable pleasures and lasting joys; read chaste books and choose associates who are pure-minded and intellectual. Let the works of Irving, Ruskin, Mrs Browning, Mrs Sigourney, &c., be your study and pleasure.

CURATIVE POWER, OR CURATIVENESS.

CURATIVENESS IS THE FACULTY THAT ENABLES ONE TO ADOPT THE MEANS AND APPLIANCES NECESSARY FOR THE RESTORATION OF HEALTH OF BODY OR SOUNDNESS OF CONSTITUTION.

The physiognomical evidences of this faculty are strength of form and healthy vigour of constitution.

1. Instead of being adapted to cure others, you are a patient in need of curative attention.

2. Those who are deficient in life forces will not be largely affected by the little strength that remains in your structure.

3. The unequal and vacillating condition of your system prevents you from becoming a successful physician.

4. Some parts of your form being defective and others strong, your success in the healing art will be with those who are weak in those parts which correspond to your strong faculties.

5. All the education of all the medical schools in the world would not make you capable of success as a physician

6. The perceptions of your nature may recognize disease in others, but your system is deficient in the surplus of strength which is necessary to supply those who are weak.

7. In the treatment of children and members of your own family, when they are not dangerously ill, you might succeed very well ; but, in severe cases, you are apt to seek the aid of those you consider more competent than yourself.

8. In the history of your experience, some remarkable instances could be related in which you have suggested or wrought out the means of relief for those in trouble, or afflicted.

9. Nature has adapted you to lend a relieving hand to the enfeebled.

10. You are wonderfully proficient in comprehending the wants of the unbalanced and diseased conditions of those in need of cure, as well as the necessary remedies that would afford them relief.

11. Morbid and ailing people find your very presence a ready relief, few could excel you as a doctor.

12. Astounding reliefs and wonderful cures have been effected by your vast powers of recuperation and validity. In these benign qualities you closely resemble Dr Newton of Boston and Dr Davis of Chicago, who have effected the greatest cures of modern times.

Curativeness large.
Capt. Samuel Staddon. Has always been perfectly healthy, and weighs 200 pounds.

A. TO CULTIVATE THE CURATIVE POWER:—Sleep much; exercise properly in the open air; breathe pure air only, night and day; live on healthful and nourishing food; avoid excessive exercise of every kind; and, above all, cultivate tranquillity of mind and purity of soul; then, when sufficiently strong, endeavour to relieve the sufferings of humanity.

B. TO RESTRAIN THE FACULTY OF CURATIVENESS:—This is rarely necessary, but when persons are constantly tampering or putting forth futile and fruitless efforts to restore others, when they are themselves sadly deficient in health and vitality, then they abuse the faculty, and it needs restraining; in this case the performer as well as the patient should learn that quackery is playing upon the credulity and likely living from the gullibility of the sick and their friends.

DESIRE OF APPROVAL, OR SOLICITUSREPUTATIVENESS.
AN INNATE WISH FOR THE FAVOURABLE OPINION OF OTHERS.

Thin-skinned or red-lipped people are always sensitive to the opinion of others about them. The head turned a little to one side, the voice low and insinuating; courteous and obliging manners are stable signs of a strong desire of approbation.

1. A perfect pachyderm, as regards being chidden, upbraided, or objurgated, as it gives you no manner of uneasiness or displeasure.

2. Not being inclined to sacrifice one jot of your ease to win flattery, you can bear to be hissed, hooted and your acts contemned; nor will you manifest any displeasure or rouse yourself in your own defence, no matter what is said of you or your acts.

3. Little you care for either the censure or admiration of enemies or friends. Detractive invectives make no more impression upon you than snowballs hurled against an iron-clad ram.

4. Though naturally discourteous and not very sensitive to blame or praise, still you will manfully withstand the attacks of the traducer, critic, or censor, sometimes very pugnaciously.

5. When the popular breeze fills your sails, your barque glides smoothly over life's breakers, yet when the winds of obloquy and scorn, and the gentler breeze of disapproval blow against your craft, you haul in sail, put on more of the steam of energy, and make course prosperously.

6. Not sensitively regardful of flattery, praise, admiration, or detraction, disapprobation or slander, yet a well merited and delicately paid compliment affords you pleasure. You would never become a hanger-on, not being panegyrical or laudatory, as you would rather deserve approbation than be fawned upon.

7. Though you would not sacrifice your honour by giving tribute of praise, yet you would strive to do well that you might merit the commendation of the just and good. Mrs Hannah More puts it well :—

> " Sweet is the breath of praise when given by those
> Whose own high merit claims the praise they give "

8. Having a high appreciation of the good graces of others, you endeavour to avoid aspersion and detraction. To your feelings, commendation, when felt to be merited, acts as salt to fish, purifying and preserving them.

9. Duly valuing and highly appreciating the respect and approbation of others on your own behalf, you occasionally pay in return a tribute of praise, and frequently become eulogistic and encomiastic.

10. So sensitive and tender are your feelings that you are often hurt even by the admonitions and criticisms of your friends; thus being too touchy you hate and shrink from detraction while you too eagerly strive for praise.

11. There is such a thirst in you for the admiration of others that the slightest disapproval or disparagement cuts your fine sensibilities as keenly as Paddy's razor—" an inch before the edge." You will admire Derozier's expression of your innermost feelings in his lines :—

> " Speak it again for it is sweet to hear
> Praise from the voice we love, and thine is soft
> And hath a touch of tenderness, as 'twere
> A gentle flower grown musical."

But read your best lesson in the fable of "The Old Man and his Ass."

12. So intensely eager are you for commendation and flattery that you will often err while endeavouring to win them, so blindly do you esteem the encomiums and blandishments of your associates. Indeed, so keenly do you relish flattery and adulation that the pursuit of it in your case more resembles in eagerness the deadly scent and eager pursuit of the blood-hound in following his prey than aught else. Lay the pungent words of Shakspeare to heart:—

> "When I tell him he hates flattery,
> He says he does, being then most flattered."

A. TO STRENGTHEN THE DESIRE OF APPROBATION:—Act honourably and be courteous and obliging that you may gain admiration; always manifest great care about cleanliness and dress; use no cutting or sarcastic language; in whatever you do, consult and counsel the good pleasure of others; guard against whatever is unpleasant in word or deed; manifest on all occasions a sensitive anxiety and desire to win the appreciation and high esteem of every one; and never say "I don't care." Finally, read "Lord Chesterfield's Letters to his Son."

B. TO RESTRAIN AND WEAKEN THE DESIRE OF APPROBATION:—Be slovenly in dress and untidy about your person and all your surroundings; taunt and sneer at those with whom you have intercourse; encounter the world unaided by friends or acquaintances; heed not the clamour, insults, and revilings you may engender. In a word, never woo public opinion and steel your mind against adulation. Otway gives you good counsel:—

> "If thou hast flattery in thy nature, out with't
> Or send it to the Court, for there 'twill thrive!"

La Rochefoucauld has well put it thus, "Flattery is a sort of bad money to which our vanity gives currency." This opinion, no doubt, inspired Tennyson's couplet:—

> "This barren verbiage current among men,
> Light, coin, the tinsel clink of compliment."

UNRELENTING TEMPER, OR INEXORABLENESS.

THE QUALITY OF BEING INEXORABLE, UNRELENTING, IRRECONCILABLE IN ENMITY.

A cross, inexorable look, an aversion to laugh, and a protruding under lip, beyond the upper, are unmistakable indications of an implacable disposition.

1. Being naturally of a sweet and gentle disposition you have a strong aversion to those of a sullen, implacable character

2. Not often petulant or fault-finding, you will regard others sympathetically, and turn away from those who wrap themselves up in selfishness and are unmoved by either the joys or sorrows of another.

3. You never will become the victim of your own gall; and so little spite is in your composition that you quite agree with the opinion of Julius Cæsar, who says that "implacability is only known to the savage."

4. Naturally possessing much kindness of disposition, warmly admiring humane goodness in others, even though you partially want it your-

self, being sometimes rancorous, you are much benefited by the companionship of the gentle and amiable.

5. Naturally disliking churlish and mordacious people, you generally make an effort not to be grim or maleficent; nor have you the graceless modesty that would make you ashamed of requiting a kindness, from the ill-natured idea that this would be a confession that you had received one.

Inexorableness large.
An Irish woman of Edinburgh, a gabbler.

6. Though your feelings towards others may be somewhat mild and without severity, yet your language will have bitterness in its meaning and tone when you are excited by a deep feeling of wrong. Generally, however, humane feeling prevails.

7. Being rather irritable and sharp, if you think there is an attempt to impose upon you, you may become sour and ireful, and this will cause your path in life to be beset with sorrows and vexations.

8. Your disposition being nasty, petulant and fault-finding, malice is often engendered in your mind. Hence your words become sharp, and give utterance to scathing satire, keen reproach, and peevish fault-finding.

9. Your inner life will be chilled sometimes by moodiness and austerity; many of your joys must be dispelled by your acerbity and waspish nature. Your peevishness is the canker worm of your whole life, tainting and vitiating what it cannot consume.

10. Intensely bitter and sarcastic in your nature, your flashes of acrid irony and sneers may pass among your friends as indications of intellectual brilliancy, while they are almost sheer implacability.

11. If you rule and domineer, you are rude, rough, and despotic; but, in subordinate positions, you are acrimonious and inapproachable. Always you are ready with a snarl, a growl, a word, and a blow.

12. Naturally intensely implacable, at the slightest provocation, your lip curls with bitterness or scorn; even to your most intimate friends you can remain cold, distant, unpleasant, and inexorable.

A. To CULTIVATE IMPLACABLENESS:—Employ the most scathing and sarcastic language to those who displease you; let trifles ruffle your feelings and cause you to take umbrage towards your friends; manifest keen resentment on all occasions; and be irreconcilable in your anger and enmity. Say with Shakspeare:—

> "Had I power, I should
> Pour the sweet milk of concord into hell,
> Uproar the universal peace, confound
> All unity on earth."

B. To RESTRAIN IMPLACABLENESS:—Never provoke another; avoid fault-finding, malice, pettishness, rancour, implacability; and cherish the more noble and irenic affections. Clap an extinguisher upon your irony, if you are unhappily blessed with a vein of it; and never let a humorous jest, at the expense of a friend, escape from your lips. How very beautifully Byron supplies a motive:—"The drying up a single tear has more of honest fame than shedding tears of gore."

CONSECUTIVENESS.
THE CAPABILITY OF APPRECIATING AND PRODUCING PROPOSITIONS IN CONSECUTIVE ORDER.

Perpendicular wrinkles in the forehead, immediately above the nose, and horizontal wrinkles, or a wrinkle across the nose, near its junction with the forehead, are unfailing signs of large CONSECUTION.

1. Rarely do you complete those subjects you attempt to study; you cannot continue a train of thought; your preference is for short stories, brief speeches, and newspaper paragraphs.

2. Being impatient and easily irritated, you cannot give the proper attention, or make the sustained mental effort, when circumstances demand close and consecutive application for days or years.

3. Your mind, ever flitting from one object to another, and your efforts being spasmodic, you are unstable, lacking thorough earnestness.

4. Not very consecutive and too easily interrupted, you are desultory and inconsequent in your writing or speeches; and pleased with variety.

5. Being rather fond of change you will evince spasmodic efforts which seem to be almost without relation to each other.

6. Though it is impossible for you to keep up a consecutive and

rational argument, being somewhat of a changeling, you give vent to many good ideas.

Consecutiveness large.
Cyrus W. Field, a projector of the Atlantic telegraph.

Consecutiveness large.
Selfish cat.

7. Though not an extremist, in this respect, you are able to change, yet caring little for it. You will meet many who are more inclined to succession than yourself.

8. One thing at a time pleases you best; you can concentrate your thoughts thoroughly upon one subject, yet you may be discursive at times.

9. Sentences and ideas, with you, jostle each other, and, unless hurried, you are fairly patient, and can confine your attention thoroughly to the labour of thought and work.

10. Being adapted to patient and continuous labour, you scrutinize everything most closely, and can concentrate your attention a long time upon one subject; but you naturally dislike to be distracted or diverted from the immediate object of interest; you are thorough, and will completely concentrate your intellectual power upon the subject under deliberation.

11. Your intellectual forces being concentrated, you maintain one position of the body for a long time; and, though prolix, you are very patient but tedious, while entering into the details of an undertaking.

12. You have, in an extraordinary degree, the power to continue and link together mental operations; but you are given to tell long stories and refer to incidents very slenderly related to the main anecdote, hence you become tiresome. Owen says, " Without consistency there is no moral strength."

A. To CULTIVATE CONSECUTION:—Closely think and reflect several hours a day; lead a settled life; steadily keep your eye on one object, and your mind the same; follow to completion everything you undertake.

B. To RESTRAIN THE POWER OF CONSECUTION:—Cease to be prolix; constantly notice new things; cultivate love of novelty; be variable and abrupt; let the series of your thoughts be disrupted; and omit all the unimportant incidents when narrating an anecdote.

CAPACITY TO SING, OR SONIDIFFUSITIVENESS.

THE CAPACITY OF PRODUCING OR MAKING A SOUND OR MUSICAL TONE WITH THE MOUTH,—VOCIFERATIVENESS.

A full throat, large thorax, open nostrils, and protruding lips, with good length from the point of the nose to the point of the chin and full cheeks, are faithful signs of the power to give forth tone, if the ear be round and prominent, so that it can first receive the tone.

1. Don't waste your time in vocalism: the culture of a lifetime could not raise you to good performance. Never venture to divert others, they will only laugh in their sleeves, and sneer when you do your best.

2. Having poor vocalization, it would be almost if not quite impossible for you to become a vocal musician.

3. You may appreciate fine music, but could not become a superior vocalist, as you cannot give intonation or resonance to your voice.

4. Lacking the power of vocality, your voice is too coarse and too sharp and harsh to produce good vocal music; music purchased would be better than you could make.

5 Having little control over your voice, you enjoy and judge music better than you can perform.

6. Never need you try to astonish the world with your music, as it must prove a useless effort. You may be taught to make music in a mechanical manner, and yet you will never excel.

Sonidiffusitiveness small.
Irish peasant, who could not sound a note correctly.

Sonidiffusitiveness large.
Pareppa Rosa, a celebrated singer.

Sonidiffusitiveness small.
A duck. The flat bill of the duck gives a flat unmusical sound, like "quack" when pronounced.

Sonidiffusitiveness large
A canary. The round beak of the canary gives a round musical sound.

7. In the execution of instrumental music, you evince some taste, if you have had some practice in it; you can sing if you possess a suitable voice.

8. In nature and art, you enjoy the harmonious; with practice you would sing well if your vocal powers are suitable.

9. You are delighted with singing, and with practice you could perform very well provided you have a good voice.

10. You can trill from high to low and *vice versa*, with wonderful grace and accuracy, and when once you have fully caught the tune, you become

in a high degree musical and able to distinguish accurately the nicest degrees and variations of tone.

11. You render variations of tone in a manner most remarkable, and noble thoughts are stirred by your grand trilling and warbling.

12. Not only is music your passion but you have become one of the best musicians in the world.

A. TO CULTIVATE THE POWER OF DIFFUSION OF TONE: While away your time in singing, humming, whistling, and playing on instruments; if you cannot sing try and keep trying; study the properties of harmonial sounds as well as their relations and dependencies: and train your voice to produce sounds pleasing to the ear.

B. TO RESTRAIN THE TALENT FOR DIFFUSION OF TONE:—Avoid the habit of everlasting whistling; turn your mind to works of a metaphysical nature; put away your musical instruments and books; throw your melody and harmony to the wind, and devote your time to the study of history or mathematics.

LOVE OF ORNAMENT, OR DECORATIVENESS.
THE TENDENCY TO ORNAMENT IN A BECOMING MANNER.

A full eye, accompanied by arching, thin, long eyebrows are emblematic of DECORATIVENESS.

1. You care far more for the necessaries of life than for any ornaments.

2. It pains you to see young people display their gewgaws, tinsel and trinkets.

3. Plain practicalness, durable apparel, substantial furniture, houses undecorated by art suit your simplicity of style better than all the embellishments afforded by the world.

4. When trinkets or jewels are given you, they might be worn, but you care not to purchase them.

5. The occupation you generally admire is one where the useful is paramount to the adornful

6. Occasionally you adorn yourself in a plain or meagre manner, but gaudy equipages, gorgeous outfits or dazzling arrays of adornments you care little about them.

7. Perhaps a plain ring or watch may be worn by you, but no gay tinselry will you ever flaunt to win the attention of the simple and unsophisticated.

8. Artistic work you admire, but would not succeed well in an occupation where ornamental work was required

9. To lay out a tasty flower garden, arrange pictures, furniture, books, or museum would be your delight, if you had the means that you wish to use in such manner.

10. Have an innate feeling as to what is becoming. As naturally men e into reasonable customs as a mouse into the cupboard, and are pleased with embellishments which render an object agreeable to the intellectual view.

11 Ambitious contemplations of viewing the decorations of Paris may thrill your being with unutterable joy; yet when you view the Elysium of Rome, or St Peter's, in the same city, your blood tingles through its life-channels and spreads its red glow of delight throughout your every lineament.

12 An Indian squaw or Negro woman could find no more delight in cheap jewellery or gay adornings than yourself.

A. TO STRENGTHEN DECORATIVENESS:—Put on jewellery; cast aside your plain utilitarian ideas; purchase fashion books; gaze into every display window; associate with those who are dressy, and imitate their styles, and soon you will enlarge your taste for adornments.

B. TO CHECK YOUR FONDNESS FOR DECORATIONS:—Throw aside your rings, jewellery, or other adornments; live in the woods by camping out; and when ornament or usefulness are the only two prongs of a choice left, decide at once firmly in favour of worth, and never again allow your mind to seek the flimsy gewgaws of fashion.

SEARCHING INCLINATION, OR HUNTATIVENESS.
THE DISPOSITION TO SEARCH FOR OR FOLLOW AFTER ANY PERSON OR THING.

Some of the physiognomical records of this endowment are, fulness in the forehead immediately above the top of the nose, good muscular and bony systems, with the head carried well forward of the body.

1. Being but feebly inclined to hunt either mentally or physically, you can refrain or avoid meeting those you do not wish to find.
2. You can abstain or not even attempt to discover that which is undesired.
3. The elusive and evasive power within your structure is sufficient to overcome those feeble inclinations, you may betimes feel, to search out and rush headforemost upon hidden vice, or fugitive criminals.
4. Caring not to pursue the concealments of life, or the refugee from justice, you would not become an able detective or administrator of executive law.
5. That which requires little or no searching to find you may obtain, yet manifest no great desire to hunt or race after unknown or unseen objects.
6. To follow up in searching for game, antiquarian curiosities, rare books, geological specimens, or facts, may not be your natural forte, yet with practise you might become an expert.
7. Searching for game simply to kill it, may not afford you much pleasure, yet when the necessities of the case demand your assistance to bring the guilty to justice your aid is of considerable value.
8. You are efficient in the pursuit of any object, whether laudable or unworthy.
9. If accustomed to the chase you may delight in diligently pursuing game, but would more likely search for ideas.
10. To hunt up old coins or curiosities is a pleasant task to one of your nature if time is found in which to engage in such pursuit.
11. The great delight of your life is to court favour or seek for something which affords you pleasure. You will likely hunt for money.
12. Angling, guning, chasing, and seeking each or all would afford you much amusement; you ever delight in hunting out something new.

A. TO CULTIVATE HUNTATIVENESS:—Buy yourself a gun and join in the chase: turn geologist, and pass much of your time in searching for specimens with which to illustrate that science; become a naturalist of some kind and seek to find new species of animal life; travel, read and examine every avenue for new thoughts; in a word, turn huntsman in mind and body.

B. TO RESTRAIN HUNTATIVENESS:—Allow facts and hidden objects to pass by unnoticed; never pry into the affairs of others; sell your gun, hunting horses and dogs, and find pleasure in literature, science, art, or the more stable industries of laborious life; never indulge in angling, and renounce all games of chance, while you strive to swell your spiritual capacity in solitary repose and elevating meditations.

SAGACITY, OR SAGACITIVENESS.
SOUNDNESS OF JUDGMENT AND SHREWDNESS ARE CONCOMITANTS OF THE FACULTY OF SAGACITIVENESS.

The short round neck is one of the natural accompaniments of sagacitiveness. Napoleon I. had an extremely short neck his head apparently resting upon his shoulders; and all Europe learned by sad experience his overwhelming sagacity.

Sagacitiveness large.
Thomas Parr, who lived to the rare old age of 152 years and 9 months. At the age of 120 he married a second wife, by whom he had issue.

1. You are as wileless as an ostrich; shallowness and dotage are your weak traits of mind, which subject you to being imposed upon by any who wish to take advantage of you.

2. Empty patedness and incapacity utterly unfit you for any path in life that requires thought or judicious ratiocination. Never could you appreciate the beautiful thoughts that spring up in the sagacious mind, and, like sweet flowers, ornament and perfume the pathway of life, and delight the soul by their never decaying amaranthine spiritual loveliness.

3. Being in your nature unprotective and always liable to imposition, imbecility and doltishness are interspersed in almost every effort of your life.

4. Having been unhandsomely dealt with in the general distribution of mother wit and acuteness when dame nature gave you in charge to your nurse, it is only by aping the sagacity of others that you manifest any wisdom or penetration in your intercourse with the world.

SAGACITIVENESS.

Sagacitiveness large.   An Asiatic elephant.

5. Not having largely inherited quickness of perception or keenness of penetration in union with practical judgment, you are unable to guard against the designs of others, and fail to turn things to the best advantage.

6. Though neither great acumen nor astuteness characterise you, yet you are not wholly simple or incapacitated.

7. You take real pleasure in connecting the links in a chain of circumstances whereby the extremes of any great events of life are connected.

8. Being protective in your form and disposition, perspicaciousness is an active trait in your character.

9. That keen acuteness which you employ when you deem it necessary to accomplish your aims, would fit you for the legal profession, trade, or politics, if otherwise well suited.

10. The ready and captious sagacity which wells up from the

Sagacitiveness small.
Ostrich.

deep and occult recesses of your subtle nature, when circumstances demand obtains with those largely gifted with shrewdness.

11. Being sagacious beyond the comprehension of most individuals, your genius is generally misnamed talent only.

12. Being so full of shrewd tact and sharpness of intelligence in management, many fear to encounter or deal with you; in this they, in their turn, likely show their sagacity, as they might only come off only second best in the contest.

A. To Cultivate Sagacity:—Mingle with the world, and especially with those who are shrewd, astute, and sagacious; learn the fact that you are doltish and slow of comprehension when others are endeavouring to entrap you with the bait of deceit; keep the eye of alertness wide open and brush away the dust of over confidence; draw full inspirations of air, and gently beat upon your chest to enlarge the lungs and heart which will assist in enlarging the neck and the capacity to carry the blood through it, thereby strengthening the neck and giving it relative shortness, while enhancing your shrewdness and sagacity.

B. To Restrain your Sagacious Tendencies:—This is not almost ever necessary; but, if you wish to become less able to cope with the accumulated acuteness of the world, you may place implicit confidence in others; exercise little in heavy work; keep to light occupations; shun people of the world; and in due time you will become as unprotective as a giraffe, and be considered a fit subject for the wards of a lunatic asylum, especially, if your relations hope to inherit any poor residue of any property of which you may still be possessed

---

PRONENESS TO TRADE, OR TRADISTIVENESS.

THE TENDENCY TO TRADE AND BARTER.

A wide, rounding jaw, rounding, short, elastic, and springy person, that is very active, are symbolic of a trading tendency.

1. Utterly destitute of any wish to trade.
2. If necessity demands it, you may buy or sell, but display no aptitude in this direction.
3. To purchase you are better adapted than to sell, yet should never enter upon the lists of exchange.
4. To traffic, peddle, or auctioneer have no beguiling enchantments for you.
5. It is seldom you read the columns of a newspaper where the various market quotations are given.
6. Commercial transactions rather weary you, and trade has no attractions except through necessity.
7. Can bargain for the plain necessities of life, but dislike to negotiate for another, yet could do so if necessary.
8. Being able to purchase those articles that are needed in your family or business with fair success, you may venture into speculations only to find remuneration
9. To barter, hawk, retail, and job you take considerable pleasure in, and, if circumstances will allow, your talent could be profitably employed in mercantile pursuits.

10. The musings of your mind picture many a bright bargain, and trading air-castles may lure you into huckstering or respectable trade.

11. The bustle of markets, the stir of the business mart, or the uproar of the money exchange lends thrilling delight to your business disposition.

12. In your youth you seemed to have an unusual aptitude for trading; and with age this inclination has widened and taken deeper root in your organization until you care little for aught else than trade.

A. To STRENGTHEN TRADISTIVENESS:—Buy and sell; deal and barter; speculate and exchange; swap and dicker in every available article; buy old horses and trade them for land or sheep; sell your old waggons for cattle, and fat up your cattle and sell them for beef, and deposit the proceeds in a savings bank at the highest rates of interest; set a price on any saleable article you possess, and bear in mind that commerce is the great highway to civilization.

B. To SUBDUE YOUR INORDINATE TENDENCY TO TRADE :—Keep out of speculations; avoid the busy thoroughfares of life; live on what you raise; always buy for cash and sell for the same; associate with professional and mechanical men, and shun the society of thrifty business men; read much and live a retired life, and time lending its assistance to this rule will aid your necessities to restrain the desire for trade.

FITNESS OF THINGS FOR EACH OTHER, OR ADAPTATIVENESS.

THE FACULTY WHICH PERCEIVES AND DETERMINES THE FITNESS OF PERSONS OR THINGS FOR EACH OTHER.

A long, narrow chin that reaches well forward, is the sign of appropriateness; and the individual possessing largely this disposition will be a good judge of the adaptation of one thing or person to another.

Adaptativeness large
Thos. Cook and wife, who were well adapted to live together, for one was as avaricious as the other was miserly.

1. Differing from every one, you cannot admire any one so much as one resembling yourself.

2. Irrelevancy so often appropriates your small stock of congeniality,

that nothing remains for good credit, or society, but discord and querulousness.

3. Discrepancies have so crowded themselves into the nooks, crevices, and crannies of your life that they jostle out the harmonies and all that is in accord with unison.

4. Occasionally the inconsistent and incommensurable will mar your harmony with others.

5. To be and do like others and agree with them in opinion would prove irksome and distasteful to you.

6. You are conservative in your disposition as far as your nature will permit, but you thoroughly dislike extremes.

7. Correspondence in every circumstance of life must be gratifying to one of so congruous a nature as yours.

8. As a diamond of the first water you look upon consistency; being completely averse to all the incompatibilities.

9. Those in society most like yourself you can best enjoy.

10. All your plans are coherent and consequential, and with those of congenial tastes you easily agree.

11. Readily you detect a want of agreement or correspondence, and often lament that such a condition should exist; but, in your general mood, your wish is for a companion similar to yourself.

12. You instantly discern what is suitable to you, and the chief desire of your life is to live with one like yourself in mind and physique.

A. HOW TO IMPROVE CONGENIALITY OF CHARACTER:—Become accordant with others; adapt, adjust, and accommodate your manner of action and power of thinking to other minds, so that you may harmonize fully with them; and associate with those who have the same tastes as yourself.

B. HOW TO REPRESS CONGENIALITY OF MIND AND CHARACTER:—Cultivate the acquaintance of those who are essentially unlike yourself in every feature and characteristic; and then bear yourself in the most incongenial manner to all mankind.

CLASS IV.

COGNIZANT CAPACITIES.

THE FOURTH CLASS OF CAPACITIES BEING LARGE, THE OSSEOUS OR BONY FORM WILL BE PREDOMINANT IN THAT PERSON.

DISCRIMINATING CAPACITY, OR DISCRIMINATIVENESS.
THE FACULTY WHICH DISCERNS AND JUDGES THE DIFFERENCE OR RESEMBLANCE OF OBJECTS OR IDEAS.

The nose that seems divided at the point into a right and left part, and has a firm appearance and a fulness of the lower brow, should not be passed by when looking for signs of discrimination.

Discriminativeness large.
Linæus, a celebrated Swedish naturalist.

Discriminativeness small.
A Chinese woman, who was very deficient in the endowment to note and mark differences.

1. In diagnosis and analysis you are very weak; accidentally, you may stumble upon some nice fields of thought, but minute investigation is a heavy drag to your mind. In descriptive capacity you are poor, while you are so slow in perceiving analogies and comparisons that a stroke of wit is lost upon you.

2. Indiscrimination and misjudgment characterize you; hence you must always remain a stranger to nice differences and distinctions, and

nothing but vivid pertinent illustrations can attract your attention. The idea of appropriateness is utterly wanting in your mind.

3. Your mind is of the undistinguishing character; hence you will often overlook and neglect slight distinctions; cannot institute comparisons readily nor perceive the meaning of figurative language.

4. The power of comparison is so weak in you that you never appreciate or utter analogies; the philosophy of things is almost without interest to you. Doubting generally your own judgment you cannot trust that of your advisers Never attempt the profession of the chemical analyst.

5. Closely scrutinizing and analyzing have no charms for you; vast differences you can notice, but little ones attract not your observation. It is a puzzle to you to draw the line of demarkation between similar objects.

6. Little heeding minute differences and distinctions, still you readily notice those that are striking. Being free from extremes, in this respect your mind is well balanced.

7. You can analyze well, and hence estimate well the forms and qualities of things and persons, thus proving that your perceptions are clear and demonstrative ability good.

8. Your ready comprehension of distinctions and differences enables you to regard with engrossing attention the affinities and diversities belonging to different persons or things.

9. Having a metaphorical turn of mind, you can ably draw parallels, and place in juxtaposition things that are analogous. Having a ready appreciation of slight differences you are a critic and a connoisseur.

10. At a glance you discover the similarities and dissimilarities; you have real pleasure in comparing the conditions and states of things; in speaking and writing you are very ready, copious in illustration, with full, pleasing, and pertinent amplifications, analogies and allegories.

11. You have a wonderful perception of nice and delicate shades of difference, and can at once detect the semblance between pretension and reality, and are not at all liable to be deceived.

12. At a glance you perceive and take cognizance of resemblances and differences, being quite remarkable for your analytical power. How you revel in parables and metaphors. You must feel an intense sympathy with glorious old Æsop and our modern Æsop, *Fontaine*.

A. To CULTIVATE DISCRIMINATION:—Examine the differences between persons and things as well as their similarities; learn to discriminate nicely; criticize; use figurative language; read ample pithy illustrations; analyze and define; then, as good practical work for promoting your power of discrimination, study chemistry and natural philosophy.

B. To RESTRAIN DISCRIMINATIVE POWER:—Be less critical; avoid taking cognizance of every little flaw and defect in mechanical and artistic work; indulge not in berating your friends or neighbours, but allow your charity to furnish abundant excuses for their excesses and perceptible defects of character; unite more and sunder less in your investigations; be pseudo observant of the universe of objects around you; and receive and trust the assertion of others without investigation.

MECHANICAL TALENT, OR STRUCTURODEXTERITY.
THE ABILITY OF FORMING AND CONSTRUCTING READILY AND DEXTEROUSLY, MATERIALS OR MENTAL PRODUCTS.

Square faces, with the bony form slightly in the ascendancy, are the requisite physical indications of a good mechanic.

Structurodexterity large.
James Watt, the celebrated Scottish mechanician.

Structurodexterity small.
P. T. Barnum, who said he never could whittle a barrel tap round

1. You are a complete mechanical void totally wanting in every qualification in this respect.

2. Being utterly disqualified for mechanical work where originality of thought or expertness of hand is indispensably requisite, your constructive incapacity and inefficiency are too evident to your friends, if not to yourself.

3. Only capable of rough-hewing whatever you attempt to fashion, you work awkwardly as a mechanic, and have precious little of constructive ability.

4. Though you may build or form, yet the work will be executed in a very poor fashion; hence you need not expect to excel as a mechanician

5. Your forte and talents are not in the mechanical direction, though you may have tolerable perceptions and comprehension of the means and resources required for accomplishing engineering operations, and adapting machinery to the objects intended, by manual labour.

6. Though you are likely to devote your attention to other than the mechanical industries, still you have fair constructive abilities, and by application and practice you might become a tolerable workman.

7. Having a natural aversion to dilapidation of any kind you would prefer building up to pulling down, and could succeed pretty well as a builder, having a fair idea of architecture.

8. Having a strong bias for plain mechanical workmanship, you would make a good artificer or artizan. For building, you have some inclination, and by determined efforts you might succeed in the contrivance of complicated structures or machinery.

9. Your inventive powers are ancillary to your automatic ability in mechanical workmanship, and with practice you would be able to manufacture and fabricate neatly many new things, that would command the approbation of the skilled and critical in such matters.

10. Having good natural mechanical and constructive ability you take much interest in machinery and mechanical appliances.

11. By application you might become an expert in the use of mechanical tools; but if you have had experience in their use you are a superior workman or amateur mechanic.

12. A mechanical inventive genius, you are gifted with extraordinary talent for invention and operation in such arts; Vaucanson-like, you either have, or should originate something hitherto unknown which would facilitate labour, in agriculture, manufactures, chemistry. electricity, mechanics, or any other department of scientific or skilled industry.

A. To TRAIN, CULTIVATE AND DEVELOP MECHANICAL TALENT:—Always endeavour to concoct your own plans; make new models or improve those of others; and recollect that mechanism is necessary in every undertaking. Industriously practise the use of tools; saw, plane, chisel, carve, form, and put together the constituent parts of a house, simple or complicated. If you are unable to handle mechanical or artistic tools, then turn your talents to literary labour, and construct sentences, form ideas and theories; and by the rightly and rationally directed use of the faculty you shall unfold its power and intensify its action.

B. To CURB AND RESTRAIN THE MECHANICAL TALENT:—Refrain from attempting to originate perpetual motion; never allow the desire for invention to become a mechanical mania or patent-right disease with yourself; never try to do anything that has not been already done; exercise other faculties, but let this one remain dormant.

PHYSICAL ARRANGEMENT, OR ORDINIPHYSICALITY.

THE DESIRE TO ARRANGE PHYSICAL SUBSTANCES, OR ATTRIBUTES.

Compressed lips of medium thickness regular and rather thin, well-defined features, accompanied with a systematic and regular pendulation of the hands, as well as precision and regularity of step, are unmistakable signs of material order. The Language of physical order is an impulse to arrange articles so that they may bear due and systematic relation to each other.

1. At home in disorder, you revel in confusion, and can never find what is wanted; your idea of the picturesque is utter confusion.

ORDINIPHYSICALITY.

2. Your books and papers, or materials of whatever kind, are in one place to-day, and somewhere to-morrow. You mix, muddle, and scatter things so much about that you have become to admire the promiscuous. Danby says: "Desultoriness may often be the mark of a *full* head." Query, did he not mean *fool's?*

3. Hodgepodge and litter will characterize the affairs under your personal superintendence. Being always in confusion, you are ever ready to jumble and disarrange the furniture and furnishings of your residence.

Ordiniphysicality large.
Edwin Booth, actor.

Ordiniphysicality small.
Miserly, flat head Indian.

4. Being rather irregular in many of your habits, your day for putting things to rights rarely comes; you are utterly reckless as to where you leave tools or implements of any kind. What a relief you must feel it to be that your limbs and members are only as a whole united and not at your own disposal.

5. In you the power of appreciating order far exceeds the power of keeping it. When you are in haste you unfortunately get into a hurry and throw your things about in all manner of ways and directions.

6 Being thorough and judicious, training may accustom you to put things in their places, but you rather dislike to spend much time in arranging your wardrobe or household.

7. Being neither fastidious nor dowdy in your dress, orderly persons have a fair share of your approbation, while your estimate likely embraces more than the apparel of those you prize.

8. Should tumult or anarchy arise in a meeting your displeasure manifests itself; but you can wait your turn (or "bide your time," as the Scotch say) if not led away by excitement.

9. As you are very precise in keeping step and pendulating your

arms while walking, you would make an excellent drill master or disciplinarian.

10. You arrange your wardrobe, bookcase, or workshop, with systematic care, and if properly trained you will display much regularity in all the concerns of life.

11. In physical materials your arrangement is perfect; hence you would make an excellent bookkeeper or librarian. In such matters remarkable method would be manifest in all details. Shakspeare's words apply to you as well as the insect you resemble:—

> "So work the honey-bees,
> Creatures that by a rule in nature teach
> The act of order to a peopled kingdom."

12. A martyr to the love of order, you are distressed beyond measure by the sight of confusion, and never feel satisfied unless everything is fittingly arranged. With Sam. Johnson your goddess, "Order is a lovely nymph, the child of beauty and wisdom; her attendants are comfort, neatness, and activity; her abode is the valley of happiness. She never appears so lovely as when contrasted with her opponent—Disorder."

A. TO CULTIVATE HABITS AND TASTES FOR MATERIAL ORDER:—In the arrangement of physical objects be regular, uniform, and unconfused; arrange articles in rows and ranks, and never place them where they do not belong; be patient in awaiting your turn at the bank, ferry, post office, and other places of business; let your steps be regular and measured; grade everything; organize meetings, schools, debating and literary societies, and benevolent associations; group pictures; parcel out packages of receipts, letters, and papers; arrange and classify insects and geological specimens; assign a place to every article of wearing apparel; and in every way, as opportunity offers, assiduously cultivate this faculty, as it will facilitate business and act as oil in all the machinery of the labours of life. Southey has expressed our ideas in the most felicitous manner thus:—"Order is the sanity of the mind, the health of the body, the peace of the city, the security of the state. As the beams to a house; as the bones to the microcosm of man, so is ORDER to all things."

B. TO RESTRAIN AND LESSEN HABITS AND TASTES FOR MATERIAL ORDER:—Give yourself more ease and naturalness; let things get misplaced and go tangled; don't trouble yourself about them, nor let yourself be a slave to your faculty for order. Your knife and fork are just as useful instruments, no matter whether they lie *orderly* on the right and left of your plate, or are found in the midst of the dishes on the table; don't mind whether the shed of your hair is in a line or not; be less precise every day; and never mind whether things are agee or turned topsy-turvy; cultivate the magpie faculty, and hide things, lest they should be lost, where neither the owner nor anybody else can find them. Abraham Tucker complained that whenever his maid-servant had been arranging his library, he could not set comfortably to work again for several days. This is the model for you!

PERCEPTION OF ANGLES AND STRAIGHT LINES, OR ANGULARITIVENESS.

THE ABILITY OF APPRECIATING THE QUALITIES AND BEAUTIES OF ANGLES AND STRAIGHT LINES.

Angular form of ear, nose, malar or cheek-bones, brows, knuckles, knees, and every part of the human structure cannot be mistaken by a natural physiognomist as the hieroglyphics of angularity.

Angularitiveness small.
Edward V. of England. Born 1470. Smothered with his brother in the Tower of London in 1483.

Angularitiveness large.
An old Cardinal, who was quite eccentric.

1. There is no part of your structure that forms an angle, and being thrown into curves you cannot comprehend or form anything in which angles abound. You feel desirous even of rounding the corners of furniture, implements, and houses, having a constitutional aversion to sharp points wherever they appear.

2. Having in your frame very little of the earthy or crystallizable material which naturally forms angles in your bones, you take no pleasure in the corners and lines of crystals and exact shapes wherein smooth planes abound.

3. The acute and crystalogenic attractive force being but feeble in your constitution, you fail to perceive and appreciate beauty in angles, preferring the blunt and round to the acute and sharp.

4. Your small bones give more of the curve than the angular to your physique; hence you prefer going in the old routine mode of life rather than darting off at a tangent in striking out new and startling thoughts.

5. Your features are neither too round nor too sharp, and rarely, if

ever, do they run to extremes in either particular as to fancy or the workmanship you execute.

6. Being harmoniously balanced in possessing a body alike free from acuteness or roundness, your form occludes inclination either to excessive curvilinearity or rectilinearity.

7. No excess can be perceived in your faculty of angularity, and yet you will evince, although slowly, good judgment of material which may be rectilineal, zigzag, crinkled, folded, or crotchety.

8. The forks of trees, corners of houses, angular plots of ground, &c., you readily notice, and can remember the shapes of rectilinear figures and the intersections of straight lines far more accurately than rivers, mountains, or clouds wherein the curvilinear line marks their flowing and waving boundaries.

9. Though to the eye of the physiognomist it is at once apparent that the inflexible largely manifests itself in your nature; yet, even the unskilled who come in contact with you must soon thoroughly understand this faculty to be your prevailing characteristic.

10. The round and flexible person will signally fail to understand you; in fact, your mind will seem to be traversing some plain and straightforward subject, when in an instant you dart off unexpectedly at a tangent, which stamps you as odd and whimsical in character.

11. From your inability to appreciate and imitate curved lines, either simple or compound, you could never become a portrait or landscape painter. The mechanical arts in which plain surfaces and angles predominate, are those for which you are by nature adapted.

12. Being angular, sharp-cornered, and crotchety, in a pre-eminent degree, you will prove of some value to humanity, if you wisely and consistently select the vocation or profession for which so rare a specimen of the *genus homo* is adapted. In social life you present to your associates many angularities of character. Frederick the Great of Prussia had no more sharp eccentricities and extreme acuteness than you possess. Mentally, you are constantly squaring every curve and bringing into line every graceful bend or waving deflection.

A. THE MANNER OF STRENGTHENING THE ANGULAR FACULTY:—Allow every intense emotion and desire to run to extremes; cultivate moral courage, energy, and decision of character, as they are good auxiliaries of knuckles, elbows, and every kind of angularity; straighten the flexures; unbend the curls; practice architectural drawing, or engage in house-building; choose your associates from amongst the most crotchety, testy, touchy, and cusp portion of society, and learn to stick out your elbows; when you jostle against another, don't say, I beg your pardon, please excuse me, but dart on and fork into everybody and everything you see and at last you will become as angular in character as a well cut diamond, if not as valuable.

B. TO RETRENCH AND CURB YOUR ANGULAR NATURE:—Sketch scenes and faces; dance reels, waltzes, and cotillions; spin a top, and watch the musical swaying curves that are so beautifully described as its curvilinear life seems about to expire; earnestly, and in the majestic silence of NIGHT, the "mother of all things," view the ethereal dome, bedecked with its myriad suns set as gems in mystery's crown; trace and draw the winding shores of the sea, and the rivers that try to appease her insatiable call for many waters; get into the region of the mountain ranges of both worlds, and in silence contemplate the grandest and most elevating objects in nature; let all the varieties of form, shade, and colour, enrapture your soul and raise you to a sphere sublime. Never plane a board or draw an angle; round off the angles of both the material and mental sharp points you encounter; curl your hair, if it is not naturally wavey; when you meet others, sweep gracefully round and past them; clap your wings (or elbows) close to your sides, and gracefully sweep past those you meet, though you abnegate your natural feeling of taking "the right of way;" and lastly, like a Nero determined to prove himself so, bend every thought to the rounding off of the sharp points and angularity of your own mentality, and, like a practised and wary pilot, steer clear of the flukes, dodges, and elbows of others.

BENEFICENCE, OR BENEFICENTNESS.
THE INCLINATION TO DO GOOD.

The long face joined to a receding forehead and a prominent nose are nature's intimation of a naturally beneficent individual. Peter Cooper has the above form of features, and he annually educates several hundred children free of cost in the city of New York.

Beneficentness small.
An Australian man.

Beneficentness large.
Peter Cooper.

1. Only actuated by some selfish aim or end. You would contribute nothing for the relief of the needy were you possessed of the wealth of the Indies. You are as innocent of charitable feeling as John Elwes or Daniel Dancer, both noted misers. As Pollok has it:—

> "With eye awry, incurable, and wild,
> The laughing-stock of devil's and of men,
> And by your guardian angel quite given up."

2. To render a service and confer a benefit would not half so much gratify you as to injure and disoblige. "The silent digestion of one wrong provokes a second" in you, as Stern beautifully hits your propensity.

3. Having little active goodness or charity in your nature, you scarcely ever perform a beneficent action, being so thoroughly wrapped up in your own sweet self. Baxter was thinking of you when he said:— "Selfishness hath defiled the whole man, yet selfish pleasure is the chief part of your interest."

4. The gifts and favours which you bestow upon those asking alms are really of no mutual value to either the receiver or yourself. They are given of sheer ostentatiousness.

5. Should your kindness of treatment be all that is requisite you will delight in making others happy, but your giving will be with a careful hand. Your feelings are larger than your beneficence when tested by your gifts.

6. Being humane and well-intentioned, and not by any means malignant, nor will venom even cause you to be barbarous, yet charitableness will not rob you of much of your means.

7. When you are certain the suppliant for charity is needy, you give ungrudgingly. At your hands, the ordinary street beggar and able-bodied mendicant will receive small assistance.

8. The secret desire of your interior life is to be good and kind. When and how much you give depends upon your early education and your means.

9. You will do much to relieve the sufferings of those around you. You desire to execute the philanthropic plans you concoct; and being propitiatory in your nature, you can overlook the faults of others and form excuses for their shortcomings.

10. The bestowal of daily food to those who are needy would afford you exquisite pleasure; your almsgiving will always assume a practical form, and hence you prefer giving food, clothing, or a home to the destitute rather than money, yet even this you will give when you feel satisfied in doing so.

11. As soon as you are convinced of the worthiness of the object, your purse is always open, and you are inclined to give largely in the promotion of science, art, discovery, civilization, or the relief of suffering humanity.

12. Like Mr Gosse of London, you would rob yourself to benefit men or animals; nor can you bear to see a brute ill-used. Your type of character is that of Henry Bergh of New-York, who is the executive head of the society in that city for the prevention of cruelty to animals. Goodness in your character is so much in excess that it may be considered almost a fault. Bacon says of goodness: "This of all virtues and

dignities of the mind is the greatest, being the character of the Deity; and without it, man is a busy, mischievous, wretched thing." "Good deeds will shine as the stars in heaven," says Chalmers. Dickens says: "There is nothing innocent and good that dies and is forgotten." As to its reward, Basil beautifully observes: "A good deed is never lost; he that sows courtesy reaps friendship; and he that plants kindness gathers love, and gratitude begets reward."

A. To CULTIVATE BENEFICENCE:—Imitate the good Samaritan; learn the golden rule and try to live by its precepts; give freely, however little; cultivate the amiable and noble; forgive all that injure you; read the lives of Howard, Oberlin, Gurney, Peter Cooper, Florence Nightingale, and Lady Coutts; do not think the world selfish; remember the widow's mite, but do not forget it was *all* that she possessed. Old Epicurus says: "A beneficent person is like a fountain watering the earth and spreading fertility." Cicero remarked: "Men resemble the gods in nothing so much as in doing good to their fellow creatures." The following sentiment given by Shakspeare should be your guide: "Great minds erect their never-failing trophies on the firm base of mercy."

B. To RESTRAIN BENEFICENCE:—Remember that charity begins at home; learn to say *no;* don't be so tender-hearted and pathetic; you should have a kind but economical partner and defer to his judgment in all your acts of charity. Remember what Shakspeare says:

> "My master is of churlish d'sposition,
> And little recks to find the way to heaven
> By doing deeds of hospitality."

Lord Halifax has also well said: "He that spareth in everything is an inexcusable niggard. He that spareth in nothing is an inexcusable madman. The mean is to spare in what is least necessary, and to lay out more liberally in what is most required in our several circumstances."

DECISIVENESS.

THE FACULTY OF PUTTING AN END TO CONTROVERSIES OR DOUBTS, BY AN ASSERTION, AN IRREFRAGABLE FACT, OR ARGUMENT.

Prominent and well defined features, in connection with a large, active brain form, are nature's records in favour of decision of character.

1. Being utterly without the ability to choose between two alternatives, the character best befitting you is identical with that of the weathercock.

2. Naturally fickle and undecided, you cannot be relied upon; hence society has been almost unaffected by your influence.

3. Ever changing your mind you show how completely you are the victim of circumstances; a frail barque on the ocean of life without a helm and tossed to and fro by every wind; your daily conduct is well indicated by your unsteady gait. "Both right and wrong being hooked to your appetite, you follow as it draws."

4. Light-minded is the designation usually applied to such characters as you; your life is one of resolutions instead of being one of resolution; hence your oft felt doubts and suspense. "Some men, like pictures, are fitter for a corner than a full light," such is yours.

5. Fickle and freakish. you are moderate in your endeavour to make a point. Keep in mind the observation of Burke:—"Those who quit their proper character to assume what does not belong to them, are for the greater part ignorant of both the character they leave and of the character they assume."

6. Inherently ready to retreat and yield rather than be stupidly obdurate, you are neither very fickle nor constant. Take the sage advice of Socrates: "Endeavour to be what you desire to appear."

7. Possessed of a nature too plastic for positions of great responsibility, though generally stable and sufficiently decided for ordinary affairs, you would do well not to assume dictatorship, ascend a throne, or mount the presidential chair. Archbishop Whately gives sound advice when he says: "Do you want to know the man against whom you have most reason to guard yourself? Your looking-glass will give you a very fair likeness of his face."

Decisiveness small.
Louis W. Jackson, an ignorant hireling, who murdered a man in Illinois for 500 dols.

Decisiveness large.
Montesquieu, an accomplished scholar, upright man, and conscientious judge.

8. Such is the enterprise of the world that your firmness and persistent determination are not a whit more than what is necessary. Remember what Virgil has so well said: "They can conquer who believe they can." This chimes in admirably with your innate being.

9. Your character has such weighty influence that others have little power over you, except it plainly appears that they should. Yours is the kind of character Milton had in view when he said: "He who reigns within himself and rules passions, desires, and fears is more than a king."

10. Possessed of remarkable inflexibility and determination of character, you have resolution, decision, and stability to give you the character of staidness and solidity. "You can govern your passions with absolute sway, and grow wiser and better every day."

11. Incapable of yielding, you have a solid unmoved resoluteness not easily thwarted. Lavater must have had such characters in his mind

when he wrote: "He who, when called upon to speak a disagreeable truth, tells it boldly and has done, is both bolder and milder than he who nibbles in a low voice and never ceases nibbling."

12. Being doggedly positive you have become perfectly tyrannical in disposition. Keep in mind what the old cynic Diogenes said: "A tyrant never tasteth of true friendship, nor of perfect liberty."

A. To CULTIVATE AND STRENGTHEN DECISION OF CHARACTER:—Let circumstances be ruled by you, but never allow them to swerve you from your purpose. However humbly, take as your models such men as Cæsar, King Alfred, Bruce, Washington, Wellington, Nelson, Andrew Jackson, and Abraham Lincoln.

B. To REPRESS AND WEAKEN DECISION OF CHARACTER:—Keep in mind that you as well as others are liable to err, and that your excessive positiveness has often rendered you offensive to others; be a little more gentle and pliable; allow the opinions and decisions of others to have more weight with you; avoid being so positive and indomitable; and shake off the onerous feeling that the world has been shifted from the shoulders of Atlas to yours. Ever keep in mind Fletcher's apothegmatic words:—

"Our acts our angels are, or good or ill,
Our fatal shadows that walk by us still."

Remember that character is as inseparable from yourself as your very being; and also, "Talents are nurtured best in solitude, but character on life's tempestuous sea." Then keep clear of the billows in order that you may ever become more undecided.

OBSERVATION, OR OBSERVATIVENESS.

THE QUALITY OR DISPOSITION TO LOOK CLOSELY AND WITH RIGID CARE AT EVERY OBJECT.

Full long arching eyebrows, which are lowered down close to the eyes, are the visible physiognomical expression of a desire and capacity for observation. Darwin is an excellent example of large observation.

1. Destitute of any desire for knowledge, you never gape, stare, or wonder, being totally incurious and unimaginative. Your knowledge must be very limited, and if you can avoid it must never much extend its boundaries.

2. Only carelessly noticing what is thrust before you, as well might you be blind for all the use you make of your eyes. Hence your few ideas of things observable must be very confused, as you can have no definite knowledge of anything; and you may often be caught with a vacant stare of unrecognition in your face when you meet your most intimate acquaintance.

3. Your observant capacity and descriptive talents are slender, hence you could never become proficient in reading or portraying character; and you take almost no notice of your surroundings.

4. Naturally inconsiderate and inadvertent, you will be seen strolling along the streets with your head down, in apparent listless meditation without taking the least notice of objects or persons. You will often be surprised by the question from some of your friends or acquaintances— "Why did you cut me the other day?"

5. Being apt to observe only the most conspicuous things; hence minor objects will very likely escape your notice; and you are rather desirous of seeing the world, though not by any means strongly characterized by this faculty.

6. Though you overlook some of the minutiæ, yet it affords you much engrossing pleasure to view the world. Articles and objects not intimately connected with your business you will often take pleasure in examining.

7. Having an insatiable thirst for knowledge. you examine very closely both persons and things, as you desire to see, know, and inspect, in order to satisfy yourself.

8. Being of an earnest, observant, inquiring nature, you carefully attend to the concerns of daily life; observe well the general appearance of men and things; and everything attracts your attention sufficiently to afford you definite ideas of details.

Observativeness large.
Darwin.

9. Having a quick, ready. observant eye, you would enjoy travelling. as you are always on the look-out, and ready to examine everything around you. Observation and experience are two of your best instructors.

10. The five reception doors of your mind are ever wide open and ready to admit their appropriate visitors. Consequently many facts and ideas gain entrance, and nothing can be concealed from you; you would excel in the natural sciences.

11. Intensely endowed with insatiable curiosity, you manifest it in your eager desire of knowledge. And having an excellent talent for observation, and an aptitude for acquiring knowledge of details, you scrutinize every object with intense delight.

12. Such is your intense curiosity and impetuous eagerness to see and

examine everything, that you know what exists, and nothing escapes your acute, keen, and scrutinizing penetration.

A. TO CULTIVATE AND STRENGTHEN OBSERVATION:—Open your eyes upon everything visible; try to see everything; let the ten thousand objects you pass in the streets be scanned minutely; be off-hand and ready. Embrace every honourable means of awaking in your mind a desire for knowledge; be inquisitive and ready to see "the sights;" interest yourself in all the natural sciences, such as astronomy, geology, chemistry, botany, ornithology, &c.; and never forget that observation is the great medium and the lever by which we gain access to their mysteries, and poise aloft for the instruction of others new stores of knowledge.

B. TO RESTRAIN THE DESIRE FOR OBSERVATION:—Don't be so inquisitive; mind your own affairs and let all those of other people alone; look after only those things appertaining to the mere business of life; and remember that your questions regarding the affairs of others and their special province will be deemed impertinent. In one word, let indifference and listless carelessness about everything be your constant characteristics; and let the motto on your banner be, *n'importe (i.e.,* It matters not.)

PERSEVERANCE, OR PERSISTENACITY.

THE DISPOSITION OF HOLDING ON, THE PROPENSITY TO PURSUE A COURSE OF DESIGNS OR CONDUCT.

The body or ramus of the lower jaw, when long, may safely be considered the certain evidence of remarkable PERSEVERANCE. *This faculty is large in the bull dog, and small in the fox and wolf.*

1. Your nature is transitional, unstable, shifting, sliding from one conclusion to another; like a wolf you snap at an undertaking and instantly let go.

2. Versatility is your paramount characteristic, hence you can adopt at a moment's notice any course of action. Convertability is a prominent trait of your nature.

3. Assimilation and transmutation are powers so equally blended in your nature that your life seems ready to change its current from one channel to another with great facility. Either your life or views you can readily reorganize.

4. Being likely to yield your grounds of argument you reasonably and consistently with your character avoid harping upon the same string and repeating your discussions.

5. The genuine verities of life you love, but you will never enslave yourself to anything requiring to be accomplished by persistent efforts.

6. Should stings and thorns lie in your path you heed them not, when you have settled in your mind that your cause is worthy of your pursuit.

7. Such sentiments as those embodied in the following words o Lucretius, you heartily admire :—

"A falling drop at last will cave a stone."

The original we may quote for those who admire this old Roman scholar and poet :—

"Gutta cavat lapidem non vi sed sæpe cavendo," literally
A drop hollows the stone not by force, but by often falling.

8. Constancy in carrying out the project of your life is a positive and prominent trait in your character.

9. No one need try to turn your life from the higher aspirations of your nature; for, unless swayed by excellent reasons, you are unshifting.

Persistenacity very large.
This gentleman has lost thousands of pounds sterling by being excessively persistent.

Persistenacity very small.
Johnny, who could not persevere in an undertaking sufficiently to succeed.

Persistenacity small.
Prairie wolf or cyote.

Persistenacity large.
Bull dog.

10. Tenacity of purpose and persistency of pursuit are your characteristics. Whatever intentions you have determined upon for your life's course in those you will continue to persevere.

11. The invariable purpose of your life is unswerving, still pursuing, you ever persist and remain inflexible.

12. Nothing could turn you from your purpose. Perseverance is the magic key that opens for you the portals of every avenue to success.

A. To IMPROVE THE POWER OF PERSEVERANCE:—Grapple with the trials and labours of life in an earnest, persistent manner; shrink not from carrying to consummation all your noble views and aspirations; and remain fixed and determined on all occasions. "If at first you don't succeed, try, try, try again."

B. To CHECK PERSEVERANCE:—Reverse, change, and let slip your former opinions; strive to be guided by your judgment rather than impulse; forget that those who hold on longest and most tenaciously are sure to win; and be mutable, versatile and fond of change.

RECTITUDE, OR RECTITUDITIVENESS.

THE FACULTY THAT INCITES HONESTY OF PURPOSE AND STRAIGHT-FORWARDNESS OF CONDUCT.

Square bones, a bony chin, prominent cheek bones, and eyes which are at right angles to the mesial line of the face, or which cut straight across the face, are signs of HONESTY OF PURPOSE.

Rectituditiveness small.
John Tetzel, vendor of indulgences a *dishonest* face.

Rectituditiveness large.
Andrew Jackson, an *honest* face.

1. Being a thorough-paced knave, the law may have some influence in preventing you from doing wrong, but much more likely it will require the prison, penitentiary, or workhouse to prevent a second act of dishonesty.

2. Naturally wanting in honesty and void of integrity, your fraudulent disposition and propensities will stamp you with disgrace and ignominy.

3. Lacking in the sound principles of honesty, you are seldom, if ever, troubled with any scruples of conscience. Though, sometimes, you may intend to be as just as others, still somehow it ends by you deeming them dishonest.

Rectituditiveness small.
Lizzie Smith, a notorious pickpocket of New York City.

Rectituditiveness large.
Wm Tyndale, a translator of the Bible and martyr for the same.

4. Your moral nature not having received the stimulating influences conferred by education, and instilled by birth and rectifying circumstances around you, such as would have moulded your character into conformity and sympathy with what is right and real; you should ever beware of temptation, lest you be inadvertently overcome and fail to withstand the wily and potent propensities within you to commit evil.

5. As self-interest will prompt your weak mind to deceive and cheat, in expressing opinions you may give an unequal distribution of merit or demerit.

6. You earnestly strive to shun the wrong and act aright, yet under great trials you may yield to temptation, but sadly will you repent the error; and having tasted the bitterness of sin, and turned from it with disgust to feel the pleasurable sweetness of virtue, the experience will cause you to become more upright in disposition and conduct.

7. You will generally act uprightly, being disposed to place great value upon rectitude and veracity; yet you may be swayed by great temptations, being almost equally balanced between turpitude and probity.

8. Having a fair instinctive perception of the difference between right and wrong, truth and error, you will encourage in the young a high sense of honour and faithfulness, and endeavour to manifest candour and plain dealing on all occasions.

9. Justice and fair play please you; you endeavour to be truthful and impartial in your judgment, and entertain a high regard for straightforwardness of conduct and character.

10. Having naturally a love of integrity and detestation of falsity and deception, in your intercourse with your fellows, your aim is to do the right, to shun and suppress the false, and on all occasions promote rectitude of conduct and character.

11. Feeling no degradation to acknowledge it when you are in fault; you are ever ready to condemn yourself in what you do, and to overcome with the right; nor will you adopt any expedient which is not sanctioned by probity.

12. Intensely honest and upright in your own nature, you resemble Diogenes who was so intent in search of an honest man that he lighted his lantern and went forth at noon-day in search of such a character but failed. You think with Pope that "An honest man's the noblest work of God." Never for a moment do you harbour a thought of evil; greatly resembling Andrew Jackson, who had such contempt and hatred for falsehood and dishonesty, that when a man told the integrified president a lie, Jackson kicked him out of his room.

A. TO CULTIVATE THE ENNOBLING FACULTY OF RECTITUDE:—This faculty depends so much on early education that every mother should begin early in the life of her child to tutor and educate this faculty by her kind advice, and moral lessons, but of all things by her example, remembering that precept *teaches* but example *draws* (*i.e., educates.*) Study the meaning of the word right (*straight*) and follow its precepts. Never tamper with rectitude of principle, but ever bear in mind that the world hates falsehood; then, in everything you say or do, be sincere, just, and straightforward. Exercise taken in the open-air, under the genial influence of the beaming sun by the young, will settle and strengthen the foundations of honesty; and the continued use of sensibly regulated exercise in open-air with associations of elevated moral tone, will tend to strengthen and confirm the basis of honour. Let the noble example of Epaminondas, the great Theban general, be your guide in honesty; whose love of truth was so great that he never disgraced himself by a lie. Allow nothing to tempt you to err, that your character may resemble that of Phócion the celebrated statesman and orator who was called by the ancients an honest man.

B. TO RESTRAIN THE FACULTY OF RECTITUDE:—Don't for one moment entertain the idea that you have committed sins unpardonable; be less critically inclined towards your own shortcomings; sneer at all your trifling sins of omission; scout the ideas of moral obligations and duty; eat freely of bread and other edibles; sleep as much as you can; and, no matter how enormously you have transgressed, offended, or sinned, *never repent.*

NUMERICAL COMPUTATION, OR COMPUTATIONUMERICALITY.

SKILL IN COUNTING AND RECKONING.

Whenever we observe the outward extremities of the eyebrows running towards the top of the ears, or horizontally backwards, it is a sure sign of a quick, ready CALCULATOR; *but when the external terminus of the brows curve downwards to, or towards, the malar bone, as in Lord Lyttleton, it is a trustworthy indication that the person, thus facially marked, sadly lacks the ability to perform accurate numerical calculations.*

Computationumericality small.
Lord Geo. Lyttleton, an eminent historian of England, who was unable to master the Multiplication Table or any of the common rules of arithmetic.

Computationumericality large
Thos. Allen, M.D., a scholar in the reign of Queen Elizabeth, the first mathematician of his day.

1. So completely deficient are you in the comprehension of numerical relations that you never can even learn the Multiplication Table. In this respect you strongly resemble the late Rev. Mr Craddock, of Dublin, who could never learn the Multiplication Table.

2 Long arithmetical problems are a great bore to you, as you are almost totally deficient in this faculty. Hence no amount of cultivation could ever render you fit to be compared with such experts in figures as Euclid, Lana, Lagny, Landen, John William Lubbock, Thomas Drummond, Sir John Leslie, Herschel, Zerah Colburn, Lagrange, Truman H. Safford, Adrien Marie Legendre, Arago, &c.

3. Being unable to appreciate nicely and readily the relations of numbers, figures are always a drag to you and repulsive. In any urgent case, being compelled to cast accounts, you cannot trust yourself without consulting your tables and using graduated instruments.

4. Being rather deficient in this faculty, you will require much prac-

tice to attain skill; but you can scarcely ever expect to take an ardent delight in the study of any of the exact sciences.

5. Though slow and uncertain in arithmetic, you may take considerable pleasure in the study of algebra and geometry.

6. Though you will probably fail in the complexities of fractions and the extraction of roots, and find yourself deficient in exactitude, still by patient perseverance you may become proficient in the simpler rules of arithmetic.

7. You have scientific inclinations and like accuracy, yet you are neither precise nor inexact in your own affairs.

8. Very well balanced as a mathematical reasoner and calculator, you will excel, especially in numbers, and yet never become insane about computation.

9. While you are not a genius in the sciences of number and measure, you have naturally a strong desire for accurate answers and conclusions in arithmetic and mathematics. You are inclined, by instinct, to calculate or ask the number of those present at a party, assembly, campmeeting, or mass-meeting.

10. In the knowledge and science of quantity, you have unerring aptitude; and having a sound mathematical judgment, you desire to determine accurately all the problems of life. In the higher mathematics you could succeed admirably.

11. Having an innate tendency to apply your calculating powers to everything, you feel great pleasure in the use of figures, and are naturally rapid and correct in calculations. Such is your instinctive feeling that you would count the windows in houses, the panes in the windows, the telegraph poles along your route by the rail, the ornamental pipes in front of an organ, the pews in a church, or, indeed, anything that may be counted.

12. Having an intuitive comprehension of numbers and quantities, with their endless and infinite delicate relations, you are a mathematical prodigy. Your scientific mathematical conclusions come "As effortless as woodland nooks send violets up and paint them blue."

A. TO IMPROVE YOUR TALENT FOR NUMERICAL COMPUTATION:— Count all you see that can be numbered; at night reckon the pulsations of your heart, the ticking of your watch or clock; study and give undivided attention to long problems in arithmetic; morning and evening think out several problems in mental arithmetic; keep a slate or calculating materials in your room, and just before retiring to rest solve a few accounts of fair length; keep the faculty in exercise and it will strengthen.

B. TO RESTRAIN THE FACULTY FOR ESTIMATING AND COMPUTING:— Avoid working in figures; cease to count objects or parts of them; turn your mind to other matters; never attempt to get rich by air-castle building in calculations alone; but turn your mind to anything else.

DISCERNMENT OF DENSITY, OR SOLIDATIVENESS.
THE POWER THAT JUDGES OF SOLIDITY OR COMPACTNESS.

When density is large it reveals itself by a firm quick step and a well balanced gait; and in the face it betrays itself by a quiet, steady, thoughtful expression of the eyes.

Solidativeness large.
J. Q. A. Ward, sculptor.

1. Your walk or gait lacks steadiness, hence you are liable to falter, fall, or be capsized.

2. Being liable to dizziness on elevated places, and wanting the power of equipoise, you are unable to balance well, and should never attempt the Blondin feat of crossing the Niagara falls upon a rope.

3. Being liable to stumble you should keep upon *terra firma;* in hurling and curling you are liable to miss the mark; you cannot become an offhand and expert judge of the weight of animals; nor can you well peer into objects sufficiently closely to tell where compactness reigns or sleaziness abounds.

4. As it is nearly impossible for you to learn by sight whether or not much matter is contained in a small space you should weigh all you purchase, if you desire to have an approximate knowledge of the weight.

5. Having but a feeble perception of the lightness and compactness of material, you would be liable to stumble and fall, unless you are doubly careful.

6. Not being very able in judging of the proportion of matter to the bulk, you must be unable to determine accurately whether or not the constituent parts of a body are closely united

7. With practice, you could roll a ten-pin ball and possess a fair idea of the laws of gravity.

8. Ponderosity or lightness rarely escape your notice; rigidity or pliancy arrest your attention, and hence you readily determine which side of a load is the heaviest.

9. Seldom do you miss your footing, and can throw a stone, pitch a quoit, or ride a horse, and could walk in dangerous places with ease and self-possession.

10. Being excellent in statics, at a glance you can judge whether a body is cumbersome or sublimated. If a thing is impenetrable or compressible, you recognize either condition with facility; and you can tell whether a peach or an apple is hard or soft without trying it with your hand.

11. Engineering would be your delight as you are excellent in dynamical skill and understand the application of mechanical forces, while you readily perceive degrees of force and keep the centre of gravity well. And besides all this you can decide whether the material is close, compact, and firm or fluid and rare.

12. Having great facility in judging of momentum and resistance, your idea of relative weight and ability to keep the balance is a superior one; being sure-footed as well as sure-sighted, you would excel at quoits and archery, while you are a dead shot. This faculty was large in Brunel, the celebrated engineer and mathematician.

A. To CULTIVATE THE FACULTY OF JUDGING OF DENSITY:—Balance yourself on one foot; balancing in dancing and riding calls out this ability. Practice shooting; suspend bodies on a point; a book upon your thumb; hold in equipoise any body you can command; and play at ball, ten-pins, bagatelle and billiards.

B. To RESTRAIN THIS FACULTY:—Use it only to a good purpose and do not play mountebank or Blondin.

SUGGESTIVENESS.
THE POWER OF FURNISHING PRACTICAL ASSISTANCE OR DIRECTION.

The annexed engraving of Mr Holcraft, of California, in which the septum of the nose is long at the place to which the index finger points, indicates an unusual amount of SUGGESTIVE FERTILITY OF MIND.

1. Devoid of freshness, your mind resembles a dead and leafless shrub unfruitful and utterly careless about the conjectural, hypothetical, or theoretical. Illusive notions and ideas never trouble your mind.

2. Inclined to travel in the beaten ruts of ages gone, pre-supposition will find little sympathy with you. Ever ready to repeat the same threadbare story or anecdote; the ideas you deal in are counterfeit and plagiarized from more original minds. You are no innovator upon old ideas, being enamoured of stereotyped customs and notions.

3. Being devoid of creative intelligence, the world will be none the richer in mental treasure from your advent, or departing mental bequest.

The very attempt to innoculate you with a fresh idea strikes pain to your heart.

4. Though you would not be presumptuous, yet you are under the necessity of accepting the logic of others, and still feel unsatisfied with what you consider baseless deductions. New ideas are not manufactured by minds of your mould.

5. Since you care little for theoretic or hypothetic ideas, not being of an intimative nature, you are somewhat feeble in the capacity of suggestion.

Suggestiveness large.
Mr Holcraft of California.

6. Though none too suggestive, yet should danger hover near, your mind will suggest the means of avoiding it. Having a taste for the novel, you enjoy fresh scenes, and are ever ready to encourage those who are making discoveries in science.

7. To your mind the old rut is not quite satisfactory, hence you venture upon suggestive hints when startling propositions present themselves to you. Though rather putative you are quite good counsel.

8. You are competent to appreciate and sympathize with an original genius who ventures to question and controvert the old philosophy, while your own cogitations are inventive and fertile.

9. As theories and conjectures are ever waiting at the portals of your mind, your putative and instinctive nature will leap to many rash and original conclusions In this characteristic you largely resemble the famous and talented Lord Brougham

10. Postulation and presumption will make you impractical; your monitions are worthy of the notice of those for whom they are intended. Many new theories occur to your mind, and the style and diction of your writings are perfectly unique, having no family resemblance to those of any other writer in the entire catalogue of literature and science.

11. Possessing many secret incitements, you profess to know much of things of which you are ignorant; still, your originality in designing and planning shows that you are the possessor of a mind of your own capable of mighty projects.

12. With a rare talent for invention ever evolving something unmatched, you imperceptibly become hortative, dogmatical, and full of false conjectures; you are constantly surmising and insinuating to the intense annoyance of those of ordinary suggestive power and imagination.

A. HOW TO STRENGTHEN THE FACULTY OF SUGGESTION:—Seize eagerly and examine whatever is new; study the wonders of nature in their uncontaminated state; and, unfetter your mind, by metaphysical research; let each day have its hours of solitary study, guided by authors of original works; while in solitude, write something unsurpassed. Great and supreme minds, such as Montague, Leibnitz, Petrarch, and Voltaire, retired from the fashions and frivolities of an apeing world, in order to evolve new thoughts. Montague says of company and bustling courts, "There is an effeminacy of manners, a puerility of judgment prevailing there, that attached me by force to solitude."

B. TO RESTRAIN OR WEAKEN THE FACULTY OF SUGGESTION:— Be quite satisfied with what you know; let the veil of superstition be your shield, and leap from premises to conclusions without one intermediate step of ratiocination; smother every original thought; ape others, and in due time your suggestions will become feeble if not altogether smothered. Keep pace with fashion, remembering it is a hard race; adopt the old foggy notions of the stagnant past, and you may fairly say I have suppressed originality.

PERCEPTION OF CHARACTER, OR CHARACTERIOSCOPICITY

THE ENDOWMENT WHICH GIVES THE POWER OF PENETRATING AND UNDERSTANDING THE CHARACTER OF OTHERS.

Prominence of the frontal bone immediately over the inner corner of the eye together with a prominent and long nose are unfailing evidences of keen perception of character.

1. Knowing or caring little about character, you are very easily deceived in individuals.
2. When in the society of others for a length of time you may learn their characters, but you are unable to discern them at once.
3. On the *second* interview, people appear vastly different to you from the *first*.
4. In a knowledge of friends or foes you should not flatter yourself.
5. Be not hasty in your judgment of those you meet, as you may be deceived by others in their peculiarities.
6. You may feel some interest in faces, yet other themes will absorb your soul more completely.
7. In the expression of the human countenance you feel a deep interest, and in human nature you have a theme of real enjoyment, while you are ever ready to interest others.

8. If you have studied physiognomy you will readily appreciate the characteristic signification of faces.

9. The appearance of individuals excites your curiosity, your presentiments about persons are apt to prove true.

10. The peculiarities of human dispositions are no mystery to you; and your perception of their dispositions are clear and correct.

11. Your talent for the study of anthropology, ethnology, ethnography, and human character, is very remarkable.

Characterioscopicity large
Rev J. G. Lavater, a Swiss poet, and author of several works on physiognomy. He was a talented divine, and became pastor of the Church of St Peter, at Zurich. His works have been translated into most European languages. Born at Zurich in 1741, where he died in 1801.

Characterioscopicity large.
J. B. Porta, a learned mathematician, and Neapolitan writer. Author of works on physiognomy, natural history, optics, hydraulics, and agriculture. He was the inventor of the camera obscura. Born at Naples in 1540, where he died in 1615.

12. Never deceived by character, you intuitively know another as if you had been acquainted for years.

A. To Strengthen the Perception of Character:—Notice and study minutely the faces of all you meet, marking carefully the dog or cat like expression of the face; read books on physiognomy and mind; and wherever you notice any peculiar look or form of face try to learn its signification.

B. To Weaken the Perception of Character:—Avoid peering into the faces of those you meet, note only the good in others and become more confiding; avoid reading such works as Reid's "Essays on the Intellectual Power of Man;" Pope's "Essay on Man;" Dugald Stewart's works on the "Philosophy of the Active and Moral Powers of Man;" "Lavater's Physiognomy;" and all works relating directly to mind.

FRIENDSHIP, OR AMICITIVENESS.

THE FRATERNAL DISPOSITION AND GREGARIOUS INCLINATION.
A broad forehead and open eye are evidential of true friendship.

Amicitiveness small.
Catherine II, who possessed great intellectual powers, strong passions, yet was destitute of true friendship.

1. As unfriendliness and estrangement are deeply rooted in your character, you are very naturally thoroughly inimical to those whom you should highly esteem.

2. Being huffish, resentful, and suspicious, you readily become alienated from your friends, and take umbrage on the most trifling occasion

3. The most trivial incidents and traits in the conduct of your friends when they happen to be displeasing to you, become an excuse for your falling out with them.

4. Possessing weak social sympathies, the least unpleasantness may cause variance and even hostility between you and those with whom you should fraternize.

5. Sociality and amity are to some extent indigenous to your nature, but still they are not sufficiently powerful to overcome any very strongly provoked and deep estrangement.

6. Although grave offences may arouse animosity towards your associates, yet the amicable and cordial impulses of your nature will triumph over the baser propensities.

7. Being naturally compassionate you enjoy much pleasure in befriending a fellow creature—man or brute Neither intense hatred nor perfect amity of feeling will occasion your ruin.

Amicitiveness large.
Mrs Lydia H. Sigourney, a talented poetess and friend to woman

Amicitiveness large.
"Greyfriar's Bobby" With remarkable faithfulness he guarded his master's grave, in Edinburgh, upwards of 13 years. For the photograph and history of this dog, and other favours, I am highly indebted to Mr W. G. Patterson, 34 Frederick Street, Edinburgh.

8. Happily mellow and genial in the glow of your innate attachments, you are truly and eminently social among your personal friends.

9. The more tried you are the more true you become; hence friendship is a strong bond between yourself and the hearts of those you relieve in sore trial.

10. A desire to be on friendly terms with the world, displaying itself in your feelings and amicable deportment towards all, causes many to wish you well and prosperous. The following lines well portray your fraternal nature and freshness of spirit:—

> " Friendship, like an evergreen,
> Will brave th' inclement blast,
> And still retain the bloom of *spring*,
> When summer days are past."

11. Full of warm and gregarious preferences you are naturally very confiding, and perhaps too readily form personal attachments.

12. Being peculiarly conciliatory and propitious towards every one, you are surrounded and admired by numerous friends, as you are ever befriending strangers and manifesting high esteem for others.

A. To CULTIVATE FRIENDSHIP:—Trust especially in friends, if judicious; constantly go into society; give up your anchoret life; never omit an opportunity to increase your friendly circle; form honourable attachments; but under all circumstances, try to prevent alienation or estrangement from cutting the cords of amity; never turn state or king's evidence; follow the example of Richard Cobden, who proved himself not only a friend to the poor of his own country, but to those of other nationalities.

B. To RESTRAIN FRIENDSHIP:—Never attempt it;—but if you will become misanthropic, keep your thoughts to yourself; avoid all close intimacies; but specially recollect that your powerful friendship may ruin you. Hear what La Fontaine says: "Nothing is more dangerous than a friend without discretion; even a prudent enemy is preferable." But be warned by what Lavater says: "He that has no friend and no enemy, is one of the vulgar, and without talents, power, or energy." Then, as a final consolation in discarding all friendships, hear what Aristotle says: "He who hath many friends hath none."

ORIGINALITY, OR ORIGINATIVENESS.

THE POWER OF PRODUCING SOMETHING NEW, UNLIKE ANYTHING PREVIOUSLY EXISTING.

Coarse, large features,—such as a large nose well raised from the plane of the face, ample mouth, wide cheek-bones, and a strong look, rather than fine and effeminate face,—are indications of originality of mind. Professor Morse, the inventor of the electric telegraph, was a good example of originality.

NOTE.—The ability to originate is always accompanied with prominent features.

1. A new idea, machine, or implement is not acceptable to you.

2. So little that is new springs into your mind that you might rather be denominated annihilator than producer or originator.

3. You are better adapted for demolition and extermination than for planning and concoction.

4. Being an old-style mind accustomed to follow, you will be rarely found in the van of enterprise, but may come pretty surely at the termination.

5. Though you may delight in useful inventions, your forte is not to originate notions or invent novelties.

Originativeness large.
Prof. Morse, the inventor of the electric telegraph.

6. The happy medium suits you best, as you are not naturally adapted to the initiation or conclusion of any important enterprise or undertaking.

7. Occasionally you have queer and new thoughts, and derive some pleasure in the inauguration of subjects and ideas.

8 You delight in leading the way, and being the primordial cause of valuable discoveries.

9. Thoroughly appreciating nascent and dawning intelligence, and original minds, your pleasure will ever be to broach and set on foot what is new and striking.

ORIGINATIVENESS. 161

10. You will invent, institute, and throw forth to the world many very valuable thoughts, though you fail to compel society to compensate you adequately for your discoveries in embryo.

11. You are one of the very few that are capable of introducing schemes and originating valuable thoughts such as are worth propagation.

12. Possessed of great originality of mind, that is ever inventing and occasioning in concert with kindred minds, you will follow your natural bent by being originatively inclined. Every sentence you utter, as well as every work you perform, will stand out as connotative and stamped with the originality of genius.

Originativeness small.
George IV., the leader of fashion during his reign.

A. MANNER OF DEVELOPING THE ORIGINATIVE POWER:—Travel, observe, and think for yourself; make, model, and fashion, but solely after your own ideas; associate with those who have thoughts of their own and dare to express them; read the works of Lord Bacon, Stuart Mill, Herbert Spencer, Denton, and other authors whose writings are characterised by originality of thought; in short, accept nothing unless your reason sanctions it, and not even then unless it is new: but at all times keep in mind that "the little mind that loves itself will write and think with the vulgar, while the great mind will be bravely and daringly eccentric, and, from universal benevolence, will scorn the beaten track."

B. HOW TO PROCEED TO CURB THE EXCESSIVE ACTION OF ORIGINALITY:—Believe all you hear even though you can't eat all you see; do as others have done before; restrain your thoughts by turning them into the dry stubble of long since reaped ideas; seek flippant and gay society, especially those of the windbag and Joe Millar class, who can never utter a sentence without repeating "By the Lord Harry;" "How jolly;" "Upon my word and soul," and such inanities; stay at home, always sleep, sit, and eat in one unchanged position and manner; read the Bible in scraps, and don't imagine that it has any meaning but that put upon it by the officiating man-made minister; sing the old version of the Psalms — but don't observe the absurdity of the first two lines of this old version of the fifty-third Psalm, when you hear the precentor boldly shout over the congregation: "The Lord shall come, and He shall not;" and then, when he and the congregation have intoned this in serious and solemn fashion, he bawls out: "Be silent, but speak out." Live on rich food; and rest assured that original ideas will no more come to you than the sun to the earth or Pallas to the moon.

DISCERNMENT OF MAGNITUDE, OR MENSURATIVENESS.

THE PERCEPTION OR FACULTY WHICH PERCEIVES AND JUDGES OF MEASUREMENTS.

A general fulness across the lower forehead, long eyebrows, with a bony and square face, are excellent assurances of capability in recognizing and judging of MEASUREMENT.

1. Not being capable of perceiving the difference between three and five miles, don't trust your eyes when an approximation to accuracy is required. Possessing very little you manifest none of this faculty.

2. Being liable to inaccuracy, you should look several times at an article of value before you make an offer to purchase, and then say, "I'll look in to-morrow, if I think well of it."

3. Being quite liable to err in estimating size, bulk, proportion and dimension, you should always take care to postpone your decisions in matters of this kind, and advise with those skilled in such admeasurements.

4. Being utterly at fault in such matters, you must fail in attempting to determine length, breadth, height, depth, thickness, &c.; hence, you are quite unqualified to superintend mechanical and architectural enterprises.

5. Inaccurate in the perception of size and distance, and, consequently, in that of dimension, you retain only crude recollections of the scenery you have been induced to behold long ago, and faces that were well known to you a few years since seem like apparitions in an uneasy dream.

6. Not very exactly can you judge the size of bodies; for accuracy, you had better take the exact dimensions; and for improvement in exactness you might well devote some of your time to working in a mechanical occupation, even as an amateur.

7. Though not deeply skilled in the perception of distance and proportion, you have fair ability in appreciating and approximating to a just conclusion when these subtle relationships are to be decided upon.

8. Having an accurate eye in judging of bulk, you seldom err in judging of volume or size.

Mensurativeness large.
John, Duke of Bedford, Regent of France.

Mensurativeness large
Chetah, or hunting leopard of India and Africa.

9. Your eye most accurately perceives relative size; and in your judgment of parallax, you are a most accurate guide.

10. Were your other natural gifts as valuable and accurate as your mechanical eye, you would excel as an engineer.

11. Distances, of whatever length, you measure with wonderful accuracy; and, perpendicular as well as horizontal dimensions, you ascertain rapidly, so that few excel you, either in this respect, or in judging of magnitude.

12. Never deceived in dimension of any kind—length, breadth height, or distance—you detect proportion or its opposite, at a glance. Your eye is too accurate to require the aid of tape or measure of any kind.

A. To Cultivate the Power of Estimating Distance:—Observe the size of every object within your observation; estimate its length or breadth; then, when practicable, measure it to discipline your judgment; always notice carefully the size of everything. Engage in surveying, designing, architecture, and civil engineering, in order to develop this capacity; measure lumber, or timber; transcribe and fold papers and books; and, if possible, engage temporarily in an occupation in which this faculty is always in exercise.

B. To RESTRAIN THE FACULTY OR TENDENCY TO ESTIMATE DISTANCE:—
Live more by your soul powers; never step across a field or by the side of a house, or the length of a block to ascertain the distance; it matters not that you do not know the admeasurement of everything you pass! Never ask the captain of a boat or the railway guard or conductor how far you are from the last place you left or the distance to your destination; you must have felt that the anxiety of the passenger to know his distances often makes him boorish and look silly. Remember that "sublimity, grace, and beauty, are the effects of distance," as Sir Walter Scott has well expressed it.

PERTINACIOUSNESS.

THE QUALITY OF BEING PERVERSE OF PURPOSE AND PERTINACIOUS OF OPINION.

The power of OBSTINACY *manifests itself by relative length in the limb of the jaw.*

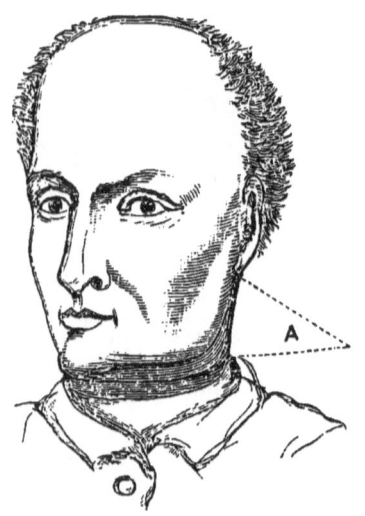
Pertinaciousness large.
Charles XII. of Sweden.

Pertinaciousness small
Ristori, a talented actress in the Italian language.

1. Yielding and conciliatory, you are always ready and willing to yield your own opinion to that of another.
2. Instinctively hating positive, mulish, and tenacious persons; you manifest entire freedom from obstinateness.
3. You will acknowledge your error, being of a persuadable and convincible spirit.
4. Thoroughly disliking the pertinacious you can easily change your mind and conform to the desires of others.

PERTINACIOUSNESS.

5. You are apt to give your assent at once by saying yes; but on a moment's reflection you may say no immediately afterwards.
6. You neither assume the opposite side for the sake of opposition simply, or the contrary, and yet you gain knowledge from the opinions of others.
7. Though well balanced in this trait of character, at times you may seem inconsistent from obstinacy.
8. Being ready to become an opponent in argument, you can say no, and adhere to it.

Pertinaciousness large.
Ass.

Pertinaciousness small.
Hunter, Horse.

9. Unyielding and headstrong, refractory and contumacious, you are too positive, and have a strong bias to the inexorable.
10. Mulish and unpersuadable, doggedness and obduracy, stiffness and obstinacy are ever causing you to be prejudiced.
11. The poet Cowper was evidently describing a character like you when he so accurately drew his picture in the following lines:—

> "His still refuted quirks he still repeats,
> New raised objections with new quibbles meets,
> Till sinking in the quicksand he defends,
> He dies disputing and the contest ends"

12. Wilfulness and stubbornness are your most powerful traits of character; and being utterly untractable, you will never repent.

A. To INCREASE YOUR OBSTINACY:—Having formed an opinion of your own upon every subject, never yield to those of others; be positive, and never say I think, reckon, or guess. Always use the superior tone, "I know;" take no one's counsel or advice; and try to imitate Charles I. of England, whose stubbornness, undoubtedly cost him his head.

B. To COUNTERACT OBSTINACY:—Always say yes, and avoid the negative; yield to others, bearing in mind how intolerable obstinacy is in others; by every effort try to repress this mulish disposition.

MECHANICAL MOTION, OR TEMPORIMECHANICALITY.

THE ABILITY TO JUDGE OF TIME MADE BY INSTRUMENTS, MECHANICAL APPLIANCES, OR DIRECT MOTIONS.

Mechanical time is known to a physiognomist by a squareness of the face joined with a large mathematical capacity. (See signs of Computationumericality.)

Temporimechanicality small.
Chinese girl.

Temporimechanicality large.
Duke of Wellington.

1. Rather unmindful of engagements, you fritter away the time.
2. Your dance betrays the graceful posturing of a poked pig; and as to keeping time to music, you will try, but be cautioned by the success that attended the efforts of the dog that attempted to bite the moon
3. You will fail in judging the time of day, but more signal will be the failure in your efforts to indicate the hour of the stilly night. Your mind is utterly helpless without an alarm or timepiece.
4. Your memory of births, deaths, and dates is very faulty; you take little interest in definite duration; the simple fact is that you should desire to be where "time shall be no longer."
5. Having no regard for the true value of time, our mightiest boon, you will often try to while away an hour or two in light reading or useless amusement. In fact, you have a liking for the old impossible murder

problem, and *try* "to kill time." Your talent not being so great as your desire, you need not kill time by meditating how to kill it.

6 You can remember only when important occurrences transpired; but you care little for a few moments.

7. In judging of periods of duration you are not much to be relied upon.

8. Though pretty good at comprehending measured duration, you could scarcely remember the exact date of a marriage, a birth, or a death.

9. When dancing or marching, you naturally keep time to the music with your step, and can tell whether the measure is or is not well timed.

10. You scarcely need to carry a watch to determine the time; you can dance in correct time only; and, with practice, you would become an expert in beating a drum.

11. In judging of the hour or minute of the hour of the day or night, you are very accurate, and enjoy that which recurs in regular succession; and you catch yourself measuring your steps.

12. No one could beat time for musicians with more accuracy than you; and, in metre, you are as steady and as true as a clock's pendulum.

A. To Cultivate the Mechanical Appreciation of Time:— Strive to remember accurately when incidents occur; trust more to your mind and rely less upon a timepiece; when dancing, keep step to the music; beat a drum, and imitate Wellington and Nelson, who were alike remarkable for their punctuality.

B. To Restrain Mechanical Appreciation of Time:—Be less particular about a few moments, and omit drumming with your feet; do not join in concert when others play or sing; let your attention be diverted by something in order that your time may pass without tedium.

PRACTICALITY, OR PRACTICALITIVENESS.

THE QUALITY OF BEING PRACTICAL—MAKING A GOOD USE OF EVERYTHING.

Receding foreheads are never found, except in persons of great PRACTICAL INCLINATIONS. *Dr John Hunter, whose genius, cultivated taste, and profound research have placed him among the most eminent philosophers and scholars of his time, had a low, receding forehead. He remarked that his first consideration of a subject was in regard to its practical usefulness, and that, if considered impractical, he abandoned it for ever.*

1. Utterly incapable of perceiving the adaptation and application of means to an end, though your theories are specious and plausible to the illogical mind, you are totally useless as a scientific guide.

2. Delighting in flighty theories, you *seem* to be able to manage a complicated subject, while you wax deep and profound in thought, revelling in speculative and metaphysical theorisation. Though there is much in you, it can never become available or of any practical value to mankind in general, unless you get a dash of common sense infused into your wild notions, so as to precipitate some practical and palpable results.

3. In your case first impressions are utterly untrustworthy, especially in material things; hence you fail to comprehend many of the useful

affairs of life, except you take time to investigate them philosophically, and pop them into the thinking crucible. Unless you look several times at an article before purchasing it, especially if it is of value, be cautious, think and pocket your purse very deliberately, sleep upon it, and then decide.

4. Incorrigibly impractical in your theories, you are nevertheless capable of discerning and comprehending the cause as well as the consequences of most subjects submitted to your investigation.

5. While theories and idealistic subjects afford you much gratification, becoming at times absorbing, yet you are able to discern the difference between the achievable and the unattainable—a valuable gift.

6. Most happily balanced you are in respect of practicality, being neither a misty theorist nor a plain utilitarian.

Practicalitiveness small.
Thomas D'Urfey, a facetious English poet, who wrote several plays and songs, yet they were of no practical value, and justly forgotten because of their licentiousness.

Practicalitiveness large.
C. M. Wieland, an elegant and learned writer and poet of Germany, whose writings comprised 51 vols. of classical and practical literature.

7. Having a natural and useful tendency in your nature to condense knowledge as well as pleasure into the most exquisitely enjoyable shapes and forms, you are quick to take a hint, and tact is your most valuable characteristic.

8. Available and practical undertakings are most readily and easily grasped by your mind; hence experience and observation will and have been your most faithful and trustworthy tutors.

9. Having an intuitive perception and discernment of the compatible, you readily comprehend the feasibility and possibility of a plan when submitted.

10. Naturally talented in applying knowledge to useful purposes, those things are most prized by you which can be turned to good account. You cannot have any sympathy with rules founded on the hypothetic

principles which are resorted to in the arithmetical rule of "supposition."

11. Replete with practicality, you advocate practical theories; idealistic and theoristic notions are distasteful to you; the first and truest scale-test to you is practicalness. The value of everything is tested by you as to its intrinsic value and utility.

12. Exceedingly practical in your very nature, your mind harbours no vague or unfeasible plans; hence the most direct mode of accomplishing your object most gratifies you, as useful ideas only are at all pleasing to you.

A. To CULTIVATE PRACTICALITY:—Look alive, act, and *observe more*, and *think* or rather *dream less;* one practical idea is worth ten thousand vague theories. Travel, hold your peace when you meet with the world, but look it straight in the face, and ask it how it gets on; never get into a brown study, but look as if everything with you was anything but brown—quite celestial bright. "Then thou shalt learn the wisdom early to discern true beauty in utility," as *Longfellow* puts it.

B. To RESTRAIN PRACTICALITY:—Don't do it; still if you wish it,—observe less and meditate more; get into the metaphysical world, and rent a house there; but never leap over the hedge of premises to the garden of conclusion. Allow the tranquillity of retirement to beckon your mind into those deep meditations that diverge from the general paths of practical life; remember that many great minds have retired from the superficial world to give scope and activity to deep thought, thereby expressing practically and developing the character that philosophers pass in a private condition. Charles V., Emperor of Germany, passed into seclusion, voluntarily retiring from the throne of Germany and Spain, to give to his mind the quickening effect of solitude and meditation, - not to say, the intense relish of sensual enjoyment, of an endless course of Epicurean pleasure. The celebrated Greek biographer and philosopher Plutarch retired from the world and its frivolous society that he might arouse and awaken the dormant ideas within him He said, "I live entirely upon history; and while I contemplate the pictures it presents to my view, my mind enjoys a rich repast from the representation of great and virtuous characters." Pericles, Phocion, and Epaminondas, in solitude drank deep of philosophy, which was the foundation of their eternal greatness. When only thirty-four years of age, Virgil retired to that beautiful city of Naples and produced the finest effort of his genius, "THE GEORGICS." Pliny the elder, who was one of Rome's ripest scholars, devoted his whole life to retirement and learning. Alexander the Great took much pleasure in reading. Cicero said, "I spend my recollective hours in a pleasing review of my past life, in dedicating my time to learning and the muses." Heracleus left his throne to devote his mind to philosophic truth. The last nine years of the life of Diocletian were spent in retirement. Reading and thinking, while freed from the cares and follies of life, will restrain practicality and seduce the human mind into labyrinthian conceptions.

REVERENCE, OR REVERENTIALNESS.

THE STATE OF AWE, HIGH REGARD, AND FELT RESPECT, EXHIBITED FOR GOD AND MANKIND.

A low coronal region and high superior front head and eyes, which naturally turn upwards on meeting another's gaze, indicate large respect; but when they stare boldly into the eyes of fellow kind and care not to turn their glance, and when it seems to require effort to do so, it indicates small reverence and no respect.

1. Apt to scoff sneer at, and derisively ridicule your best friends, you are as impudent as a monkey, as pert as a parrot, as upsetting as a jackdaw, as provoking as the mocking bird, and as packyderm as the pig. Carlyle catches your character beautifully and graphically when he says: "Against stupidity the very gods fight unvictorious."—"It says to the gods try all your lightnings here, see whether I cannot quench them!"

2. An inbred characteristic of your organization is to slight, disparage, and disrespectfully treat others. Lavater says: "A habit of sneering marks the egotist, or the fool, or the knave, or all three."

3. Your harsh and unsubdued voice indicates that you care little for the aged and antique specimens of mechanical, artistic, or natural relics; hence you would not manifest much interest in antiquities, and would never become an antiquarian.

4. Though radical and sometimes supercilious, you may at times reverence the feelings of others; still you are generally very gruff and not very serious in the affairs of life.

5. Although you are no worshipper of high-sounding titles, still you consider it a humane duty to treat others with proper decorum and respectful esteem, and you will look up to and venerate the aged.

6. Being happily balanced in your reverential feelings, you are alike free from extreme awe or derision. "Such minds as yours can only negatively offend, but cannot positively please"

7. Neither ceremonious nor disrespectful, you will reciprocate civilities, and not despise even obsequiousness.

8. Though disposed to treat the aged with respectful tenderness, still you are anxious to have a reason for everything.

9. You have due deference for friends, honour for the good, esteem for all the noble and worthy, and reverence for God. Shenstone puts your nature well when he says: "Deference is the most complicate, the most indirect, and the most elegant of all compliments, and before company is the genteelest kind of flattery."

10. The ennobling sentiment of veneration expands within you and raises you to a respectful and yielding deportment towards those whom you consider your superiors.

11. Not only are you imbued with sincere adoration of the Supreme Being, but you have a passionate reverence for ancestry as well as your superiors in society, being inspired with the sentiment of broad respect for your fellow man.

12. Being highly reverential and devotional, you are liable to become an unreasonable and bigoted devotee and your character is well drawn by Daniel O'Connell: "When she moves it is in wrath; when she

pauses it is amid ruin; her prayers are curses; her god is a demon—her communion is death—her vengeance is eternity—her decalogue is written in the blood of her victims."

A. To ENLARGE AND STRENGTHEN REVLRENCE:—Never permit yourself to speak irreverently of sacred things or of old age; cultivate respect towards all superiors; read books written by respectful authors, and associate with persons of good moral character. "*Verbum sat sapienti.*" Travel. and visit the mountains crowned with everlasting snow elevated in sublime purity towards heaven; stand by the thundering cataracts and become inspired by their deep but elevating diapason; traverse rocky ravines where old Sol can never penetrate the mysterious shade; emerge into the valleys, quiet and soft, where the god of day first bids his gentle and reluctant adieu; wend your way silently along the meandering stream beneath the impressive shadow of the dark forest; calmly observe in earnest contemplation the roseate and golden hues and soul inspiring tints flung across the prairie, landscape or mountain barriers that kiss the sky; and then reverently feel and say: "If these are but atoms of the vast universe how much more grand and glorious must be the Almighty Creator." After this open the page immortal penned by Cowper and read:—

> "Not a flower
> But shows some touch in freckle, streak, or stain,
> Of His unrivalled pencil. He inspires
> Their balmly odours, and imparts their hues,
> And bathes their eyes with nectar, and includes,
> In grains, as countless as the seaside sands,
> The forms with which He sprinkles all the earth:
> Happy who walks with Him! Whom what he finds
> Of flavour or of scent in fruit or flower,
> Of what he views of beautiful or grand
> In nature, from the broad majestic oak
> To the green blade that twinkles in the sun,
> Prompts with remembrance of a present God."

B. To RESTRAIN, MODIFY AND REGULATE REVERENCE:—Avoid blind devotion to persons or things, and remember that to work is as necessary as to pray; don't frown at every joke and pleasantry, as if they were mere levity. for there is a proper time to laugh, dance, and worship. Remain at home, bind up your thoughts in yourself; heed not the grandeur of the vast mountain range and sea-like prairie, the mighty ocean or magnificent vault of heaven, and in due time you will fully accomplish the restraint of the finest faculty of your nature—which, if rightly directed, leads to respectful deportment towards our fellow man and an elevated appreciation of the wonderful power and goodness of God.

CLASS V.

ELEVATIVE ENDOWMENTS.

THE ENDOWMENTS OF THIS CLASS ARE LARGE WHEN THE BRAIN AND NERVE FORM PREDOMINATES.

MENTAL SYSTEM, OR ORDINIMENTALITY.

THE QUALITY OR ENDOWMENT THAT INCLINES ONE TO ARRANGE AND SYSTEMATISE THOUGHTS, OR IDEAS.

Mental order gives its indication in physiognomy by a square head and forehead, with a prominent, straight nose.

1. As to system of thoughts and mental arrangement, you exhibit strong symptoms of idiotcy.

2. By your acquaintances, you will be generally referred to as a little touched in the upper storey, so constantly you manifest utter confusion and incoherence of ideas,—a rambling, desultory, hair-brained creature — a "wee bit cracket, ye ken," as the Scotch beautifully express it.

3. You never manifest any grasp of a subject under discussion; ideas are always looming in the distance, but they generally turn out vapour, or a bag of moonshine.

4. All the operations of your substitute for a mind are jargon and confusion. Like the poet Gray's boat:—

> "Borne down adrift at random tossed
> Its oar breaks short, its rudder's lost"

5. Should you ever have the misfortune to venture to mount the stump, or hold forth as a preacher, your utterances would beautifully remind your audience of the sounding brass and the tinkling cymbal— total jargon.

6. Feeling always easy as to the manner in which you put forth your ideas, you may often detect yourself presenting first the thoughts you should reserve for the last part of your discourse.

7. Though you are no adept in the orderly and consecutive arrangement of your ideas, yet you can admiringly appreciate a systematic, consequential thinker.

8. You have the acuteness to discern whether your mental subject is dominated by order or reigned over by old Chaos.

9. Those who possess mental order in a large degree will feel much pleasure in your arrangement of ideas and subjects

Ordinimentality large.
Alfred the Great, the noblest and wisest of the kings of England.

10. Possessed of a comprehensive and grasping mind, you can appreciatingly appropriate and assimilate every part of a subject for debate, essay, or treatise, as to its æsthetic and artistic arrangement.

11. A speech of yours would be as consequential as the hours of the day, as well arranged as the fixed stars, and as methodical as William Penn's small clothes, or Voltaire's ruffles and peruke.

12. Being intensely methodical in your notions you are considered by the silly a perfect oddity. You never throw down your pearls in heaps, expecting the hearer or reader to pick them up and string them. With Johnson's idea you thoroughly sympathize, that "Order is a lovely nymph, the child of Beauty and Wisdom."

Ordinimentality large.
Ambroise Parr, who first tied arteries with ligatures.

Ordinimentality small.
Ratasse, Prince of Madagascar.

A. TO CULTIVATE MENTAL ORDER: - In every essay or speech you make, have a prescribed order and consecutive arrangement; before delivering a lecture study, plan, and write out the whole in logical and consequential order; let the occurrences follow consecutionally; in referring to noted persons, refer first to those who earliest occupied the stage of action, as the first to give the impulse in the life-drama, and then freely give expression to every thought you hear and utter, in established, logical, and philosophical succession.

B. TO CURB AND RESTRAIN THE TENDENCY TO MENTAL ORDER:— Let your ideas, if so they may be denominated, gurgle out like the babbling brook over the pebbles, or as beans, peas, or shot from a measure, never heeding which falls first; jot down the thought which first presents itself, but never mind consecution; choose as your companions those who disregard method in any relationship of life; recollect you are squeamish about intellectual arrangements; let your even tenor and uniformity of thought and utterance give way to disorganization and irregular effusions of words and ideas.

PRESCIENCE.

THE FACULTY WHICH ANTICIPATES AND GIVES KNOWLEDGE OF EVENTS BEFORE THEY TAKE PLACE.

Prescience is most readily discovered by its producing a dreamy eye, high forehead, and bending the entire body forwards, immediately at the arm-pits.

OBSERVATION:—Few persons possess this faculty in any great degree, as it is a power which is rarely developed in mankind.

1. A complete idiot you are as regards the eras and events yet unrolled by TIME, the GREAT REVEALER of all things.
2. The power of foreseeing in you resembles a dry river-bed—no life or motion there. You may have excellent back-sight for reviewing the past, but cannot look into futurity.
3. No power have you for anticipating impending phenomena, being short-sighted and without foreknowledge.
4. Merely living on memory and the absorbing present, you never or rarely attempt to prophesy. Though you have many joyous reflections, yet no forecast flings delightful raptures into your soul.
5. The future is a dull, fleecy, dark, void, unknown to your mind. The murky shades hang between you and *that* and *those* coming.
6. You live only in and for the past and present, and deem it sufficient to know what has transpired.
7. Cloudy visions momentarily dart across your mind; and if you would eat that food containing the life-principle, you might enlarge your sybilistic powers.
8. You experience dim precognitions and foresights which unveil the important unoccurred mysteries.
9. That which is remote in the hereafter, you anticipate as clearly as unclouded noonday rays penetrate pure air; and your presentiments prove to be very good and truthful.
10. The clear prevision with which you comprehend that which to most minds lies shrouded by the future tense is highly gratifying and instructive to yourself.
11. Approaching scenes and occurrences seem as it were, spread out before you, like a vast chart or map of the future. You possess this faculty almost or quite equal to the old prophets.
12. Your knowledge of the future is remarkable. The events of to-morrow and many years to come you can foresee with almost divine power, while prophetic wisdom suffuses your whole nature and overflows with sublimity of god-like prevision.

A. TO CULTIVATE PRESCIENCE:—The first of all and the most momentous requisite is to eat sparingly of wheat, beans, fruit, and life-containing material; avoid narcotics and sedatives; breath pure air and no other; visit the summits of mountains; and there pour out your thoughts in solitary reverie while you imbibe soul-enlivening influences while communing with boundless nature; utter your thoughts regarding the morrow, however crude and incorrect they prove to be; try to divine the inevitable fortunes of your friends, and of the leaders and rulers of nations; endeavour to previse and forewarn; and study proleptics.

B. TO RESTRAIN PRESCIENCE:—Abstain from predicting about the weather; relinquish your habit of prognosticating of everything; cease to exert your proleptic inclinations, and they will become enfeebled; and utter no more fortunes or prophecies.

SUSCEPTIBLENESS

SUSCEPTIBILITY OF BEING INFLUENCED BY SURROUNDINGS.

Large eyes, sharp features, quick step, with sudden movements of the head, indicate an excitable nature.

Susceptibleness small. Susceptibleness large
Charles James Fox, an illustrious M.P.   John Elwes, an extraordinary miser of
of England in 1769. London.

1. Having true composure, and the calmness of a quiet lakelet, placidity and gravity are evinced by you in an extraordinary degree.
2. Nothing ruffles you; imperturbable and composed, you are as calm as a May morning.
3. Inexcitable, undisturbed, cool, calm, and serene, you are deemed of a good disposition, because you seem so placid and collected.
4. You possess a certain tranquillity of disposition which exercises a composing and gratifying influence.
5. Being free from great agitation of spirit, you possess a healthy share of patience.
6. Ennui will not venture to claim you as her slave, as she perceives you are so equally balanced between tranquillity and its fierce antagonist, excitement.
7. Somewhat restive, though not violent, you are fond of volatility, and cannot relish the even humdrum of life.

8. Being at times irritable, you may occasionally flare up, while agitation and restlessness make you appear excitable.
9. Being too mercurial, touchiness and disquiet make you somewhat impetuous. Unrest is your besetment.
10. Apt to chafe and fret, easily stirred to action in any of your faculties, you naturally become tremblingly alive to excitement of whatever nature.
11. Few, if any, are so marked for mobility as yourself. You can laugh or weep with equal facility, according to the manner in which you are affected by surrounding circumstances. There is much champagne in your character
12. Giving way to your intense susceptibility, you must soon consume your life principle. The brilliant vivacity of your nature wastes away all insensibility, and renders you very impatient and impetuous. Instantaneously your nature responds to stimulants or excitants.

A. TO ACCELERATE EXCITABILITY:—At every trivial matter explode; let your feelings bubble up without restraint; be excessively funny and facetious about trifles and intensely sad at funerals—even to audible sobbing; on the slightest feeling of displeasure, wriggle and stamp with impatience; and at the climax acceleration; ostentatiously enter into all the political, social, and religious excitement of the day.

B. TO RETARD EXCITABILITY:—Let nothing affect or perturb you; court coolness and composure; collectedness and sedateness are excellent exercises, in your case; when mirth or sadness encompass you, retain your equanimity, making every effort to repress your feelings; when excited, utter no sound, remembering that, when the dominating citadel of the Will is closed, all is quiet and safe within. So it is with the mouth, since it is the gate whence rush out the passions, as they are roused and urged on by excitement.

MENTAL IMITATION, OR MENTIMITATIVENESS.

THE POWER THAT COPIES MENTAL EFFORTS.

Superior width across the top of the forehead, when compared with the rest of the face, can safely be considered an indication that that person desires to copy, and is capable of IMITATING *the* INTELLECTUAL *and worthy efforts of others.*

1 Being quite incapable of copying or doing in an intellectual manner as others do, or be like others in mind, you are strange, and may be considered deranged.
2. Weakness in the imitative arts will mark all your intellectual efforts; you cannot counterfeit, being possessed of imitative powers in a very slender degree, especially relating to mental rather than bodily imitation.
3. You may be able to personify or turn into ridicule another, but it is beyond your powers to copy and reproduce the good and noble ideas of the great of this or any other age.
4. Incapable of becoming a fine artist, you would make poor representations, your inclination would hardly induce you to make speeches or write books.

5. Parody or paraphrase are beyond your abilities; hence you copy no particular style of speaking or writing when you bring forth your original ideas.

6. Your ideas are unequalled, springing from your intellectual genius. Hence when you do give forth your thoughts they have the true ring of your original mind; and you dislike the spurious and counterfeit mental coin of those minds of the baser sort.

Mentimitativeness large.
Elizabeth Canning.

Mentimitativeness small.
Mary Squires, the gipsy.

7. Your delight is to diverge and stray from the beaten paths of science made and trodden by others; hence diversity will characterize your life

8. In following a pattern or model you show fair ability, and try to reproduce great and good mental labours, and hence in quotations you are apt.

9. It is irksome to you to diverge from your early teaching, your capacity being rather to receive what you are taught than to venture to originate new ideas. This is the general characteristic of the Celtic mind.

10. However poor or excellent they might prove, you could make a speech or write a book; and with practice you could become a good penman or a fair artist.

11. The wise sayings of others you readily catch and make them your own, and try to make duplicates of inventions. Hence you are naturally expert in copying opinions or in transcription; thus showing that your intellectual imitative propensities are large.

12. The intellectual doings, thoughts and designs of those who can originate, you can copy with unusual skill and readiness; and the thoughts of others you flatter and enhance by the style in which you copy them.

A. To Cultivate Intellectual Imitation:—Do as others do in speech-making and editing newspapers; paint, draw, transcribe, calculate, teach, lecture, copy mechanical designs, make duplicates of machines; but during your spare hours engage in an entirely mental occupation. Emulate the excellences of the intellectual and good.

B. TO RESTRAIN INTELLECTUAL IMITATION:—Let originality and suggestion lead you to cultivate the inventive faculty; imitate nobody; and, should you engage in a purely mental occupation, or in one in which mind performs the chief part, be yourself and think for yourself. Goldsmith gave the following line, which you should bear in mind:—"The great mind will be bravely eccentric and scorn the beaten road, from universal benevolence."

AFFABLENESS.

COMPLACENCY OF DISPOSITION WITH THE NATURAL CONSEQUENCES, INVITING MANNERS WITH EASE AND ELEGANCE IN CONVERSATION.

A long thin neck, in mankind, will ever testify as indicative of AFFABILITY; *while a short necked person will care little for grace or affability of manners.*

Affableness small.
Rulof, hung at Binghamton for murder, in 1871.

Affableness large.
Mrs Josephine A. Prosch, a talented elocutionist of New York City.

1. Naturally rude and uncivil, you have no attractiveness in your nature, being as boorish in your manners as you are repulsive in your aspect.
2. Innately untoward, you fail to ingratiate yourself with those who possess the finer feelings of humanity, being destitute of all that renders intercourse easy and inviting.

3. Being sadly perfunctory in affability of manner, you have no winsome ways about you, and you are unjustly underrated on these accounts by many who do not understand you.

4 Having no innate desire to please, you evince no desire to do so, especially to strangers; still, among your intimates, you may be easy of access and sufficiently attractive.

5. With culture your manners and deportment would become graceful and charming.

6. Being happily balanced in your feeling and exercise of affability, you are freed from ridicule in regard to your use or abuse of this attractive characteristic

7. Though not distinguished for politeness, still you can assume just enough of it when your interests require polished deportment.

8. On the principle that all present have a right to justly merited compliments you naturally admire the mild and accessible person who carefully avoids harsh personal remarks.

9. When so inclined you can assume pleasing and persuasive manners and become attractive in conversation by saying everything in the most pleasant manner to your friends.

10. Being strongly imbued with the duty of civility and courteousness, you are much pleased with good manners, and are rather complimentary to those around you, but you have an instinctive abhorrence of ill-breeding.

11. Possessed of an insinuating and winning style of address, you are exceedingly gaining and courteous in your receptions, easy in conversation, as free and unreserved with strangers as with friends whom you take a genuine pleasure in having in your society. Fuller says:— "As the sword of best tempered metal is most flexible, so the truly generous are most pliant and courteous in their behaviour to others."

12. Grace and affability are so natural to you that they resemble the tendency of water to find its level and the power of sunlight to dispel the morning dews. Hence the ease and attractiveness of your manners have a perfect charm in them. Perfect grace and elegance are the characteristics of your bow and smile, and the delicate touch of your hand is sufficiently impressive to electrify your friends with a feeling never to be forgotten.

A. To CULTIVATE AFFABILITY:—Read books on politeness and manners; mingle with polished society; discard the uncouth, and shun the awkward and boorish; try to please; avoid speaking on unpleasant and disagreeable subjects. If you live in a city try to imitiate the affability and elegant attractive manners of those noted for such qualities. Enter cheerfully into conversation with those you meet, and humour them in their peculiar notions and manners; and be respectful, and manifest an interest in every one you engage in conversation.

B To RESTRAIN AFFABILITY:—Discard all "blarney;" utterly ignore and discard all the winning ways of the French; be curt and sharp in your remarks, questions, and replies; and keep always in mind that others have an idea that your courtesy and affability are mere sham.

WIT, OR SALITIVENESS.

THE POWER OF SEIZING ON THOUGHTS AND OCCURRENCES, AND PRESENTING THEM IN A LAUGHABLE MANNER, CHIEFLY DEPENDING ON QUICKNESS OF FANCY.

A face very wide in the upper portion, and tapering downwards like an inverted pear or pyriform, always denotes the very witty person, provided the health is good, and no bad habits exhaust the vitality.

Salitiveness small.
Ute Indian, of Salt Lake.

Salitiveness large.
"Mark Twain."

1. Fine, pleasant, and condensed aphorisms are utterly lost on you. Sir John Davies says—"It is the soul's clear eye," but you have put your finger in it.

2. You cannot make a pun, and, of course, are very slow to comprehend one from another.

3 Sadly deficient in facetiousness, you do not possess that condensed and compact thought that can pun and play upon words in a kaleidoscope fashion. You cannot sympathize with Ben Johnson, when he says:— 'I love teeming wit as I love my nourishment."

4. Though you cannot admirably use words in a witty sense still you can appreciate the terse and epigrammatic use of words and sententious construction, when the result is laughter and fun; still, nevertheless, you do not possess the power to use words so, and construct your sentences in such a manner. When reading Pope, you fully agree with him when he says:—

> "True wit is nature to advantage dressed,
> What oft was thought, but ne'er so well expressed;
> Something whose truth convinced at sight we find,
> That gives us back the image of our mind."

5. You had better avoid any attempt to pun, or play upon words, as your *failures* will excite more laughter than your *hits*. Your jokes, like the priming in the pan of the old musket—merely fiz, and are ineffective—neither fun nor death ensues.

6. You can discern the difference between witticism and atticism, and can enjoy the quick-witted whom you meet; yet you are neither a wit nor a flat.

7. You may be able to put words together in such a manner as to produce a pleasant surprise.

8 You highly enjoy pleasant pictures, which are unusual and provocative of unexpected thoughts, which are highly enjoyable.

9. Having a strong feeling as to appropriateness of time and place, you never object to pleasantry and jocularity when they are likely to be somewhat epigrammatic and facetious.

10. You can give a laughable keenness and force to language which will arouse pleasant thoughts in others.

11. Yours is the happy ability of giving new applications to ideas and words which form new and ludicrous relations. "Wit is a mighty, tart, pungent ingredient, and much too acid for some stomachs," says Washington Irving. But, says Johnson, "Wit will never make a man rich; but there are places where riches will always make a wit."

12. Your uncommon mental tact in giving funny surprises in concentrated language, constitutes you keen in wit and most acute. Burnett admirably portrays your character thus:—" Your uncommon reach of vivacity and thought is an excellent talent very fit to be employed in the search of truth, and very capable to discern and embrace it."

A. To CULTIVATE WIT:—Joke whenever you can; think of something which will have a patness of application; devise keen, intense remarks, and never smother a funny thought; give full vent to the original ideas that spring up in your mind; associate with those who are quick at repartee, and witty; read and copy the oral and written lectures of such men as Sterne, Voltaire, Charles Lamb, Dr Valentine, Artemus Ward, Albert Smith, &c. But remember there is a perfect consciousness in every form of wit, using that term in its general sense—that its essence consists in a partial and incomplete view of whatever it touches. We get beautiful effects from wit—all the prismatic colours—but never the object as it is in fair daylight. Also recollect that a pun, which is a *kind* of wit, is a different and much shallower trick in mental optics, throwing the shadows of two objects so that one overlies the other.

B. To RESTRAIN WIT:—Poke no more pleasantries at others; suppress every funny thought; never allow yourself to say new or fanciful things which will incite ingenious turns of fancy in others, especially before your company, should they be aged, grave, and serious, and try to be earnest and as plain as possible. Milton's grand advice is:—" Imagination's airy wing repress, thy thoughts call home and put to rest."

ADMIRATION OF THE SUBLIME, OR SUBLIMITASITY.

THE EXPANSIVE SWELLING OF THE SOUL THAT APPRECIATES THE ELEVATED GRANDEUR OF NATURE AS WELL AS THE ELEVATING, LOFTY EXPRESSION OF THOUGHT AND FEELING—"ALL THAT EXPANDS THE SPIRIT YET APPALS."

This quality or faculty of the mind largely abounds in a fine organization in which the upper portion of the face is larger and wider than the lower. Also the towering form, if well cultivated mentally, indicates nobleness of character.

1. Being naturally unromantic, you are perfectly indifferent towards whatever is wild or weird.

2. Only very faint conceptions arise in your mind from viewing the majestic grandeur of nature, and her beautiful themes stir no responsive echo in your soul.

3. Fearing much more than enjoying the impetuous tempest, you naturally shrink from it, shuddering.

4. The sublime sights of nature do not largely affect you with that awe and astonishment which are experienced by those gifted largely in this quality of mind.

5. Far from being enthusiastic, you much prefer and enjoy realities.

6. You can maintain a calm composure when the grand and sublime phenomena of nature are playing God's great dramas.

7. You admire the transcendent mind. Eloquence permeates and thrills your imagination, and you thoroughly enjoy the racy and glowing utterances of the impassioned orator.

8. Lofty sentiment expressed in a corresponding elevated style, you admire in a speaker. Elevated places, grand old towers, extensive battlemented castles, frowning aged rocks battling back the mountain waves eternally surging against them from the restless ocean, the towering, snow-clad mountain, all stir the depths of your soul and arouse you to fresh endeavours of exalted excellence.

9. Possessing naturally a sublime comprehension when grand subjects are presented for your consideration, you appreciate the magnificent in everything.

10. The noble spirit you possess gives you a lofty manner and bearing and elevates your mind above meagre and petty thoughts.

11. Mountain scenery and whatever is romantic and terrific or awe-inspiring, you enjoy, so that your inner life often leaps out in quest of thoughts majestic.

12. Such is your nature that a storm at sea, vivid lightnings in the midst of appalling darkness, the fearful and deafening crash of the bursting thunderbolt, with its devastating electric discharge, flashing and pealing along a grand mountain chain, afford you intensest pleasure

A. TO CULTIVATE NOBLENESS OF CHARACTER:—Study those authors whose language and thoughts are grand and elevating, such as Shakspeare, Milton, Byron, Edgar A. Poe, Ruskin, Longfellow, &c.; visit sublime and magnificent scenery; listen to the grand swelling and dying notes of nature's orchestra, the howling wind, reverberating thunder, and the everlasting notes of the mighty ocean as it rolls the deep eternal bass in nature's anthem. Take Plutarch's Lives, Macaulay's History of England, or some other well written history of ancient or modern times, and seek some retired spot beneath the jutting rock or hid under the shade of some peaceful tree or vine, and there read daily for hours until grand conceptions of noble lives expand you into nobleness of character.

B. To RESTRAIN EXCESSIVE NOBLENESS OF CHARACTER:—Cultivate a practical every-day feeling; avoid bombast and high-flown sentences; go down with the spade rather than up with the balloon; enter into all the petty and trifling details of ordinary jogtrot life, and worry yourself by meddling in everybody's little quarrels and squabbles.

DESIRE FOR FUTURE LIFE, OR FUTURITIVENESS.
THE DESIRE OF A FUTURE LIFE.

The stooping form, thin chest, wide and high top head and upper face, narrow superior and inferior maxillaries or jaws, thin and well defined nose, and a thin ear, are palpable indications of a desire for future life.

1. About a future life you care utterly nothing, and, if it could be so, would be quite satisfied to dwell on this earth for ever.
2. When persons pass from earth-life, you often imagine it is the last of them.
3. Were it possible, you would readily cling for ever to the joys and sorrows of this world.
4. Though you care little for the future life, there are terrors in death you would shun if you had the power.
5. By the "*Fates*" you are willing to abide, in regard to spirit-life; hence you never trouble yourself about it.
6 Regarding this ancient belief in immortality, you often question yourself.
7. In your pathway to the future, bright hopes cast pearls of untold splendour, and lure you on.
8. As a pleasure, long anticipated, you expect a post existence; and joyously hail futurity.
9. To be for ever blotted out of existence, to you seems terrible. By the hope and assurance of a hereafter, the dark veil of death is rent away.
10. With the hopeful assurance that you only change at *death*, you are anxiously looking forward to glories of a future *life*.
11. As ephemeral insects vanish at the approach of winter, the sensual pleasures which you may have enjoyed are utterly forgotten as you muse upon the beauties of immortal life.
12. In your soul, an abiding and deep assurance of spiritual life has pillared itself. Nothing affords you so much pleasure as the life beyond physical death. The most sublime example of this state of anticipation in the fruition of future happiness is that which is recorded by the apostle to the Gentiles, where he says:—" Death is swallowed up in victory. Death! where is thy sting? Grave! where is thy victory?"

A. To INTENSIFY THE DESIRE OF A FUTURE LIFE:—Appeal to every means of learning of another world. Let not your early education debar you from seeking light respecting spirit-life. Learn from nature that though the seed falls it perisheth not, but in a brief time springeth into a new life. "It is sown a *natural* body; it is raised a *spiritual* body. First was that which is natural, and afterwards that which is spiritual." Cicero, though a heathen, and not believing in the revelation of a future state, has said that, "from the consent of all nations, we conclude that the soul survives the body." From ancient history we learn that the Egyptians (in the time of Menes, the first Egyptian King, who lived more than 2000 B.C.) believed in the immortality of the soul.

B. TO REPRESS THE DESIRE OF A FUTURE LIFE:—Live only for to-day, and heed not to-morrow. Cast your thoughts away from the spiritual to the physical. On the beauties of spirit-life muse and dream no longer. But forget not the man in the parable to whom it was said, while he was contemplating present aggrandisement, "This night shall thy soul be required of thee."

APPRECIATION OF THE BEAUTIFUL, OR ÆSTHETICALNESS.

THE APPRECIATION OF THE BEAUTIFUL IN NATURE AND ART, AS THE RESULT OF THE POSSESSION OF THE ÆSTHETIC FACULTY.

A high, or prominent nose, is nature's evidence of a love and appreciation of the beautiful.

Æstheticalness small.
Kettle, a selfish and cunning Indian chief.

Æstheticalness large.
Charlemagne, a great warrior and promoter of science and art.

1. Possessing scarcely a particle of this faculty, you fail to manifest any of its action ; hence you esteem homely objects as highly as those of the most exquisite beauty.

2. Naturally devoid of taste, and incapable of appreciating the higher beauties of the world or of art, you are fitted for only a low condition in life. This is indicated by the flatness of your nose, which well bespeaks the almost utter absence of æsthetic feeling.

3. To you the miserable donkey seems as attractive in form and action as the purest barb of Arabia; the beautiful rose, the sweet, modest violet, the grand ethereal bow in the clouds, present no more beauty to your unappreciative eye than the dog-daisy, the sunflower, or the common cabbage.

4. The power of appreciating beauty is perfectly alien to your structure; hence your imaginings are plain, homely, flat and unattractive rather than graceful. In the finer, rounder, and more elegant forms there is little that attracts your interest where elevation of taste is displayed in the world of art, mechanics, science, or literature.

5. Being moderate in your desire and appreciation of the beautiful, you like plain clothes, people, and houses, as well as all the ordinary appliances of life. Fine paintings you admire, and beautiful scenery will afford you some pleasure; even the ever changing tints of the gorgeous sunset may be fairly appreciated, yet you would not sacrifice many selfish interests for the enjoyment of such beauties.

6. Possessing the æsthetic faculty in its incipiency, you may often notice beauty in minor objects, and yet you may fail to perceive the grand and sublime beauties which the divine wisdom has spread over every department of the vast universe.

7. The plastic or decorative arts seldom engage your mind or occupy your attention, when more utilitarian and important themes present themselves for your consideration.

8. Your dormant genius unfolds, in the contemplation of the planetary orbs in the solar system, the illimitable extent of the universe, the myriads of fixed stars in the vast expanse of the celestial dome; also in the contemplation of the rounded and graceful forms on earth, the multitudes of beautiful natural productions that present themselves on every side, your conceptions are elevated and pure delight renders your joy ineffable.

9. Being yourself of a beautiful form, you can readily appreciate the round and harmonious objects which present their beautiful proportions to your view.

10. The sight of assembled graces and symmetrical parts united in one whole, thrills your inmost being with delight ecstatic.

11 The wide and flat-nosed stupid, vulgar individual, who is nearly devoid of the love of the beautiful, is repulsive to one possessed of your æsthetic taste.

12. Being an accomplished connoisseur in the fine arts, the beauties of nature arouse the delight of your mind and the admirations of your whole soul.

A. To CULTIVATE THE LOVE OF THE BEAUTIFUL:—Study æsthetics or the science and philosophy of beauty; follow its suggestions and precepts; choose your associates from the refined and cultivated; read works on the beauties of nature and the fine arts; devote time to the arrangement of furniture and household ornaments, that they may present an agreeable view to the eye; contemplate the beautiful everywhere; and, at length, this silent, ever pleasing educator will arouse your sluggish taste and by degrees inspire perception and appreciation. Remember what *Keats* has so beautifully said:—

"A thing of beauty is a joy for ever."

B. To RESTRAIN THE ÆSTHETIC FACULTY:—For the spade, forsake the palette; devote your attention to agricultural pursuits; but do little work, and if possible eat all your farm produce; keep on clumsy boots and wear ungainly clothing; seek the company of flat-nosed people; and, in due time your fine tastes will descend to the level of those of the Chinaman.

CAREFULNESS.

SOLICITOUSNESS, GUARDEDNESS, WARINESS, AND CIRCUMSPECTION IN ALL THE TRANSACTIONS OF LIFE.

The palpable manifestation of caution is a long nose. The elephant is the best example of this, as his nose extends to the extreme end of his trunk.

Carefulness large.
Flavius Josephus, an eminent and illustrious Jewish historian, an exceedingly careful and correct author.

Carefulness small.
Thomas Hudson, the most unfortunate of all men. He was ever blundering into misfortunes.

1. Careless as an infant, you have remained heedless and unconcerned in all the affairs of life.
2. An unsuspecting dupe, you are ever blundering into mishaps, and from your own carelessness may likely die earlier than you should.
3. Fearing nothing, you get often into trouble; are luckless, unmindful, inattentive and improvident.
4. Before calculating the cost and consequences, you are apt to plunge into the enterprises of the world.
5. Having an inclination to trust to luck or chance more than thoughtful foresight, you manifest little anxiety in regard to future occurrences, and, when not excited, you may evince a fair degree of care even prudence.
6. Being usually careful in a sensible and rational degree, neither anxiety nor heedlessness will likely mar your happiness.
7. Evincing a fair amount of prudence, you are inclined to penetrate the motives and intentions of others.
8. Circumspection and discretion characterise the acts of your life, and being possessed of forethought, you are deliberate and not venturous, unless your prudent and deliberate judgment discerns the way clearly.
9. Provident for the present and solicitous for the future, you would make an excellent protector, as you have a good and clear comprehension of danger that may be approaching, whenever it may become perceptible to the human mind.
10. Being apprehensive of dangers and difficulties, you will generally manifest forethought and discretion in an able and effective manner.
11. Fearful and hesitating about entering into extensive enterprises, you will naturally fish or sail as near the shore as possible, if you ever do risk your precious life in a small boat or craft.
12. A perfect martyr to your imaginary troubles, groundless fears and anxieties swarm around your boding imagination like flies around a putrid carcass.

A. To CULTIVATE THE WARY TENDENCY OF MIND:—Always think twice before you act, or better pause and don't act; your rashness may ruin you; consult those who have careful deliberation and judgment, and act according to their advice; study the motives of others; and ever keep on the alert. Never depart from the principles you have received when you feel that sound and solid reasons are their bases; and consider that by deviating from this advice you may occasion some of the worst evils that can befall human society and may cause ruin to yourself.

B. To RESTRAIN THE CAUTIOUS TENDENCY:—Be more self-possessed; jump at conclusions; act with promptitude and decision; don't keep putting off; never fear to-morrow's advent; foreboding and procrastination may thwart every effort of your life; press and drive, on ever looking ahead; banish fear, be confident, and let hope ever preside over your counsels. "Fear is the last of ills; in time we hate that which we often fear." "It is also the white-lipped sire of subterfuge and treachery." Then be reckless and cast aside caution, wariness, and circumspection as you would nightmare.

SPIRITUAL HOPE, OR SPEMENTALITY.

THE FACULTY THAT DESIRES SOME MENTAL OR SPIRITUAL GOOD.

Spiritual hope may be known as large when we see a large open eye and high forehead, with great comparative measurement from the point of the nose to the hair of the forehead.

Spementality small.
An Indian of California attired for an annual war dance.

1. No bright rays from the spiritual life flit across your soul, and that which lies beyond the grave is as little desired by you as ice is by fire.

"Where no hope is left, is left no fear."—*Milton.*

2. No aspiration ever escapes your bosom with the desire of meeting those friendly forms that have shaken off their mortal coil and ascended to a higher sphere.

3. The inertness of your spiritual nature presses out almost every desire unconnected with your bodily wants. Shakspeare gives your portrait to the life:—"A man that apprehends death no more dreadfully, but as a drunken sleep; careless, reckless, and fearless of what's past, present, or to come; insensible of mortality, and desperately mortal."

4. Forebodings of a dark abyss of unknown and undesired mystery often cast deep gloom over your mind.

" What see you there,
That hath so cowarded and chased your blood
Out of appearance?"—*Shakspeare.*

5. Your spiritual hope is developing slowly, but it needs much more nourishment. It resembles the taper that flickers in the socket when the oil is exhausted.

6. Hope in your constitution justly holds aloft her scales and shows them equally depending from the horizontal beam with *excess of hope* in the one scale, and *deficiency* in the other, of perfectly equal weight.

7. Circumstances or education has slightly unfolded your inner light, which, the more it illumes, the more exhaustless are its resources.

Spementality large.
Milton.

8. Not being very sanguine in spiritual desire, it might seem strange that nevertheless cheering reflections and wishes do often enter your mind, still you give but little heed to the kindly monitors.

9. Permeating your nature there are many strong and high-toned spiritual desires.

10. The beautiful hope you entertain of the future will assist and invigorate you in preparing for the spirit-life. Still, you feel with Mrs Hemans, that—

"Dreams cannot picture a land so fair,
Sorrow and death may not enter there,
Time doth not breathe on its fadeless bloom,
'Tis beyond the clouds and beyond the tomb."

11. Steady and enduring desires about the higher life will cheer you along the pathway of mortality.

12. The mighty, bright, and beautiful hope with which your nature is blessed may well be envied by intelligent mortals. No doubts of a future ever enter your mind

A. To ENHANCE THE ACTION OF SPIRITUAL HOPE:—Select for your associates those who live more for the future life than for this; read books by authors who have no doubt about the life beyond the grave; partake sparingly of beans, peas, oatmeal pudding, Scotch broth, vegetables, Graham bread, ripe fruits, &c. Discard from your bill of fare such soul-depressing articles as pork, mince-pie, rich puddings, sausages, &c. Never use tobacco or alcoholic liquors in any form; and shun a materialist as you would the cholera, or small-pox, or black-death.

B. To REPRESS SPIRITUAL HOPE:—Measure every spiritual desire by the rule of physics; ask for material demonstrations of a future life, and if you are favoured by the good will of God with what you desire, don't believe a word of it, but denounce it as the work of the devil; and last of all quote Scripture profanely, sneer at all that is considered sacred, but take heed to what Carlyle has said so well:—" There is but one thing without honour; smitten with eternal barrenness, inability to be or to do —insincerity, unbelief. He who believes *no* thing, who believes only the shows of things, is not in relation with nature and fact at all."

PURITY OF MIND, OR PURITATIVENESS.
THE VIRTUE OF CHASTITY AND INNOCENCE UNDEFILED.

A clear, bright eye, a broad, high forehead, evenly developed lips, with refined and intelligent countenance, are some of the signs of purity of mind.

Puritativeness small.   Puritativeness large.
Patagonian.   Lucretia Mott.

1. Corruption enters largely into your composition, so much so, that you may aptly be likened to a cesspool—the receptacle for any filth.

2. Impregnated with sin and iniquity, your natural depravity renders you liable to misdemeanour or any culpable act.

3. Being liable to stumble and trip into indiscretions, from the natural pollution of your mind, you require to edulcorate your propensities with pure and unsullied thoughts.

4 The amount of artificiality in your character speaks weakly on virtue's behalf.

5. Though not at all past reclamation, yet the tendency to corruptness and depravity steals often into your constitution.

6 So constituted, you should emulate and imitate the noble life of Madame Roland, Mrs Fry, Madame Guizot, and John Howard, in their *public* characteristics.

Puritativeness small.
Samuel Hunter.—This portrait was copied, by permission, from a very interesting work entitled "Characters of Glasgow," published by John Tweed, 11 St Enoch Square, Glasgow, Scotland.

7. While you really admire natural purity and chastity, still concinity may not be your strong trait.

8. As you are ever trying to practice virtue, you will shun the vulgar, and endeavour to live a praiseworthy life.

9. Correctness of deportment and love of the high-toned and the good, will leave their stamp on many portions of your life.

10. Your natural antipathy to the low and vulgar is as strong as your love of defending the high-minded and pure.

11. Such spirits as yours were in the mind of Shakspeare, when he indited the line—

"For unstained thoughts do seldom dream on evil."

Your soul, untainted by the world, is as pure and unspotted as that of an innocent child.

12. Truly pure and immaculate as the snow fresh from the heavens, your every form is angelic and god-like.

A. To Promote Purity:—Let no vulgar ideas enter your mind or intermingle with your thoughts; it is better to remain unsophisticated than impure; use chaste and purely elegant language, and associate with the refined; and studiously eschew all indecorum and corruption.

B. To REPRESS PURITY:—Put on airs, as this is a sure sign of the absence of mental and bodily purity; cultivate slovenly, dirty habits, and your thoughts will soon bear the filthy impress; read books which vividly portray the passions, such as the fast novels of the present time; associate with saloon loafers and idle persons, and you shall soon find that your surplus innocence and purity is gone, is nowhere; associate with catiffs, varlets, and blackguards, and your dove-like impeccability will soon vanish like the mists of a June morning, as they melt before the rising sun. Not a "rack" of purity can survive this prescription.

INTUITION, OR INTUITIVENESS.
CONSCIOUS KNOWLEDGE PRIOR TO EXPERIENCE.

The signs of the **FACULTY OF INTUITION** *are a high forehead, with large, open eyes.*

Intuitiveness small.
Simon Fraser Lovat, a Scottish chieftain and rebel, who was beheaded in the Tower of London in 1747.

Intuitiveness large.
Giuseppe Mazzini, the great Italian patriot, brilliant author, and co-worker with Garibaldi for republicanism in Italy.

1. Were it possible that you have any knowledge of first principles, they must have been acquired at second hand or by dim and unsatisfactory inductions. No ideas obtrude themselves into your mind like bats that dart into the cottages during the fading light of day.

2. Knowledge is very wary in approaching your mind, feeling no doubt that her precious time might be much better spent in entering where she is welcome. Though she is a modest dame, she likes a hearty and ready reception.

3. Direct and instantaneous reception of ideas and their apprehension are almost inappreciable by you, and so feeble are they that you had better not trust them.

4. The astonishing and illimitable grasp of some minds is quite incomprehensible by you; for most of your limited knowledge has been attained in quite an asthmatic fashion by slow, laborious and panting efforts

5. Into your mind few intuitive ideas flash rays of undeduceable intelligence, hence they are scarcely ever comprehensible or trustworthy.

6. By right living and giving due heed to your intuitions you would more readily recognise truth; hence you gain some knowledge without long processes of reasoning.

7. Being slightly intuitive, instantaneous perception of realities may occasionally illumine your mind.

8. Without any perceptible cause ideas and notions often start into your mind, but in due time you learn they were verities.

9. Many true presentiments cast their illuminating rays into your susceptible mind, and the recognition of knowledge is often instantaneous with you.

10. Many primary truths you have intuition of by immediate cognition, and instantaneous mental perception and penetration.

11. Possessing a remarkable intuitive judgment you are capable of becoming of invaluable service to the world.

12. Most wonderful. strange, and new ideas and fancies are continually pouring into your mind, and time and circumstances prove them to be thoroughly veritable and practical. This subtle and wonderful capacity is in you equal to the same in Swedenborg and Humboldt.

A. To FACILITATE THE INTUITIVE CAPACITY:—Notice every impression you have, and in perfect faith accept it until disproved; sit quietly in a certain situation regularly every day, and throw up the rein to your thoughts; discard no impressions unless your reason or circumstances disprove them; live sparingly on light diet, and associate with intellectual and intuitive people; read the works of Swedenborg, Herbert Spencer, and Stuart Mill; and reject no new idea until thoroughly investigated.

B. To DISCOURAGE AND REPRESS INTUITIONAL CAPACITY:—Spend most of your time in gay, fashionable, thoughtless society; live sumptuously on eggs, oysters, pork, butter, honey, cake, pie, Devonshire cream and pudding; drink tea, coffee chocolate, wine, stout, ale, gin, rum, and whisky; use tobacco and opium; sleep ten or twelve hours each day, and you will soon smother the babes of intuition in their lovely innocence. By following the above directions, you may crush out the intuitional capacity, as is daily done by thousands, but bear in mind that it is seldom necessary to restrain this power.

WRITTEN LANGUAGE, OR LITERATIVENESS.

THE SKILL OF PRODUCING WRITTEN LANGUAGE.
A full broad high forehead with a pyriform face are signs of excellence in written language.

Literativeness small.
Mr Thomas Bogerson, a very good speaker but poor writer.

Literativeness large.
John Ruskin, a brilliant author and art critic.

1 The more you try to write the oftener you expose your inability; the productions of your pen lack body, clothing, and style; and are only an agglomeration of misconstructions and improprieties.

2. Your ideas being muddy, misty, and hazy, your words consequently are ill chosen, sentences badly constructed, and hence you are a poor writer.

3. From the barrenness and vacuity of your writings they contrast in a very unfavourable manner with those produced by men who have become eminent from their full brilliant, grasping style, utterly free from the meagreness that pervades your every paragraph.

4. You should make no more essays to appear in print as we have already many miserable writers.

5. Though your inherent weakness in matter and style may, by practice, be partially removed, yet it will be a hopeless task to eradicate it thoroughly.

6. The excitement of conversation or public speaking may supply you with a much larger vocabulary than you have when trying to write.

7. Your forte is not in writing, though you may be a fluent talker; and you will find composition rather an irksome business.

8. With careful practice you could write passably well; but without this you will make a jumble of it, from the tendency you have to allowing your thoughts to get the start of your pen.

9. You possess the power of setting forth your ideas more completely and satisfactorily in writing than most speakers can do. Your writings with constant care and practice might exercise an important influence over human affairs.

10. If you practice writing, the effusions from your pen will be such that the sentences, in harmony with the ideas, will flow on with æsthetic and mellifluous softness, grace, smoothness, and beauty.

11. Your phraseology is classic and most perspicuous, and your love of the beautiful, in idea and expression is manifested in your passion for polite literature. Hence your tendency to give the most copious and fascinating expression to your thoughts. Elegance is your characteristic in style.

12. Being pre-eminently gifted in the use of symbolical and figurative language, you will likely write better than you speak

A. To CULTIVATE WRITTEN LANGUAGE:—Study well your subject, revolving it in your mind, then write down your ideas as they occur; the next morning fresh from sleep revise or re-write, and continue this practice until you acquire an easy natural style. If you are an observant person, your best plan is to describe that which you saw, and narrate what you have heard; to increase your vocabulary or stock of words, constantly refer to Crabbe's or Mackenzie's synonyms, and Roget's Thesaurus of English words; but of all true sources of the accurate value of words and their copious bearings study the etymology of the language, in such books as Wood's Guide to the Etymology of the English Language, or Oswald's Etymological Dictionary. Nothing will enrich your vocabulary or instil into your mind the true value of words and their delicate shades of meaning so much as this. But during your acquirement of all these stores of fundamental knowledge, practise on every occasion the putting your thoughts on paper; no matter how varied are the subjects, keep at it, and success according to your powers and knowledge will be the result. Then when you have acquired these fundamental stores and have practised carefully, take studiously for your models in prose such authors as Washington Irving, Ruskin, and Baron Macaulay, Samuel Johnson, Addison and Steele. In poetry you need no advice, for that is an art that must be in your own idiosyncrasy. Imitation in this divine art annihilates the poet.

B. To RESTRAIN THE TALENT FOR WRITTEN LANGUAGE:—Do not be jotting down on all occasions your thoughts; the less you write the better. In a word, never write when you can possibly avoid the task.

CLEANNESS.

THE DESIRE TO BE FREE FROM FOULNESS AND IMPURITIES.

Fine hair, as in the rabbit, is a sure sign of NEATNESS, *while coarse hair, as in the hog, may be known as nature's testimonial of a dirty animal.*

Cleanness large.
The Duchess of Kent, the mother of Her Majesty, Queen Victoria, the noble Queen.

Cleanness small.
Nathaniel Bently, the dirtiest man of England.

1. Unkempt, bedraggled, and bedaubed, your appearance is slovenly, and generally you beslime and bespatter your apparel.

2. Ever dusty and dirty, you are likely to smear and contaminate all you touch.

3. You are apt to soil your clothing and begrim your face; you wash only when the dirt can be easily seen, and it becomes painfully necessary.

4. Through mud and mire you will stamp rather than incommode yourself by avoiding it, and yet can admire neatness.

5. Not being too particular about a trifle of dirt, you will clean up occasionally. A little smut or mustiness incommode you not.

6. Neither nasty nor yet unstained, you are alike free from the extremes of tidiness or slovenliness.

7. You are rather particular about washing, combing, and cleaning yourself as well as about the things with which you come into personal contact.

8. Slovenly persons are repulsive to your fine-grained nature, and what is coarse in things or persons you intuitively avoid.

9. Rancidity and mustiness are repulsive to you; all impurity and filthiness your nature abhors.

10. You will try to keep tidy and neat by brushing and washing in order that purity of body may be yours.

11. One grand aim of your life is to render everything clean and neat. Small particles of dust and dirt readily annoy you

12. Personal purity and immaculateness are your prominent characteristics; and your constant attention to scrubbing, ablutions, and ventilation is remarkable.

A. To PROMOTE AND ACCELERATE CLEANLINESS:—Wash and scrub; often change your clothing; brush away dust; scrape off the mud; cast away the tainted; wipe away all slime and rise above the corrupt; harbour no filthy thoughts in your mind nor allow uncleanliness to remain on your person.

B. To RETARD AND DISCOURAGE CLEANLINESS:—Don't be so squeamish about a trifle of dirt, it is only that of which you are composed; bear in mind that your attention to neatness in trifles is wearing away your life.

PITIFULNESS.

TENDERNESS AND COMPASSION FOR SUFFERING MANKIND, THE LOWER ANIMALS, AND EVERY LIVING CREATURE.

An eye that looks upon an object with lingering softness is an evidence of large PITY. *When this quality is strong, it bows the head forwards, and softens the manners.*

1. Nero-like, you are hard-hearted and merciless.

2. No feeling of tender sympathy moistens thine eyes with dew-drops of sadness at the apprehension of suffering innocence.

3. Pitiless, stony, and cold, your eyes bear marked resemblance to the ruins of Quin Abbey in Ireland

4. In you, the sentiment of sympathy is like the felled and decaying tree, unfeeling, rotting, and every day "becoming small by degrees, and beautifully less."

5. Rarely, yet occasionally kindly, compassion viridifies the tender sympathies of your inhuman heart by showers of calid tears.

6. Alike free from obduracy of spirit or extreme tenderness in sympathy, you are almost evenly balanced between intolerance and its antithesis forbearance.

7. Though depressed when sadness casts her sable mantle over the social circle, yet, when all around are merry you are calmly thoughtful, and every feature of your pitying visage relates the tale of your inmost thoughts.

8. Yours somewhat resembles that tender and great spirit whose tears of joy rush spontaneously from the eyes when suffering and sorrow have been relieved.

9. The melting anguish of suffering innocence kindles within you the fires of compassion, which burn, yet consume not, which purify while they nourish and improve the soul.

10. Concessions and benefactions you are ready to make where it will result in good, all eleemosynary projects afford you pleasure; you will grant a pardon if asked by an enemy; and you are always very lenient and indulgent towards others.

11. Much you resemble the nature of the great Pompey, who was noted for his noble generosity. No narrow, sharp lines of sectionality limit or

confine your spontaneous feelings of clement consolation which well forth unbidden whenever you are cognizant of distress.

Pitifulness very small.
Nero, one of the most cruel Emperors of Rome —Copied from the bust in the British Museum.

Pitifulness very large
Miss Coutts, of London, England, the most compassionate lady of the present age.

12. Complete abnegation of self is your distinctive quality; pity's ripest fruits are brought to perfection in you, and manifest themselves by the terribly convulsive throes of your heart when sympathizing with the woes and agonizing anguish of others. When your tenderest feeling of mercy is excited by distress, it runs through every fibre of your being with the rapidity of lightning, and with redoubled force endeavours to render assistance to the unfortunate by its divine impulses Shakspeare had such qualities as you possess in his mind when he penned the following lines:—

> "The quality of mercy is not strained;
> It droppeth as the gentle rain from heaven
> Upon the place beneath; it is twice blessed;
> It blesseth him that gives and him that takes:
> 'Tis mightiest in the mightiest; it becomes
> The throned monarch better than his crown.
>   * * * *
> It is an attribute of God himself."

A. To CULTIVATE PITY:—Visit the abodes of the poor and lowly and there enter into close communion with their troubles, however small; try to render consolation while they complain; lend an attentive ear to the voice of need and penury; from the laboratory of your tenderest compassion take the balm of commiseration, and pour it over their miseries and sorrows; entertain tender feelings for every one, and expel, as demons, all cynical suggestions and emotions; shun the egotist, as he can love himself only; avoid the ostentatious, and those whose hearts are steeled against pity by the armour of worldly gain and worship of mammon; and bear in mind that it would benefit your soul more to perform the acts of earthly kindness to a poor man, than to toast the rich man at his wedding. Sheridan says:—

"Soft pity
Hallows every heart he once has swayed;
And, when his presence we no longer share,
Still leaves compassion as a relic there."

B. To Restrain Pity:—Though it is rarely necessary to repress the action of this god-like virtue, yet, for the benefit of those who sympathise with objects of distress so as to affect them deleteriously by injuring their health and destroying their happiness, the following directions are appended:—Live sumptuously; heed not the complainings of others; turn coldly away from the poor and needy; associate with the unmerciful and selfish; shun death-bed scenes and dramatic acts that arouse the tender sympathies; read not any accounts of railway accidents, and loss of life by shipwrecks; in a word, live sedulously for yourself only, and soon you will be perfectly free from the mawkish feeling of pity. But remember, "Cruelty is an insult on the majesty and goodness of God," as Jones of Nayland says. And Cowper says:—

"I wou'd not enter on my list of friends the man
Who needlessly sets foot upon a worm."

IMAGINATIVENESS.

THE PLASTIC POWER OR FACULTY OF CREATING IMAGES IN THE MIND, THE HOME OF FANCY.

Remarkable intelligence evinced by facial expression, denotes vivid imagination.

1. Being of a low, barren, blunt, bestial mind, you have no fancy to produce scenes of beauty or poetic diction.

2. Lacking inspiration, liveliness, and refinement, yours is a plain, tame, terse, unpolished, matter-of-fact comprehension.

3. Your spiritual nature—if such it may be called—is devoid of the playful fancy that willingly lingers around the airy ideal that is seen in playful pictures. You are very concise.

4. Not being poetically inspired, you are free from the propensity to indulge in day dreams, nor can you feel much sympathy for the liveliness of the French, or what they call *le bel ideal*.

5. Writing poetry will hardly prove remunerative to you; solitude has never, in your case, united with deep meditative studiousness in order to develop an enthusiastic imagination within you and bring your passions into obedience to her dictates.

6. You enjoy the beautiful, but do not fly off at a tangent; and though

IMAGINATIVENESS.

Imaginativeness small.
A Plodding Scotchman.

Imaginativeness large.
M. Lamartine.

you are interested in works of beauty, when the idea of practical value is connected with them you are more readily appreciative.

7. Your imagination may occasionally become wearied with the common place jog-trot world of mere utilitarianism, and for relief, make ethereal excursions on lightning wings to expansive fields and worlds of beauty and splendour. However little others may guess your true character while in retirement, you are nevertheless vividly and chastely enjoying your silent reveries.

8 Though you may not be a critic, connoisseur, or virtuoso, you readily discern the elegant, and hence you are tasteful and enjoy the refined, shun vulgarisms and appreciate dilettanteism, and delight in the study of æsthetics.

9. Being enthusiastic and prolific in the combination of old forms and images into new structures of beauty and grandeur, which you place in sequestered landscapes of loveliness, as so many Edens adorned with resplendent glory, your excursions in space become like the fire in its resistless impetuosity sweeping over the dry prairie lighting up, consuming, and purifying everything it embraces.

10. Your expansive and vivid fancy produces ample results in your enchanting air-drawn pictures. Thus is your liveliness of fancy portrayed:—

> "Do what he will, he cannot realize
> Half he conceives: the glorious vision flies.
> Go where he may, he cannot hope to find
> The truth, the beauty pictured in his mind."

11. Possessing a vigorous imagination, your taste is of a superior quality, and gives you a rich pleasure in the fine arts. With an excellent conception of what is elegant and pleasing, everything that is beautiful, delicate, and refined you embrace with pleasurable emotions. There is a diffusiveness permeating every act of your life.

12 You feel intense delight in the beautiful; your conversations possess much buoyancy and sprightliness; you enjoy gazing upon the rippling, silver-footed waters; so much so that your ideas often take wing, flutter, and whirple round mystic themes, usurp the throne of reason, and feast on angelic visions. "The necromantic power can conjure up glorious shapes and forms, and people solitude with brilliant visions."—*Irving*.

A. TO CULTIVATE IMAGINATION:—Betake yourself to study, reading, and writing in solitude, constantly exercising your imagination; visit deserted ruins and old castles in Ireland, Scotland, England, Wales, Italy, Spain, and Syria, while you read their history. Sit on the tombstones in the old trellised abbeys of those countries, and wile away brief hours in imaginary pictures of the old monks and friars who in the olden time reigned supreme. Study ancient history, eloquence, painting, geology and astronomy; use choice, elegant, picturesque language; adorn your rooms with works of art and paintings; and ever remember what Lord Byron has so beautifully said:—

> "The beings of the mind are not of clay;
> Essentially immortal, they create,
> And multiply in us a brighter ray
> And more beloved existence."

B. TO RESTRAIN THE IMAGINATION:—Always call a spade a spade; avoid all ornament in dress; never mind the fashions; let your words be all literal; metaphor, and all figure of speech, score out of your vocabulary; specially avoid hyperbole; use no exaggeration; remember that though the cabbage is not so beautiful as the rose, yet it is much more useful; never betake yourself to solitary meditation; turn away from ruins of palaces, cities and castles, abbeys and druidical relics, unless surrounded by thoughtless friends, who seek to feed idle curiosity; never read novels or poetry; avoid all chances of deep and soul-stirring meditation, by light social converse with plain, practical people; and when any one speaks to you figuratively, turn sharp upon him, saying—" I want the facts—nothing but facts."

MEMORY OF FACTS, OR FACTIMEMORIATIVENESS.
THE FACULTY OF RETAINING PREVIOUSLY ATTAINED KNOWLEDGE.
Memory of incidents and general affairs manifests itself by general fulness of the forehead.

Factimemoriativeness large.
Frederick H. A. Baron von Humboldt

Factimemoriativeness small.
Miss Catherine Dunn

1. Prone to forgetfulness, and destitute of the ability to think over the past, the occurrences of your life never trouble or delight you.

2. Such is the poverty of your memory that it is impossible for you to recollect what or how much you have forgotten. As quick silver thrown upon glass rolls off in numerous little globules, soft and divisible so do facts when put upon the tablets of your memory.

3. Important occurrences are apt to fade from the canvass of your memory: hence you can give only a vague account of historical incidents long since read.

4. So misty and enveloped in haziness is your power of recollection, that you cannot readily dispel the uncertain gloom, so as to enable you to present the images of the past in a clear light.

5. Generalities you can recollect, but minutiæ you cannot recall; and hence you fail to relate an anecdote well, and at times are absent-minded.

6. Through the reticulations of your mnemonic net small facts escape; but by taking extra trouble, sustained by vigorous efforts, you may retain ideas or facts that are important and necessary.

7. Though the minor matters are in danger of fading from your memory, you will sufficiently recall important things; and though not capacious, your retrospects are pretty much to be trusted for accuracy.

8. By nature your capacity for recollection is very fair, and by careful culture it would become expert. But trifles are apt to slip your memory, and ideas you forget except you take more than ordinary care to retain them.

9. From the treasure-chambers of your memory shoot forth rays of intelligence at the behest of your volition; and hence few equal you in the ability to recall historical facts and events in connection with all their minute details and concomitant incidents.

10. So deeply impressed are facts and incidents on your memory that they seem to live in it; and so trustworthy are your recollective powers, that you can retrace the occurrences of your life with unfailing accuracy.

11. Your memory is exceedingly active and clear; hence your extreme fondness for taking cognizance of character, events and active phenomena; of enjoying anecdotes, possessing great quickness of apprehension. You retain life proceedings with wonderful accuracy, collect items of information; and garner your gathered facts with scholarly aptitude.

12. Such is your broad and strong power of retrospection that the impressions received by your mind are retained like pictures carved on agate. The facts engraven there are as safe as in a cyclopædia and equal in their fidelity. Hence, no wonder you are referred to as a "walking dictionary."

A. To CULTIVATE MEMORY:—After retiring to rest every night think over all the transactions and incidents of the preceding day; read the works of Cuvier, Leibnitz, Gœthe, Humboldt, Lyell Agassiz, Liebig. Sir Walter Scott, Prescott, Alison, Macaulay, as well as other scientific and historical writers; and at least once every day repeat all the events of importance which have transpired during the last twenty-four hours; and business negotiations, as well as every ordinary incident of life; commit condensed portions of history to memory; impress all leading incidents firmly on the mind by giving intense and concentrated attention to them when they come to your notice; associate much with those of superior memories. Employ the memory and it will give you retentive power. The Greeks continually exercised their memories by treasuring in their minds the works of their poets, the instructions of their philosophers, and the problems of their mathematicians; and such practice gave them vast power of retention. Pliny informs us of a Greek called Charmidas who could repeat from memory the contents of a large library. One should write out every speech or whatever it is desired to retain. This practice is recommended by Cicero and Quintilan. Memory is facilitated by regular order and distributive arrangement of facts, and by conversing on the subjects you wish to remember. Themistocles, Cæsar, Cicero, and Seneca were possessed of very great memories. Themistocles mastered the Persian language in one year, and could call by their names all the citizens of Athens, when its population was 20,000. Cyrus knew the name of every soldier in his army. Julius Cæsar was able to dictate to three secretaries at the same time and on perfectly distinct subjects. Portius Latro, as Seneca informs us, remembered everything that he committed to writing and wrote very rapidly. Hortentius attended a public sale which occupied the whole day and gave a full and particular account in the evening from memory of every article that was sold as well as the name of each article with the name of the purchaser; and when compared with the notes of a clerk they were found perfectly correct. Themistocles possessed such powers of retention that when one offered to teach him the art of memory he rejected the proposal, and remarked that he had "much rather he would teach him the art to forget." Justus Lipsius was able to repeat every line of Tacitus' works, *memoriter*. Josephus Scaliger committed Homer's Iliad and his Odyssey entirely in twenty-one days, each being about the same length—the Iliad containing thirty-one thousand six hundred and seventy verses. Seneca could repeat two thousand names in the order in which he heard them, and rehearse two hundred verses on different subjects after once hearing them read. Mithridates, the celebrated King of Pontus, ruled twenty-two countries, and was enabled by his faithful memory to converse with the various ambassadors in the proper language of the country which they respectively represented. St Austin's works are sufficient to fill a large library, and yet Dr Reynolds mastered them all, being able to repeat any portion of them from memory. Dr Jewel, Bishop of Salisbury, could repeat anything he had written by once reading it, and never forgot a line of what he read; but his astonishing memory he attributed to industrious cultivation of that faculty. Jerome of Prague, who was martyred for the Protestant religion by a sentence of the Council of Constance, was famous for an excellent memory, of which Poggius, in his epistle to Leonardus Aretinus, gives the following occurrence in illustration:— "After he had been confined three hundred and forty days in the bottom of a loathsome tower, where he was wholly without light either to see or read; yet, when he was called to trial, he quoted so many testimonies of the most sagacious and learned men in favour of his own principles, as if all that time he had been immured in a good library, with all the conveniences of studying." This is a remarkable example, especially if we consider the afflictive circumstances of his case, and how sadly trouble weakens and impairs the memory. A young Corsican, while in the Law School of Padua, in Italy, could repeat forwards or backwards thirty-six thousand names, and a year after could repeat anything remembered. He instructed Franciscus Molinus, a nobleman of Venice, who had a very poor memory, in less than eight days, to repeat five hundred names in any order he pleased. Mr Thomas Fuller possessed a memory sufficient to remember all the signs on both sides of Cheapside and several other streets in London. Instances could be related of other memorists equally as noted, but the limited space of this book will not permit an extensive article on this subject. Sickness, fright, or slothfulness may seriously impair the memory, as the following instances may show, viz., the orator Messala Corvinus forgot his own name—caused by sickness. Artemidor ous, the grammarian, having been frightened by a crocodile, the fright caused an entire loss of his learning, that he never afterwards recovered. Calvisus Sabinus, from the habit of slothfulness and neglect of his memory, became so forgetful that he could not recollect the names of Ulysses, Achilles, and Priamus, yet he knew those men as well as one man can well know another. Germanus, who was a clerk under the reign of Frederick II., having been bled, lost the entire use of his memory; yet one year subsequently, having been bled again, he recovered the full use of his former memory. Examples could be enumerated wherein forgetfulness could be attributed to the fact of not cultivating and employing the memory. The mathematician Wallis, while in bed and with his eyes shut, extracted the cube root of a number consisting of thirty figures, not making a single mistake. Dr Timothy Dwight, of Yale College, was in the habit of taking seven texts, and at the same time dictating to seven amanuenses seven distinct sermons. A celebrated London dramatist laid a wager that he would, after once reading a page of advertisements in *The Times*, repeat them verbatim and in order; and he won the wager. He also undertook to walk along one of the main business thoroughfares, the Strand, in which every house on each side has an elaborate signboard and number, and to repeat the names, numbers, and businesses of each, taking in both sides as he walked along only once. Mr Miller, a talented lawyer of Keokuk Iowa, who was formerly member of Congress, has a remarkably retentive memory. He has been known to write out in full an entire sermon, without taking notes, and when the bishop who preached it called upon him, and observed that Mr Miller had changed only one word. In reply, he mentioned the very word, and gave as his reason for the change that the word used by the bishop was incorrect. The bishop thanked him, and pocketed the paper in which the reported sermon appeared the morning after it was delivered. Mr Miller remarked to me that it was by his concentrated and earnest attention at the time of hearing that he was enabled so unfailingly to remember. A Miss Foster of London has also this remarkable retention of memory. A clergyman, of local note for his terse, epigrammatic style of sermonizing, was asked by his congregation to print and publish one of his telling, cogent discourses; but on his assuring them that he could not reproduce accurately what he had preached, Miss Foster, then about sixteen years of age, proffered to write it out verbatim, and did, perfectly to the preacher's satisfaction. Dudley Waller, a boy in the American States, when entering his teens, learned long lectures by hearing them read once or twice. He has been known to repeat accurately half a newspaper column, and tell where the punctuation points appeared, as he had been told them when hearing it read. Writing out one's thoughts gives tenacity to the memory. Then write out your own thoughts, as well as what you learn from books, teachers, and conversation. Keep a diary or note-book, and at the end of the day note down in chronological order every transaction that occurred within your cognizance during the whole day. Special care should be taken, however, in the exercise and cultivation of memory, not to overtax it. It is a fact well attested by experience that the memory may be seriously injured by pressing upon it too hardly and continuously in early life. Whatever theory we hold as to this great and wonderful function of our nature, it is certain that its powers are only gradually developed; and that, if forced into premature exercise, they are impaired by the effort. A regulated exercise short of fatigue, is improving to it; but we ought carefully to refrain from goading it by constant and laborious efforts in early life, and before this wonderful, God-like faculty is strengthened to its work, or it decays in our hands. The following interesting incident, related by James Beaty, may serve as a warning to those having the care of the young. A boy whose over-zealous and indiscreet mother obliged him to commit sermons to memory, lost his other faculties, and became stupid and idiotic. Let us ever keep in mind what *Coleridge*, in his rapturous appreciation of this power, exclaims:—" Memory, bosom-spring of joy." Then *Basile:*—" Memory is the cabinet of imagination, the treasury of reason, the registry of conscience, and the council-chamber of thought."

B. TO RESTRAIN THE MNEMONIC POWERS:—Should this faculty or powers of retention be leading the mind to matters of a painful nature, turn the thoughts to something else, avoiding whatever will in any manner depress the spirits; cast off past troubles; never recal the past, but live for the day and the future.

PRUDENTIALITY.
WISDOM APPLIED TO PRACTICE.

PRUDENCE *partially closes the eyes, which are usually also found somewhat settled in the head, but never seen in persons with very short noses. Hence children who almost invariably have short noses, are very imprudent. Open mouths are also evidence of natural imprudence.*

Prudentiality small.
Restless, loquacious, ignorant and saucy boy of Jacksonville, Illinois.

Prudentiality large.
John Sherman, U.S. Senator from Ohio.

1. Stolid, dolti **h**, shallow minded and short-witted, you are only a dolt and a driveller.
2. Being soft, obtuse, and feeble, your acts will be ill-advised and inconsistent, frequently.
3. Being somewhat infatuated, you may be considered rather dull and asinine.
4. Being almost destitute of acumen, your perspicacity will not make you noted.
5. Though you resolve and re-resolve you will not likely commit many deeds of indiscretion, yet you will at times evince precious little wisdom or penetration.
6. Consistency in your endeavours will prevent the weeds of imprudence from smothering the genuine plants of your better desires.
7. Though rather prudent, judicious, and discerning, yet you are not remarkable for perspicaciousness.
8. Those who are intimate with you, will know that you are considerate, politic, and provident.
9. Being deemed apt, clever, and astute (not to say "canny"), your mind is fraught with penetration, discernment, and discretion.
10. The subtlety and archness of your disposition will earn you the reputation of being long-headed and penetratingly sagacious.
11. An unusual sagacity in your nature shows that you possess shrewdness and acuteness rarely equalled.
12. Since you arrived at years of maturity and discretion, an imprudent act you rarely or never committed.

A. To ACCELERATE AND STRENGTHEN PRUDENCE:—Allow no foolish thoughts to enter your mind; avoid the company and associations of the weak-minded; shun the society of the injudicious; give a true self-education to your own mind, and you will feel that this is the most valuable of all training. The self-educated are invariably the most successful in life.

B. To RETARD PRUDENCE:—Be silly and nonsensical; become unwary; discard discretion and circumspection; be constantly unmindful of the precautions and warnings of others; let extravagance and unreason have full sway over you—give them rein—let the egregious and preposterous dominate your life; and give full swing to every absurdity.

CREDULOUSNESS.

THE ENDOWMENT WHEREBY ONE IS ENABLED TO RECEIVE AS TRUE, THAT WHICH IS UNPROVEN.

The eyebrows when elevated far above the eyes, and present a large intercilar space as in Harvey, are certain signs of large faith.

OBSERVATION:—In an early era man lived in the *stomach age*, which age rose to the summit of its glory during the days of Gracchus and his sons, Tiberius and Caius, Crassus, Caligula, Claudius, Nero, Vitellius, Severus and his cruel son Caracalla; when Rome was the home of thousands of similar unfeeling wretches who gormandised in her banquet halls; later Rome in her glory lived in the *muscular age*,—when muscle was king; in process of time printing presses, railways, telegraphs, schools and appliances to arouse sensation and thought developed the brain and nervous system and produced a *brain age*, in which the civilized world lives to-day, when sensations command a higher premium than sense. The next and purer age, the millennial era, will be the *spiritual age*, the light of which is already appearing.

Credulousness small.
Voltaire, who had no respect for God or man, and tried to destroy all religious faith.

Credulousness large.
Wm. Harvey, M.D., discoverer of the circulation of the blood.

1. Doubts and infidelity are masters in your nature and sweep away every ray of confidence about the unseen as the river in flood carries off buoyant *debris*

2. This faculty, which is the avenue for the admission of unproven truth into the human intelligence, in you is a narrow, dark, and difficult way; its walls and ceilings are corresponsively rusty, and should be lubricated with spiritual culture.

3. Being extremely sceptical and unable to give credence to strange things, you can only, if at all, experience feeble glimpses of a future life by faith as you naturally wish practical assurance of everything.

4. You require tangible evidence or solid reasons, before admitting general or strange questionable matters, nor are you credulous in new theories.

5. Being slow of belief in matters of rare and wonderful appearance, wherein complicated mystery is connected, you will question and disbelieve a long time.

6. Being apt to discredit what you deem unworthy of credence, your faith would hardly be sufficient to preach from, since its moderate strength would scarcely gain for you the reputation among your neighbours of a sincere and earnest believer.

7. Cock-and-bull and sea-serpent stories you cannot take in unless well vouched for by some one in whom you repose implicit confidence.

8. You delight in conversations on the immortality of the soul, as that species of converse is to you spiritual food.

9. In your nature there is implanted a deep love of novelty which renders you susceptible of sudden emotions of wonder and surprise.

10. Having naturally a craving love of novelty, you entertain romantic ideas, and may think you see phantoms or ghosts. Your dreams often prove true; and you can receive upon trust, cherish and nurture what others assert, though it should be bordering on the miraculous.

11. Accompanied with an insatiable desire for the wonderful and mysterious, you have implicit confidence in your friends.

12. So inordinately strong is your faith that you are liable to be duped by giving credence to whatever you are told; hence the attractive faithfulness and fidelity you possess will mantle and screen many faults of your friends, and prepare your mind for a ready assent to the truth when declared by another.

A To Cultivate Faith:—Avoid everything that tends to materialism; never doubt the wonderful and mysterious because you can't understand them; you are finite while the universe is infinite; and your reason may deceive you as it has been deceptive to the sages of all times. Learn, and daily repeat the subjoined beautiful lines from the pen of Longfellow:—

> "Life is real, life is earnest,
> And the grave is not the goal;
> Dust thou art, to dust returnest,
> Was not written of the soul.
>
> "Not enjoyment and not sorrow,
> Is our destined end or way;
> But to act that each to-morrow
> Finds us farther than to-day."

B. To Blight and Extinguish Faith:—Never read or think of ghosts, demons, fairies or witches; study the laws of nature and metaphysics; try to account for all that is strange and wonderful by appealing to natural phenomena or natural magic; think of the havoc science has already made among the superstitions of the middle ages; and finally, determine to believe in nothing that is not palpable to one of your senses, but don't forget that these avenues or gates of knowledge may also be snowed up or beclouded. The shortest indeed would be to believe nothing, and then doubt your own personal identity and existence.

COURTEOUSNESS.

THE STATE OR QUALITY WHICH LEADS TO CIVILITY OF MANNERS, POLITENESS, AND ELEGANT DEPORTMENT.

This winning power of outward attractiveness manifests itself in fine features, high, open forehead, graceful form, and a large, animated, and prominent eye.

1. Intensely crabbed and captious, you are impolite and uncourteous, spleeny, moody, scowling, and dogged—displeased with everybody and everything.

2. Sulkiness, churlishness, bluntness, and bluffness of manner characterise you. Try to rub off your corners by polished associations.

3. Towards your friends and acquaintances it requires much effort for

you to be civil or persuasive; and, if imposed upon, you are almost certain to be rude.

4. Though none too much inclined to the courtesies of life, you may at times be civil and humane.

5. Were one to judge by the little use you make of your back in courteous intercourse, he might suppose that it had been spoiled in the manufacture.

Courteousness small.
D. Fernando VII. a tyrant, who started the Inquisition, and was devoid of fine feelings.

Courteousness large.
Count De Orsay, the most polite man of the world.

6. To bow and scrape like a French Fop is unnatural to you: nor are you likely to relish it in others.

7. Recognitions and greetings you return respectfully, and you make an effort to be polite, but are none too much given in that direction.

8. Though not unusually polished in your manners, in the drawing-room, you can receive, and do the honours of the table.

9. If it is your whim, you can be quite polite, since you possess civility, though not overflowing with compliments.

10. Amenity and suavity render you obliging, and you are generally esteemed amiable.

11. Nothing do you enjoy much more than good manners. Many hearts are won by your politeness and attractive deportment.

12. You can bow and stoop very gracefully and pleasingly, and must be esteemed as one of the most obsequious of the human family.

A. To IMPROVE IN COURTEOUSNESS OR COURTESY:—First of all, never forget that all mankind inwardly love that latent flattery called politeness. Secondly, try to use suavity of manner and fair words (as delicately as possible), because it renders others respectful to us and on good terms with themselves. Thirdly, to be tractable and attractive is a duty we owe to society as well as to ourselves. It invests happiness at a high rate of interest, and is the best stock in the market of social intercourse, as it carries joy to others and brings success to ourselves.

B. To DETERIORATE YOUR COURTESY:—Be careful to carry to excess your foppish and conceited airs; be bland, refined, and courteous, but use less palaver, and you will be less sickening to others. You have too much of what the world have generally too little—you are too polite.

ATTENTIVENESS.
THE QUALITY OR POWER OF GIVING HEED TO OBJECTS OR THOUGHTS.

ATTENTION, *when large, carries the head forwa d in the same manner that one bends forward when thoroughly interested in a new book, held in the hand, as shown in the engraving of Hugh Miller, Scotland's talented geologist.*

Attentiveness large.
Abbey Kelley Foster, an able advocate of the abolition of American slavery.

Attentiveness small.
His Majesty Pomarre, King of Taheite.

1. Unbending and diverting the mind you thoroughly enjoy; being easily distracted you are wandering and fitful in your efforts.
2. Even important events and subjects you can gloss over, and overlook numerous good things.
3. Being listless and cursory, rather dreamily you skim the surface.
4. Not being very attentive, things of rare interest may engross you, while commonplace occurrences are passed without consideration.
5. It is hard work to engross your mind ully and absorb your undivided attention.

6. **You** give heed to things about you in so careless and uninteresting a manner that you may be easily diverted from your purpose.

7. You are unmindful of interesting subjects or those upon which duty calls you to take an interest.

8. Inspection and inquisitiveness will characterise you as you give due regard to important subjects.

Attentiveness very large.
Hugh Miller, Scottish Geologist.

9. With pleasant advertence, you heed the affairs of life; but thoroughly you attend to things to which your attention is directed.

10. You are apt to become absorbed for the time with the matter in hand.

11. Having a remarkable power of noticing and observing objects around you, everything receives your close, observant attention.

12. Being intent on every subject with a remarkable power of close and searching heed, you are mindful and largely gifted with introspection.

A. To CULTIVATE ATTENTION:—Examine closely every object or person; note minutely every condition of their surroundings; give earnest heed to whatever you do; be intent and live as if life were a battle and not an evanescent dream.

> " Tell me not in mournful numbers
> Life is but an empty dream!"
> * * * * *
> " In the world's broad field of battle,
> In the bivouac of life,
> Be not like dumb driven cattle!
> Be a hero in the strife!" —*Longfellow.*

B. TO BECOME LESS ATTENTIVE:—Let life glide away like a smooth stream; relax your mind and turn away from whatever interests you; proudly dash on in your conceit, and allow no thought to have an abiding place in your mind.

SYMPATHY, OR SYMPATHETICALNESS.

THE VIRTUE OF FEELING WITH OTHERS WHETHER IN THEIR WOES, TROUBLES, AND ANXIETIES, OR IN THEIR PLEASURES AND JOYS.

A long narrow face, with full lips, are testimonies of true and heart stirring SYMPATHY. *But besides these there are several other signs, such as a long head, from forehead to crown; round commissure of the eye; narrow nose, in its lower portion; long nose, long and slim fingers, &c.*

Sympatheticalness small
Robespierre, a bloody and cruel tyrant.

Sympatheticalness large.
Eustache, who saved his master and others from massacre.

1. For another's sorrows your stony heart never melts.
2. To your unmerciful soul, compassion and commiseration are strangers.
3. Worlds of woe may expand around you and yet not a spark of pity scintillates from your hard eye.

4. Being almost devoid of the sympathetic nature, you are not adapted to compassionate another in grief.

5. Having been somewhat tutored in suffering and sadness, you do smile and weep with others; and yet you are only mechanically transfused or affected by their weal or woe.

6. Occasionally, tender feelings may agitate you, yet you are not easily swayed or unbalanced in this respect.

7. Though neither unfeeling nor often melted to tears by pitiful sights, you may, and no doubt do often feel, more than you express.

8. When others suffer, with a yearning heart, you try to render consolation, and express a proper amount of sympathy.

9. Being of a relenting heart, the tender and kindly feelings are readily enlisted in you.

10. Being possessed of tenderness and forbearance for others, you have abundant pity for the unfortunate of human-kind.

11. Tender-hearted, you be well termed, as you will try to console and comfort the afflicted.

12. With the best interests of all mankind, your heart ever beats in unison, while you are instinctively lenient and merciful.

A. To IMPROVE IN SYMPATHY:—Let the lovely and pellucid fountain of secret sympathy well forth its tiny stream until its use strengthens it into a mighty river. Sympathise with the sorrowing and wretched of every clime; lament with the weepers, and shame not the tear of compassion back into its hiding-place.

B. To DETERIORATE OR MINIFY SYMPATHY:—Harbour malice against those with whom you once sympathised; enter less into and compassionate not so much the feelings of the afflicted; with steel, encase your heart, and let not its door even stand ajar to the suffering world; keep steadily in view that your well-meant clemency will rob you unjustly; and never do an act of private charity; but always stipulate that the donation you grudgingly doll out must appear in the next day's issue of the best circulated daily paper.

CLASS VI.

PERFECTIVE QUALITIES.

THE SIXTH CLASS OF CHARACTERISTICS ACCOMPANY AN EVEN COMBINATION OF TWO OR MORE OF THE FIVE FORMS.

GRACEFULNESS.

BY GRACEFULNESS IS MEANT THE QUALITY OR FACULTY RESULTING IN EASE AND ELEGANCE OF MOTION AND AGREEABLENESS OF MANNERS. THE GRACEFUL MOVEMENT IS PERFORMED IN LONG CURVES, AND THE GRACEFUL MANNER IS SEEN IN THE SWEEPING CURVE OF THE GESTURE AND BOW.

The apparent structural form which accompanies graceful movements and manners is the slim and pliable structure that bends with apparent ease.

Gracefulness large. The swan.

1. As ungraceful as a stump, your figure presents no curves that would bespeak any graceful trait in your character. To you the swan would appear no more graceful than a toad shivering on a cold stone.

2. The waddling of a duck, or a turtle, resembles your gait. The irregular movements of your body may be compared to a broken sea; you jog along like a donkey under a ton of hay.

3. Your ordinary movements are characterised by stiffness, awkwardness, and uncouthness.

4. Though pliability and suppleness of body may interest you, still they afford you no great pleasure.

5. The undulations of a wheat field waving in the breeze. the flying of the swallow, the swimming of the swan, or the gyrations and swoop of the vulture or the eagle, as it descends upon its prey, seldom raise you into ecstatic enthusiasm.

6. The stiff and perpendicular motions characterise you generally; hence flowing and sweeping garments are rarely admired by you.

7. By diligent cultivation and assiduous attention, ease of movement and elegance of attitude may characterise your actions and give you graceful and winning manners; but without cultivation you would be graceless

8. Innately loving beautiful motion, your attention will be arrested and your sympathy enlisted by the carriage that rolls easily along. the body or bird that glides, the person that easily skates, if they exhibit in their locomotion numerous long smooth curves.

9. So enamoured are you with easy, graceful curvilinear motion that time seems to glide away pleasantly while you are beholding the rolling billows or the wreathing smoke in its gyrations heavenward.

10. The toddling gait, being unnatural to you, displeases you wherever you observe it; hence you instinctively avoid it, and pay considerable attention to your gait, manners and figure.

11. Your bodily attitudes are always graceful; hence your natural carriage and bearing are always distinguished by the elegance of refinement.

12. Wavy motions are your delight. The swaying of a fire balloon; the unlimited epicycloidal curves marked by the course of a kite; and the wheeling and bounding of a spirited horse, will all afford pleasure to your graceful mind and fancy.

A. To Cultivate Gracefulness:—Measure each step you take with unfailing accuracy, and always make your steps of uniform length; read the works of graceful authors; associate with those who have a particular regard to their special, general appearance; study how to move in a bending easy manner, and endeavour to improve your gait and manual attitudes. Watch the liquid swaying of the neck of a swan, and introduce a similar easy grace into your own movements; roll a hoop, spin a top, learn to waltz, skate, and never allow yourself to perform an awkward movement. Remember what Pope says of ease in writing; and his words are quite appropriate here:—

"True ease in writing comes from art not chance,
As those move easiest who have learned to dance."

B. To Restrain Gracefulness:—Eat heartily; sleep much; be stiff in your movements, and less bending, bowing, scraping, and nodding in your salutations and deportment; pay less attention to gracefulness and more to the ordinary necessities of life; and you will thus render yourself sufficiently ungainly and boorish to repel the esteem and admiration of all that admire elegance of manner and the charms of gracefulness.

PROSPEROUSNESS, OR PROSPERATIVENESS.
THE POWER OF ATTAINING THE DESIRED OBJECT.

The curved line running round the corners of the mouth is nature's stamp or trade-mark on the visage of a person who has succeeded or can do so in some department of life.

Prosperativeness large.
Jacob Strawn, an extensive farmer, cattle dealer, and business man of Illinois, who began life poor.

1. Almost all your efforts prove abortive; hence your life has been a succession of failures, mistakes, and botches.

2. Allowing your latent energies to rust and corrode in idleness, the myriad circumstances and opportunities occurring around you are not turned to self advantage, partly arising from your being a bad planner as well as spending your force in passional indulgence.

3. By economizing your life force your old age may not be one of want and misery; many of your plans are incomplete, and cause disappointments to cluster along your path as thickly as grapes on an arbour in autumn.

4. To you the beatitude, "Blessed are they that expect nothing, for they shall not be disappointed," is likely to prove about correct; hence build not high your expectations lest the sad truth sap their walls some day.

5. Being alike free from the extremes of thrift and ineffectiveness, you require to labour attentively in order to flourish and prosper, as well as to carefully regulate your passions with the due amount of reason and common sense.

6. Being moderate in your requirements, you will never become as rich as Crœsus, Dives, Astor, the Rothschilds, Stuart, or Vanderbilt.

7. By striving earnestly in a good cause, the great struggles of your life will result successfully.

8. You will make excellent progress in life, should your path among mankind not prove very rugged and steep.

9. Your ability to accomplish what you undertake is so good that you generally succeed in your projects; so rarely are you disappointed that people call you lucky; yet should misfortune occur, it will be only a stimulus to fresh effort, and you will continue the struggle until success perches upon your banner.

10. Prosperity mostly waits upon you along the whole of your pathway in life; but should a failure occur in any of your undertakings, it will be occasioned by circumstances over which you have no control.

11. So remarkably fortunate are you that everything you touch seems to turn to your advantage.

12 Having first-class natural ability and endowments, aided by just the proper amount of energy, your wishes gain ready responses, so that you conquer and come out best in every undertaking. The world would seem to be made for you, and quite to your liking, judging from your good fortune and success.

A. To CULTIVATE THE MEANS THAT LEAD TO SUCCESS:—Be regular in your habits; calculate everything deliberately and accurately; keep cool; lead a steady life; be merry and cheerful; but above all take care of your health; depend as little as possible upon others, trusting mainly to self-exertion; think, act, and control your passions. Keep well in mind what Longfellow has so well said of the talent for success: "It is nothing more than doing what you can do well, and doing well whatever you do, without a thought of fame."

B. To RESTRAIN AND OBSTRUCT SUCCESS:—Earnestly avoid every attempt in this direction, it is only too easily done; but if you need a hint or two in this undesirable work, here are a few:—Dive into projects without premeditation; make no calculations; give full swing to your impulses; dismiss earthly thoughts; learn that worldly achievements may ruin your soul; make no effort, therefore, to succeed, and console yourself with the oft repeated absurdity, so neatly expressed by the indolent Addison with his pot of beer by the arm of his easy chair: "'Tis not in mortals to command success."

PHYSICAL HARMONY, OR PHYSIOHARMONITIVENESS.

THE POWER WHICH APPRECIATES THAT PHYSICAL CONDITION IN WHICH ALL PARTS OF THE BODY ARE ROUNDED AND IN PERFECT ACCORDANCE.

When one part of the body is equal, in due proportion, to every other part, in strength and no feature seems to dominate the others in size, and all are rounded, the individual who is so happily framed, so essentially harmonious throughout, should feel grateful, and endeavour to assist others to like harmony in their natures.

Physioharmonitiveness large in Sarah and John Bovin, aged respectively 164 and 172 years of age.

1. You are utterly devoid of the concord which invites tranquillity and happiness.

2. Jarring and clashing elements are in the very essence of your nature, and the moth and cankerworm of discord are eternally gnawing at your vitals.

3. The cause of almost all your trouble is the jarring disproportion of your strong and weak faculties — constantly at war, superinducing an incessantly irrelevant condition of mind.

4. Being never fully in accord with yourself or others, misunderstandings are constantly arising, and as with a broom of discord sweep away all concord and unanimity between yourself and friends.

5. Though generally of a well balanced mind and disposition, yet you are liable to be out of sorts sometimes.

6. Your head being neither too large nor too small, is fairly proportioned to your body. The balance between your physical organs generally gives you attractive harmony; yet when disturbing causes arise you are inharmonious.

7. Though perfect harmony may not exist in your composition, yet one faculty accords well with another.

8. The tranquillity of your nature, arising from your usually untroubled state, diffuses peace around you.

9. Acting and living in unison with others affords you pleasure. Hence you have a natural aversion to discordant people.

10. Possessing strong compatibility, you are at all times consistent, and the entire unison of your mind's action casts out all jar.

11. In your mentality, one faculty adapts and adjusts itself to another, so that, enjoying concinnity, no discord creeps into your nature.

Physioharmonitiveness small.
Cut Nose, an Indian, who, in the massacre of 1862, in Minnesota, murdered 18 women and children and 5 men.

Physioharmonitiveness large.
G. F. Handel, a talented musician, whose life was occupied in promoting harmony.

12. In all your mental faculties there is perfect concord, a beautiful, harmonious equipoise pervading every organ, and every mental attribute, and all your emotions

A. To ADVANCE AND IMPROVE HARMONY:—Cultivate and enjoy music; encourage your weak and restrain the strong faculties; allow nothing to disturb the quietude of your mind; avoid everything disagreeable, and permit no one or nothing to disconcert you.

B. To RETARD AND LESSEN HARMONY:—Flare up and rile at everything unpleasant; become excited and storm at the veriest trifle; make no concessions or attempts at conciliations; throw your nature out of gear by constantly clashing and disagreeing with others; when others sing throw in a discordant note or two; bear in mind that your grating and stridulous nature is rasping itself out apace.

PROPORTION, OR PROPORTIONATIVENESS.
RECOGNITION OF THE TRUE RELATION OF PARTS TO EACH OTHER.

The physiognomical manifestations of PROPORTIONATIVENESS *are a due symmetrical proportion of one feature to another joined in a body whose parts and features are in harmonious accord, producing beauty of form.*

Proportionativeness large.
Petrarch Zortan, 185 years of age.

Proportionativeness small.
A flat head Indian, of Vancouver Island, British Columbia.

1. Your ill-assorted members predispose you to be fond of exotic, outlandish objects and persons, and gives you by inclination a readiness in affiliating with persons of unmatched faces, and badly assorted features.

2. Irrelevance and disproportion lend a pleasure to one of your nature, as soon as you observe them, or recognize the incomparable.

3. Some of your features are too large to bear due proportionate size to the others; hence your character is marked with unsuitableness to itself.

4. Certain of your characteristics possess so much more strength than others, that it seems as if one part of your being was unallied to the rest. Hence you are a peculiar person—an oddity, in short.

5. When one in whom due proportion abounds views your features, he or she will perceive an incommensurable difference in the size of the parts; the consequence of this disproportion is that you evince both very strong and very weak traits of character.

6. Being free from extremes in any of your forms you are thus prevented from excesses in disposition.

7. Fair symmetry spreads her heavenly mantle over your organization and protects you from the cold discords resulting from disproportion.

8. Having a clear perception and comprehension of the correlation and homogeniousness of one portion of a body to another, you are enabled to discern where pertinency or fitness reigns in another's character.

9. The identity is excellent in your physical proportion; hence analogy and relevancy are manifested in your form.

10. The due proportion which one feature or part of your face and body bears to another is no less remarkable than is that of the happy relation and balance existing in your mental endowments.

11. Remarkable relation and adaptation characterise your whole being. You are an excellent judge of proportion or disproportion in persons or materials.

12. The exactitude with which the physical of your structure plays upon another, and produces or accompanies an equality and fitness of mind is worthy of remark and high commendation.

A. To Improve Proportionateness:—Notice the relative size of the wing to the upright of a house; study architecture; do not allow yourself to run to extremes in politics, religion, business, profession, or sociality; and in whatever you do be regardful of the proportion that one thing bears to another; be considerate of correlations; associate with those who are cognative, proportionate, and balanced in character; study books by mathematical and mechanical writers; observe and study those buildings, bridges, and machines in which proportion and due relation of size exist among the various parts; when writing make each letter sufficiently large to correspond with other letters on the same page; study the rule of proportion in arithmetic, and proportional logarithms; use compasses. dividers, and proportional scales; observe every suitable and comparative relation; and become symmetrical.

B. To Restrain Proportionateness:—Rarely does this inclination need restraint; yet in cases of derangement it may become necessary. In such case, the following rule will be efficacious:—Shun the rule of proportion in arithmetic, and the fifth and sixth books of Euclid as well as every book on mensuration; heed not the adaptation of any one thing to another; avoid endeavouring to bring into suitable comparative relation, every deed, object, or thought you happen to know; be incommensurable in every one of life's affairs and circumstances. And lastly, set down as sheer bosh what Professor Upham says:—" I have come to the conclusion, if man or woman either wishes to realize the full power of personal beauty, it must be by cherishing noble hopes and purposes; by having something to do and something to live for, which is worthy of humanity, and which, by expanding the capacities of the soul, gives expansion to the symmetry of the body which contains it."

REASON, OR REDUCTIVENESS.

THE LOGICAL FACULTY OF DEDUCING CONCLUSIONS FROM PREMISES.

In the human physiognomy, the ratiocinative faculty discovers itself to the observer by a well defined and prominent nose and broad face. No person has been ever known as an original and correct reasoner who had a low flat nose like that of the Chinaman.

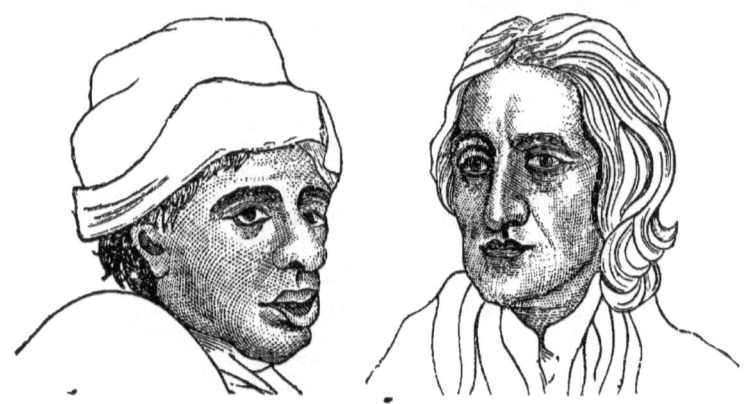

Deductiveness small.
Foolish Sam.

Deductiveness large.
John Locke.

1. Being a complete fool, you leap, frog like, at every conclusion.

2. Never caring to know the reason why, but only the fact or assertion, you will not make a good grammarian.

3. You possess more available talent than becomes manifest by your attempts at reasoning; and you are slow in comprehending any complicated system or line of argument.

4. You can pick up knowledge quickly, and your plans, though not extensive, may be practical; still you are not very thorough in tracing out the relations of arguments to subjects under consideration.

5. Naturally slow and heavy in reasoning, you will require much time to adduce the *pros* and *cons* of your argument upon any subject.

6. When deep and intricate subjects come under your consideration, you may fail thoroughly to comprehend them, as you are not invulnerable in argument.

7. Though you manifest no very decided desire for the ascertainment and study of principles, yet you give sufficient assurance of fair reasoning talent.

8. From the thinking powers of your mind being logical, when you grasp principles accurately, your inferences are usually to be trusted.

9. The origin of things, ideas, and systems as well as the rationale of them afford you great pleasure; hence your ratiocinations and inductions

are profound and extensive. You possess the spirit of the following lines by Cotton:—

> "'Tis Reason's part
> To govern and guard the heart,
> To lull the wayward soul to rest,
> When hopes and fears distract the breast;
> Reason may calm this doubtful strife,
> And steer thy barque through various life."

10. Being, if educated, capable of deep thought and fair penetration, your ability will be good in discovering the principles upon which anything new depends.

11. Though you may not be able to elucidate and exhibit your cogitations so well as you understand them, nevertheless, being capable of deep abstract thought, you readily discern the causes that underlie and precede a change.

12. Possessing an exceedingly profound and comprehensive mind, the reason why is always arising in your times of cogitation, and the same word ever ready in your interrogatories. The Aristotleian method as well as the Baconian govern, guide, and pervade all your investigations. Over all your thoughts and researches, Reason presides as the lord-chief-justice.

A. To CULTIVATE THE RATIOCINATIVE POWERS OF MIND:—Muse, ponder, investigate; debate, cogitate; seek for the wherefor of everything; study Mathematics in all its branches, as well as Astronomy, Geology, Natural Philosophy, and even Metaphysics; read the writings of Socrates, Hippocrates, Plato, Aristotle, Bacon Cuvier, Herschel, Owen, Darwin, John Stuart Mill, &c.

B. To RESTRAIN THE TENDENCY TO RATIOCINATE:—Cast away your fine spun theories; shun arguments with any one; trouble not yourself about the systems and doctrines of Plato, Pythagoras, Epicurus, Aristotle, or any great philosopher; do not peruse the works of Plutarch, Cicero, and Seneca; keep along the beaten path well paved with facts, from it carefully sweeping away any stray probability that some unwary speculator may have dropped in your path; be practical, keeping your observing faculties wide awake and hard at work.

The Following Tables for Marking were

FILLED UP FOR

M..

Marked by ....

Date of Marking,..

The Place where the Marking was done,..................

COLUMN I. Name of the Faculty or Power.	COLUMN II. Page in this Book in which the Faculty or Power commences.	COLUMN III. Size of Powers and Faculties, marked on a Scale of 1 to 12.	COLUMN IV. Culture of the Power or Faculty marked A Restraint of the Power or Faculty marked B.
Abdominal Form, ...	8		
Thoracic Form, ...	11		
Muscular Form, ...	12		
Osseous Form, ...	14		
Brain Form, ...	17		

TABLE OF MARKING.

COLUMN I. Name of the Faculty or Power.	COLUMN II. Page where the Faculty commences.	COLUMN III. Size of the Faculty.	COLUMN IV. Culture marked A, Restraint, B.
The Stomach................	19		
" Liver..................	21		
" Kidneys................	22		
" Heart..................	23		
" Lungs.................	24		
" Color.................	25		
" Texture...............	26		
" Health................	27		
Mind, Activity of.........	28		
FACULTIES, Class I.	30		
Contentment.............	80		
Animal Imitation..........	31		
Love of Liquids...........	33		
Physical Hope............	36		
Rapacity.	39		
Appetite for Food........	41		
Revengefulness...........	44		
Social Disposition........	45		
FACULTIES, Class II.	47		
Desire to be Sentinelled...	47		

TABLE OF MARKING.

Column I. Name of the Faculty or Power.	Column II. Page where the Faculty commences.	Column III. Size of the Faculty.	Column IV. Culture marked A Restraint, B.
Moral Courage............	48		
Tendency for Elevation..	50		
Sense of Smell...........	52		
Resistance...............	54		
Disposition to Attack.....	55		
Wakefulness.............	56		
Suspicious Disposition....	58		
Propensity for Locomotion	60		
Inquisitiveness...........	62		
Ambitiousness............	64		
Self-Estimation...........	67		
FACULTIES, Class III.	69		
Appreciation of Natural Motion................	69		
Physical Courage.........	71		
Sophisticalness...........	74		
Playfulness..............	75		
Locative Habits..........	76		
Substitution..............	78		
Reception of Tone........	79		
Secrecy..................	82		

TABLE OF MARKING.

Column I. Name of the Faculty or Power.	Column II. Page where the Faculty commences.	Column III. Size of the Faculty.	Column IV Culture marked A Restraint, B.
Economy	85		
Judgment of Curvature	86		
Desire of Possession	88		
Monogamous Love	90		
Will	92		
Merriness	93		
Providentness	96		
Contrariness	98		
Polygamous Love	100		
Memory of Names	1 2		
Perception of Colors	104		
Inclination to Destroy	106		
Love of the Young	109		
Spoken Language	111		
Physical Pleasure	114		
Curative Power	115		
Desire of Approval	117		
Unrelenting Temper	118		
Consecutiveness	120		
Capacity to Sing	122		

TABLE OF MARKING.

COLUMN I. Name of the Faculty or Power.	COLUMN II. Page where the Faculty commences.	COLUMN III. Size of the Faculty.	COLUMN IV. Culture marked A Restraint, B.
Love of Ornament........	124		
Searching Inclination.....	125		
Sagacity..................	126		
Proneness to Trade........	128		
Fitness of Things for each other................	129		
FACULTIES, Class IV.	131		
Discriminating Capacity.	131		
Mechanical Talent........	133		
Physical Arrangement....	134		
Perception of Angles.....	137		
Beneficence..............	139		
Decisiveness..............	141		
Observation..............	143		
Perseverance.............	145		
Rectitude................	147		
Numerical Computation.	150		
Discernment of Density..	152		
Suggestiveness...........	153		
Perception of Character..	155		
Friendship...............	157		

TABLE OF MARKING.

COLUMN I. Name of the Faculty or Power.	COLUMN II. Page where the Faculty commences.	COLUMN III. Size of the Faculty.	COLUMN IV. Culture marked A Restraint, B.
Originality..............	159		
Discernment of Magnitude	162		
Pertinaciousness..........	164		
Mechanical Motion.......	166		
Practicality..............	167		
Reverence................	170		
FACULTIES, Class V.	172		
Mental System...........	172		
Prescience...............	175		
Susceptibleness...........	176		
Mental Imitation.........	177		
Affableness..............	179		
Wit.....................	181		
Admiration of the Sublime	183		
Desire for Future Life....	184		
Appreciation of the Beautiful..................	185		
Carefulness..............	187		
Spiritual Hope...........	189		
Purity of Mind..........	191		
Intuition................	193		

TABLE OF MARKING.

COLUMN I. Name of the Faculty or Power.	COLUMN II. Page where the Faculty commences.	COLUMN III. Size of the Faculty.	COLUMN IV. Culture marked A Restraint, B.
Written Language	195		
Cleanness	197		
Pitifulness	198		
Imaginativeness	200		
Memory of Facts	203		
Prudentiality	207		
Credulousness	208		
Courteousness	210		
Attentiveness	212		
Sympathy	214		
FACULTIES, Class VI.	216		
Gracefulness	216		
Prosperousness	218		
Physical Harmony	220		
Proportion	222		
Reason	224		

Professions, Trades, Occupations, Callings, etc.

Those Professions, Trades, Occupations, Callings, and Business in which you would best succeed are marked with a dash, made by a pen or pencil, in the following list:—

Accountant.
Actor.
Actress.
Accoucheuse.
Administrator.
Æronaut.
Agent, R. R. Ticket.
" Insurance.
" Express.
" Concert.
" Lecture.
" Circus.
" Theatre.
" Telegraph.
" Goods.
Ambassador.
Amanuensis.
Anatomist.
Angler.
Angiotomist.
Analyst.
Anamalculist.
Apiarist.
Artist.
Architect.
Artificer.
Artizan.
Astronomer.
Assessor.
Astrologer.
Attorney.
Auctioneer.
Author.
Authoress.
Baggage Master.
Baker.
Banker.
Barrister.
Bar Maid.
" Tender.
Bazaar Maid.
Barber.
Barberess.

Bellmaker.
Blacksmith.
Bleacher.
Biologist.
Billposter.
Biblist.
Bishop.
Biographer.
Botanist.
Bookbinder.
Bootblack.
Boatswain.
Boatman.
Brakeman.
Brewer.
Broker.
Butcher.
Builder.
Butler.
Bugler.
Buyer.
Captain, Steamer.
" Company.
" Mines.
Carpenter, House.
" Ship.
Cashier.
Caricaturist.
Clairvoyant.
Chandler.
Chemist.
Chronologist.
Chorister.
Chambermaid.
Clerk of a Bank.
" Hotel.
" Shipping.
" Steamer.
" Store.
" County.
" Town.
" City.
Clown of a Circus.

Colporteur.
Comedian.
Compositor.
Conductor, Railroad.
Cooper.
Confectioner.
Colonel, Military.
Counsellor at Law.
Councillor.
Colourist.
Courier.
Correspondent.
Cook.
Constable.
Congressman.
Commodore.
Commissioner.
Critic.
Cricketer.
Dentist.
Designer.
Detective.
Dean.
Debater.
Demonologist.
Demonstrator.
Diplomatist.
Doctor, Divinity.
" Law.
" Medicine.
" Horse.
" Cattle.
Draughtsman.
Drayman.
Dressmaker.
Druggist.
Dyer.
Doctress.
Editor, or Editress
" Scientific.
" Literary.
" Political.
" Local.

TABLE OF PROFESSIONS, ETC.

Electrician.	Jobber, Stock.	Merchant, Hardware.
Electroplater.	" Mechanical.	" Books.
Electrotyper.	Justice.	" Clothing.
Elocutionist.	Kilnworker.	" Seed.
Engineer, Civil	Laundry Maid.	" Liquor.
" Mechanical.	Lawyer.	" Retail.
" Topographical	Lecturer, Literary.	" Wholesale.
Engraver.	" Popular.	" Flour & Feed
Engine Driver.	" Scientific.	Miller.
Entomologist.	" College.	Medium.
Entozoologist.	Legislator.	Marshal.
Ethnologist.	Lecturess.	Milliner.
Equestrian.	Librarian.	Miner.
Equestrienne.	Lieutenant, Army.	Minister.
Epitaphist.	Linguist.	Musician, Instrumental.
Farmer.	Livery-stable Proprietor	" String Inst't.
Florist.	Logician.	" Wind "
Financier.	Locksmith.	" Vocal.
Finisher, in Machinery.	Lumber Dealer.	" Treble.
Fisherman.	Lumberman.	" Alto.
Fruit Grower.	Manuf., Boot and Shoe	" Tenor.
" Dealer.	" Machinery.	" Basso.
Foundry Worker.	" Locomotives.	Moulder.
Gardener.	" Carriages.	Naturalist.
Geographer.	" Clothing.	Navigator.
Grammarian.	" Harness.	Nurse, Children.
Glassblower.	" Leather.	" Sick.
Glove Maker.	" Bricks.	Novelist.
Gun Smith.	" Furniture.	Nosologist.
Guardian of the Young.	" Cotton Goods.	Needlewoman.
Geologist.	" Woollen "	Officer, Army.
Haberdasher.	" Farming Implts.	" Civil.
Harness Maker.	" Tapestry.	" Customs.
Hatter.	" Musical Insts.	" Executive.
Hagiologist.	" Surgical "	Orator.
Health Seeking.	" Watches.	Overseer, Orna. Works.
Historian.	" Safes.	Painter, House.
Horseman.	" Tinware.	" Scenic.
House-keeper.	" Earthenware.	" Sign.
Hotel-keeper.	" Silverware.	" Landscape.
Hunter.	" Type.	" Portrait.
Huckster.	" Cheese.	" Caricaturist.
Horse-tamer.	" Indus. Machines	Pedlar.
Hostler.	Mayor of a City.	Penman.
Inventor.	" Town.	Philosopher.
Instructor.	Marketman.	Photographer.
Ironmonger.	Mathematician.	Physiognomist, Student
Janitor.	Mechanic, Machinist.	" Examiner.
Jailer.	" Foundry.	" Lecturer.
Jeweller.	" General.	" Teacher.
Judge.	Merchant, Dry Goods.	" Discoverer.
Juror.	" Groceries.	" Practical.

TABLE OF PROFESSIONS, ETC.

Physiognomist, Author.
Physician.
Plasterer.
Piano Tuner.
Postmistress.
Policeman.
Politician.
Postmaster.
Prophet.
Prophetess.
President, Bank.
" Trustees.
" Committee.
" Council.
" Meeting.
" Nation.
" Railroad Co.
Pawnbroker.
Pattern Maker.
Printer, Practical.
Prison-keeper.
Proof Reader.
Public Speaker.
Publican.
Publisher.
Ploughman.
Pontonier.
Quarryman.
Quartermaster.
Rag-picker.
Reporter.
Registrar of a County.
Sailor.
Senator.
Servant.
Salesman.

Saddler.
Saloon-keeper.
Sculptor.
Sheriff.
Seamstress.
Songster.
Stationmaster.
Stone Mason.
Soldier.
Speculator, Cattle.
" Lands.
" Money.
" Grain.
" Patent Rights
" Real Estate.
" Fruit.
" Merchandise generally.
" Stocks.
Statesman.
Stock Dealer.
" Grower.
Student.
Superintendent, Schools.
" Railroad.
" Sab. School.
" Public works.
" Men.
" Charitable Institutions.
Supervisor.
Surgeon.
Surveyor.
Telegraphic Operator.
Tailor.
Tavern-keeper.

Teacher, Gymnastics
" Music.
" High School.
" Primary "
" Dancing.
" Calisthenics.
" Mathematics
" Philosophy.
" Languages.
" Painting.
" Drawing.
" Colouring.
Teamster.
Tinker.
Traveller.
Tragedian.
Tobacconist.
Topographer.
Tailoress.
Toxologist.
Tollman.
Type Setter.
Undertaker.
Upholsterer.
Violinist.
Volunteer.
Wine Grower.
Weaver.
Whitewasher.
Waiting Maid.
Yachtsman.
Zoologist.
Zincographer.
Zoographer.
Zootomist.

Choice of a Companion for Life.

THE choice and selection of a life-companion "for better for worse," is the most important step in the career of either man or woman. Hence it becomes to every member of the community the vital question, as affecting both parties, not only during their own mortal and eternal destiny, but as influencing the offspring of such unions down to the latest generations. The principal things to be carefully considered and pondered well before entering into such binding relationship are chiefly the following:—

1. Our mental and physical organization as to compatibility. This can only be ascertained in a trustworthy manner by each one candidly and unreservedly consulting the skilled physiognomist, so that there may remain no particle of doubt as to congeniality and reciprocity of the natures of the intended partners for life. The *first step* towards securing happiness is the cultivation of INTELLECTUAL CAPACITY, which enables us to judge for ourselves and others; to reap and exchange mental benefits; to discriminate between right and wrong; to adopt advantages as they offer; and to promote that cheerfulness which will best sustain us through our earthly pilgrimage. The *next essential*, towards the attainment of the objects of life is *physical condition*. This judiciously attended to produces health and strength; the former fitting us for our gratifications and duties; the latter for our labours. But in no particular is the advice of the skilled PHYSIOGNOMIST more needed than in reference to the cultivation of the affections and the regulation of the passions, by which we acquire the esteem of others, and establish on a small scale that sympathy, harmony, and social consideration which in an advanced state will become general.

Now it ought to be observed that our natural progression from friendship to love, is to MATRIMONY. This is the position in which the object of the contracting partners should be to bind each the other as a faithful congenial participator in each other's joys for life. In this happy union the development of the warmer feelings is secured without shame or danger. Then consider well that the last grand ambition of humanity is progeny. Having surrounded themselves with children the married couple have accomplished the most exalted of their privileges, by securing to themselves a circle of companions, friends, and assistants, and by giving their race new creatures for its perpetuation; and thus establishing for themselves claims on creation.

Finally, then, personally submit yourself to the examination of a competent physiognomist before selecting your life partner. He will then give you not only a full analysis of your own faculties and powers, but will also state, for your guidance, the looks, features, colour of hair and eyes, complexion, form, and character of the one best suited as a husband or wife for yourself.

The following abbreviated description, when it is marked by an examiner, will serve as a guide to a safe, happy, and blessed wedlock.

CHOICE OF A COMPANION FOR LIFE.

You should marry, or have married, such a person as is described opposite the following dashes made with a pen or pencil by the examiner:—

Tall in Height.	Fine in Bodily Texture.
Medium "	Medium "
Short "	Coarse "
Slim of Build.	Light in Complexion.
Medium "	Blond "
Stout "	Fair "
Large Abdominal Form.	Brunette "
Medium " "	Very Dark "
Small " "	Pointed Chin.
Large Thoracic "	Broad "
Medium " "	Flat "
Small " "	Dimpled "
Large Muscular "	Indented "
Medium " "	Receding "
Small " "	Far-reaching "
Large Bony "	Double "
Medium " "	Round "
Small " "	Square "
Large Brain "	Full Cheeks.
Medium " "	Medium "
Small " "	Thin "
Large Mouth.	Thick Lips.
Medium "	Medium "
Small "	Thin "
Prominent Nose.	Black Eyes.
Straight "	Brown "
Depressed "	Blue "
Long "	Hazel "
Short "	Grey "
Aquiline "	Protruding "
Small "	Full "
High Forehead.	Medium "
Medium "	Sunken "
Low "	Large "
Broad "	Small "
Narrow "	Black Hair.
Bold "	Brown "
Receding "	Auburn "
Wide Upper "	Flaxen "

If you are a *male*, your partner should be from three to ten years younger than yourself; if a *female*, your husband should be from three to ten years older than yourself.

If you prize happiness in married life, do not marry one who is old enough to be your father, or as young as children should be, if you have them. Ann Hathaway was seven years Shakspeare's senior, and they were very unhappy as a married couple.

OPINIONS OF THE PRESS OF AMERICAN CITIES
Where the Author has Delivered Courses of Lectures for 30 Years.

SCIENTIFIC LECTURES.—The renowned and eloquent lecturer, Dr J. Simms, has been lecturing on Physiognomy, during the past two weeks, in the city of Boston, to large and attentive audiences. The lectures are not intended as advertising mediums for the sale of quack medicines, or as ear ticklers to catch pennies with, but are given to advance science and the general welfare of mankind. The lectures are largely illustrated with paintings, and being interspersed with wit and humour make them very attractive.—*The Waverley Magazine, of Boston.*

PHYSIOGNOMY.—A novel and instructive course of lectures on this ill-understood science is now being delivered by Dr Simms, whose striking delineations of character and startling revealments of the connection between form and character are creating a great amount of interest in this community. The lectures are free from all objectionable features, not being intended as advertisements for medical practice. We recommend all to hear him who would add to their stock of knowledge of human nature.—*Chicago Tribune.*

Dr J. Simms, the renowned Physiognomist of New York, has delivered a course of lectures at Platt's Hall in this city, which have proved a perfect success, as they have been attended by an immense audience of ladies and gentlemen every evening. The lectures are illustrated with a very large collection of oil paintings of noted men and women who live in the world's history. The lectures are moral, amusing, scientific and instructive. During each day the Doctor had an unusual business in the way of charts and examinations, which proved very satisfactory to those who obtained them.—*San Francisco Evening Bulletin.*

LECTURE.—Dr J. Simms lectured last evening to a large audience. The lecture was amusing and interesting. The Doctor, having been a popular lecturer for several years, is eminently qualified to make a lecture entertaining. The late discoveries in the system were clearly set forth by paintings and illustrations.—*N. Y. Sun.*

Dr Simms concluded last night one of the most interesting and instructive courses of lectures ever delivered in this city, and through them has given an impetus to Physiognomical investigation that cannot fail of lasting good. They were scientific, practical and amusing, and elicited the warmest commendations from the large and intelligent audiences who attended them. We bespeak for these lectures, in whatever community delivered, crowded—as they are sure to be—and delighted audiences.—*Indianapolis Journal.*

SCIENTIFIC LECTURER.—Dr Simms has been lecturing all this week in Brewster Hall, on the exhaustless subject of man. No lecturer has ever visited New Haven who has given so many original ideas as Dr J. Simms. He works for the good of mankind, and his fearless and independent manner has won him a perfect success in this city. The attendance each evening, (several evenings having been rainy,) has been very large, and his audience gave the closest attention to his every word and gesture. Hundreds have obtained charts and delineations of character. The Doctor will leave with the best wishes of the citizens of New Haven, for his success in the great and good work in which he so nobly labours.—*New Haven Daily Register.*

SCIENTIFIC LECTURES.—Dr J. Simms of New York, has been lecturing to the medical students of the Old Medical School in this city. Last evening four hundred students and several professors were present at his lecture, and all speak very complimentary of his efforts. The late discoveries in anatomy and physiology which the Doctor presents are charmingly well supported by sound logic and stern facts. The Doctor has been invited by a large delegation of citizens to extend his lectures in this city.—*Nashville Daily Gazette.*

Dr J. Simms, the popular lecturer on physiognomy, physiology and anatomy, has recently delivered a course of instructive and entertaining lectures in the city of New York. The audiences, always large and intelligent, were apparently much impressed with the truths of nature and science described by the learned lecturer. These lectures are rendered more interesting by the valuable paintings and apparatus by which they are illustrated. Dr Simms proposes, during the summer, to make a Western tour, visiting Chicago and other cities, where he is deservedly a favourite.—*Frank Leslie's Illustrated Newspaper.*

PHYSIOGNOMY.—No man, we think, ever stood on a platform in Portland who could read character so well as Dr Simms. Large audiences attend his lectures each evening at Lancaster Hall. To-night he lectures on "Physiognomy," and how to read character. Go to the hall during the day and obtain a chart and learn how to make your life most useful to others, as well as yourself.—*Daily Eastern Argus, Portland Maine.*

THE LECTURE LAST EVENING.—Dr Simms' lecture on "Physiognomy" drew an audience last evening which crowded the Academy of Music in every part. The lecture was instructive and highly interesting, much more so than many of those present had anticipated from the subject.—*Sacramento Daily Union.*

LARGE AUDIENCES.—The lectures of Dr Simms are admirable and pleasing, and none should forego the pleasure of hearing them. You can obtain a chart in the Doctor's private room in the hall to-day, and learn thereby what you are by nature best adapted to do, to render most service to the world and yourself.—*Illinois State Journal, Springfield Ill.*

THEATRE HALL.—Dr Simms' lectures at the old Theatre Hall continue to increase in interest. The room was filled last night to its utmost capacity. His lectures are amusing and instructive, which, together with a high moral tone, serve to make them popular among our best citizens. His examinations are very clear and accurate, thereby establishing the practical utility of Physiognomy.—*Wisconsin State Journal, Madison Wis.*

MECHANICS' INSTITUTE.—Mechanics' Institute was crowded to suffocation. Long before the proper time the large hall was densely packed, every seat being full and all standing room occupied. Dr Simms is a physiognomist. His lecture is on physiognomy, and to call his lecture of last night a complete success is scant justice. Every variety of face was illustrated; every moral and mental condition was portrayed to life. Dr Simms deserves and will receive the patronage of our citizens.—*Daily Journal of Commerce, Kansas City, Mo.*

PHYSIOGNOMICAL LECTURES—A CARD.—CHICAGO, JAN. 30, 1869.—Dr Simms' lectures are highly instructive and entertaining, and we think all who attend them will be benefited as well as amused. The Doctor is full of sparkling wit and sound sense, and as a scientific gentleman we heartily endorse him. We hope the Doctor will again visit our city at no distant period and deliver another course of lectures. We regret that he did not make a longer stay here. (Signed) H. Olin, M.D.; John S. Bement, Flour Merchant; Thomas Wilce, Builder; James McGraw, Builder; R. K. Swift, Banker; Harrison Akley, M.D.; L. Lewis, M.D.; T. S. Peters, M.D.; A. L. Hunting, Merchant; A. C. Beers, Merchant; B. O. Sullivan, Merchant; V. R. Allen, Engraver; T. B. King, M.D.; Louis M. Andrick, Lawyer; S. L. Hendrick, M.D.; T. H. Trine, M.D.; B. Davis, M.D.; L. B. Elner, M.D.; William Thiras, Editor; S. W. Lee. Medical Student; William H. Crooker, Insurance Agent; G. B. Smith, Travelling Agent; A. Dinsmore, Printer; G. H. Acker, Printer; D. A. Davis, Insurance Agent; M. T. Summers, Commission Merchant; T. Buck, Broker; M. W. Winter, M.D.; Thomas J. Lewis, M.D.; A. H. Davis, Real Estate Agent; J. G. Trine, M.D.; Rev. A. R. Wynkoop; J. H. Fry, M.D., and many others.—Clipped from the *Chicago Tribune.*

PHYSIOGNOMY.—Dr Simms, who has been lecturing for a week past in the city, to crowded houses, on the subject of Physiognomy, has just closed his course. He has been requested by a large number of medical and business men of the city to repeat the course, and has signified his intention of doing so at some future time. The lectures have been well patronized by the public, and will be sure to be when the Doctor visits us again.—*Chicago Times.*

Dr J. Simms has been lecturing to large audiences in this city. His lectures are scientific and relate to medicine. They have awakened great interest. Dr Simms makes a lecturing tour West this spring.—*Harper's Weekly.*

NOTICES OF DR. SIMMS'S LARGE BOOK.
Sold by Murray Hill Publishing Co., 129 E. 28th Street, New York.

The ablest book we know on physiognomy is that of Dr. Simms, the greatest living reader of faces. His work is scholarly, logical, incisive, and profound, and should be read by every one.—*The Evening Telegraph*, Philadelphia, Pa., Aug. 26, 1880.

Dr. Simms has been known for more than twenty-five years past as the most profound physiognomist, instructive lecturer on faces, and unequaled in Europe and America as an author on Physiognomy. At present his large work is in the third edition and selling rapidly. It is esteemed for its purity of style and its wisdom presented in logical and original form.—*The Daily Critic*, Washington, D. C., Aug. 24, 1880.

Dr. J Simms, the great traveler and leading physiognomist, has published a large book on Physiognomy. It is a faithful and able exposition of the system of physiognomy, which is the first published, yet the book is in the third edition, which proves that it has a ready sale. This is a most valuable science to the world, and Dr. Simms, who has devoted his life to it, being its ablest exponent, has produced a work of intrinsic, and we think of lasting, merit.—*The Examiner and Chronicle* (a religious paper), New York, Sept. 2, 1880.

"Physiognomy Illustrated," is a valuable and enchanting work on physiognomy by the learned, extensive traveler, and popular lecturer, Dr. J. Simms, of New York. It seems to be the first time this ill-understood subject has been treated in a systematic and scientific manner by a scholar. Here we find the cause fully explained why one man is firm, another courageous, the third selfish, the fourth musical, the fifth irritable, and others moral, logical, benevolent, careful, friendly, agreeable, etc. The signs of character, as they reveal themselves in face and form, are here given so plainly that none can fail to understand them. The work is the outgrowth of a mind naturally adapted to the study, and not only raises the subject to the level of a science, but must lead to great and lasting benefit to the public.—*The Evangel*, a religious paper, San Francisco, Cal., May 27, 1880.

The great traveler and special scientist, Dr. Simms, has written the first book giving a complete and reasonable system of physiognomy to the world. The work shows how the mind of man is influenced by preponderating bones, repugnant muscles, excess of brain, strong aerating organs, and powerful nutritive apparatus, and wherein lies the key with which to unlock all characters. The reasonable and clear manner in which the Doctor has treated his subject is worthy of high commendation. The book is the production of a mind having a taste for the study of nature, and like Descartes and Newton he takes a vast stride forward and formulates a new science, involving acute observation, wide experience in traveling, and vast research for truth in all departments of life. The book presents hundreds of signs of character, and cannot fail to give undying fame to the writer, and great practical and moral benefits to society.—*The Methodist*, a religious paper, New York, Sept. 4, 1880.

The present book by Dr. Simms, on physiognomy, illustrated, we think, while propounding a system of character-reading altogether new, is the fruit of a mind highly moral, keenly perceptive, logical, and well ripened with extensive travel and wide experience in dealing with the public for more than a quarter of a century. There have been but few authors on this subject. Aristotle, Porta, Lavater, and Dr. Simms are about all the original writers worthy of mention, and as Dr. Simms is the only one of this number who has devoted a life time to this study alone, he therefore offers to the world the first system of physiognomy, elaborated and illustrated in his large book, "Nature's Revelation of Character." The book is interesting reading, clear, thoughtful, and evincing great observation and study of all departments of life and forms in which it is domiciled. It is masterly in its treatment and should be in the hands of those who would know their friends and their natural enemies.—*Chicago Evening Journal*, Sept. 14, 1880.

The cultivated eye of a "student of human nature" can read the meaning of human faces and features more easily than Champolion could interpret the hieroglyphics of the Egyptians. An ordinary observer can tell at a glance whether one is in an amiable or an angry mood while experts at this sort of "translation of signs" can penetrate the secret arcana of the mind and divine the very thoughts and intents of the heart. We have just closed a remarkable volume of some 600 pages, with 270 illustrations, on "Nature's Revelations of Character," by Dr. J. Simms, which gives a new interest to the occult science of physiognomy. Dr. Simms has devoted many years to this great work, into which he has condensed whole libraries of facts and arguments, linked together with the inexorable logic of natural philosophy. The one great primal law of cause and effect is everywhere reverently recognized and illustrated. We do not propose to write a review or attempt an exposition of the book before us, only to call attention to it, and especially commend it to the study of our cosmopolitan readers. It is simply a "book of nature," a conscientious effort on the part of the author to interpret the "revelations" of Nature. And all such works are welcomed warmly by those who simply seek to gather facts and learn the truth, and get hold of the endless thread of creation—the everlasting chain of the logic of life and death. From a mere practical consideration there is no knowledge half so important as what is popularly called the "knowledge of human nature," the art of reading the character in the face. Dr. Simms, in his "Revelations," gives us the key to interpret human faces and expressions, so that "he who runs may read" and make no mistakes. What infinite miseries would have been spared to mankind, and especially womankind, if they had always been in possession of this key to character.—*The Cosmopolitan*, London, Paris, and New York, London, England, June 24, 1875.

Continued from 2nd page, cover.

RELIGIOUS PRESS.—"The lectures were highly instructive."—*The Baptist*, London, England.

"His character reading is simply marvellous."—*Freemen's Journal*, Sydney, Australia.

"Dr Simms is drawing large crowds every evening. He has been wonderfully successful in delineating the character of well-known citizens."—*Protestant Standard*, Sydney.

"One who sincerely seeks the promotion of truth and all human good."—*The Standard*, Chicago, U. S. A.

"The perfection which Dr. Simms has attained in reading character by viewing faces is surprising."—*Pacific Churchman*, San Francisco.

"The charts of health and character issued by Dr. Simms are highly estimated."—*The Evangel*, San Francisco.

"Physiognomy is a most valuable science to the world, and Dr. Simms, who has devoted his life to it, is its ablest exponent."—*Examiner and Chronicle*, New York.

BRITISH PRESS—"Dr. Simms is known as a most skilled practical physiognomist." *Pictorial World*, London.

"Will amuse, instruct, and enlighten the mind, and purify the affections."—*The Rock*, (a religious paper), London.

"In describing character from the form and face, Dr. Simms stands unequalled in the world."—*The Free West*, London.

"He certainly reads character with great facility. His is no guesswork."—*Anthropologia*, London.

"The author is a true physiognomist, and is known as one of the most interesting popular lecturers we have."—*Human Nature*, London.

"He is the most able and the most popular exponent of physiognomy among living men."—*The Monetary Gazette*, London.

"Dr. Simms is one of the most successful exponents of this science, and has done more than any of his brother scientists to render it popular and attractive. He is the author of a very learned and elaborate work on the subject, entitled Nature's Revelations of Character, or Physiognomy Illustrated, which has been very favorably received in literary and scientific circles, and, though he is by no means unknown in the United Kingdom, it has prepared for him, on the occasion of his present visit, a specially hearty welcome. It is a subject on which society needs much teaching, and none is better able to impart that teaching than Dr. Simms, or to convey it in a manner more agreeable and attractive."—*Northern and Eastern Examiner*, London.

"On Friday evening, Dr. J. Simms, the most able and profound living physiognomist, delivered his fifty-second and closing lecture of a very successful series in London, on physiognomy and physiology, to an audience that occupied every portion of the large gallery and the body of the spacious room in South Place Chapel. As soon as Dr. Simms entered the lecture-room, on the occasion of his last lecture, there was a general outburst of cheering, that continued until he made his bow and was ready to speak, when perfect silence reigned throughout the evening, excepting the hearty cheering often elicited by the jokes and quaint remarks of the Doctor regarding love and marriage, the subjects of the lecture. The vast magnetic and mental influence which Dr. Simms exercised over the audience can be obtained by long practice only, with a taste for the work. The lecture contained advanced ideas."—*Daybreak*, London, March 26, 1875.

NEW EDITION NOW READY.

"Physiognomy illustrated" by J. Simms, M.D. Large, handsomely finished, muslin bound, octave demy, of 624 pages, and illustrated with about 300 engravings. An extensive exposition of the principles and signs of a complete system of physiognomy, enabling the reader to interpret character by outward physical manifestations, and the forms by which character is disclosed. Price by mail, postpaid, $2.00. Address Murray Hill Publishing Co., 129 East 28th Street, New York.

BRITISH PRESS NOTICES.—"To all who wish to study and understand the human nature which passes before them daily, we can with all confidence recommend Dr. Simms' volume."—*North British Daily Mail*, Glasgow.

"Originality characterizes this voluminous book, while every page is replete with scientific observations that at once make it one of the most interesting and valuable publications produced in modern times."—*The Northern and Eastern Examiner*, London.

"This is one of the most important contributions to the science of physiognomy which has appeared for many years. It records many hundred useful observations, illustrated by a large number of woodcuts. It is popular and simple in style, and well worth its cost."—*The City Press*, London.

"The author is a great observer and a great traveller, well versed in science in its various departments, and is known as one of the most interesting lecturers we have. There is nothing in this book which offends against good taste. It is a harmless as well as valuable contribution to literature, and one which should be in the library of every student of human nature, every phrenologist and physiognomist"—*Human Nature*, London.

The Cheapest Popular Medical Book in English or German. Profusely Illustrated.

AN ENCYCLOPAEDIA OF MEDICAL KNOWLEDGE.

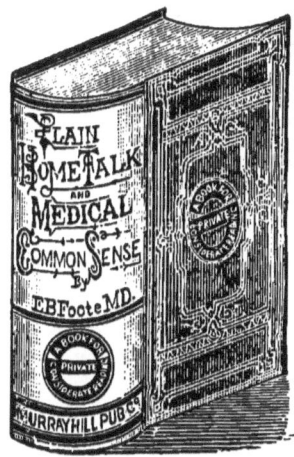

POPULAR because over 500,000 copies have been sold, and 25,000 testimonials received from its enthusiastic readers.

CHEAPEST because no other bound book, medical or not, containing 1,000 closely printed pages is offered at the price.

READABLE because it treats of the life, health and reproduction of the human race, in plain language.

USEFUL because it teaches of the human system in health and disease, and makes known "Common Sense" remedies.

VALUABLE to all invalids or those "out of health" because it marks out new paths for self-cure and permanent relief.

THOROUGH in its warnings of the follies of youth, the penalties of ignorance, and of the mistakes of hasty marriages.

RELIABLE because based on the knowledge and experience of a physician of unusual natural ability and thirty years practice.

ENDORSED by hundreds of editors, physicians, clergymen and scholars in America, Europe, Germany and Australia.

DR. EADON, of Edinburgh, Scotland, graduate of three Universities, and retired after fifty years' practice, writes: "*Your work is priceless in value, and calculated to regenerate society. It is new, startling and instructive.*"

AGENTS given liberal discount, make $2.00 an hour in leisure time, and lay up money when devoting their whole time to it.

PLAIN HOME TALK is now embellished by the addition of a series of Beautiful Anatomical Charts, in five colors; the most Instructive and Handsome Illustrations that have ever been put into a popular medical work, giving a clear idea of the relations and positions of the vital organs of the human system.

CONTENTS OF THIS EPITOME OF MEDICAL, SOCIAL AND SEXUAL SCIENCE:

PART I—TREATS OF DISEASES AND THEIR CURE.

Prevention and Cure, Common Sense Remedies and Doctors of all sorts; including chapters relating to food, clothing, bad habits of children and manhood, excessive study and labor, sleep, cleanliness and healthy babies.

PART II—TREATS OF CHRONIC DISEASES.

Especially of Diseases of the breathing organs, of the liver, stomach and bowels, of aches and pains, bilious affections, headaches, neuralgia and rheumatism; affections of the eyes and ears; diseases of the heart, kidneys, bladder and private parts. Then come important chapters on "Private Words for Women," "Hints to the Childless" and "Private Words for Men;" with essays on cancer, scrofula, syphillis, etc., and their treatment.

PART III—CONSISTS OF PLAIN TALK ABOUT

The natural relations of the sexes, civilization, society and marriage. Here are answered in plain language a thousand questions that occur to the minds of young and old, of men and women, of a nature that they feel a delicacy in consulting a physician about. Chapters are devoted to the history of marriage in the old world and the new, its defects and their remedies, to sexual immorality and numerous interesting subjects concerning marriage and the sexual relations from a physiological standpoint, which make the book a superior guide to the actions of men and women in and out of marriage.

PART IV—TREATS OF THE IMPROVEMENT OF MARRIAGE.

Adaptation, mental, physical, magnetic and temperamental; mental marriages, physical marriages, and "Lucifer Matches." Then come chapters on the intermarriages of relations, philosophy of elopements, essays for married people, concerning jealousy, sexual indifference, sexual moderation, food for pregnant women, etc., etc. The philosophy of child-marking and essays for young and old, conclude a book of which we have only been able to give a bare outline. *A 16-page complete Contents Table, with author's portrait, sent free.*

STANDARD EDITION—Elegant, Substantial—For the Library, by mail, $3.25
POPULAR EDITION—American Cloth Binding, thin paper, " $1.50

Address, **MURRAY HILL PUBLISHING CO., 129 E. 28th St., New York**

MURRAY HILL PUBLISHING CO.
129 East Twenty-eighth St., New-York,
Issue the following Valuable Books on Medical, Social and Sexual Subjects:

PLAIN HOME-TALK and MEDICAL COMMON SENSE.
By Dr. E. B. Foote. In one handsome 12mo volume of nearly 1000 pages; fully illustrated. In English or German. Cloth..............$3.25
A new cheap edition at only... 1.50

SCIENCE IN STORY; or, Sammy Tubbs, the Boy Doctor, and Sponsie, the Troublesome Monkey.
By Dr. E. B. Foote. Five vols.; set, $5; each, $1; 5 vols. in one, $2 00

HOW TO READ FACES; or, Practical and Scientific Physiognomy.
By Mary O. Stanton. 350 pages, cloth-bound...........................$2.00

SEXUAL PHYSIOLOGY FOR THE YOUNG.
The fifth volume of "Science in Story." 250 pages, illustrated and cloth-bound..50c.

DR. FOOTE'S HEALTH MONTHLY.
Devoted to hygiene, sexual and social science and allied subjects, tenth year. Specimen copies free. Per year, with premium............50c.

MOTHER'S MANUAL.
Comprising "Advice to a Wife on the Management of Her Own Health, especially during Pregnancy, Labour and Suckling" and "Advice to a Mother on the Management of Her Children in Infancy and Childhood." Two books in one volume; 528 pages...$1.00

HAND-BOOK OF HEALTH HINTS AND READY RECIPES.
By Dr. Foote. A valuable reference pamphlet of 128 pages............25c.

HOME-CURE SERIES. (DIME PAMPHLETS.)
By Dr. Foote. "CROUP," "OLD EYES MADE NEW," "COLD FEET," "RUPTURE," "PHIMOSIS," "SPERMATORRHŒA." Each, by mail......10c.

SEXUAL-SCIENCE SERIES. (DIME PAMPLETS.)
By Dr. Foote. "PHYSIOLOGICAL MARRIAGE," "PHYSIOLOGICAL IMPROVEMENT OF HUMANITY," "A STEP BACKWARD" (successor of "Words in Pearl"), "REPLIES TO THE ALPHITES," 128 pages, discussing the pro and con. of the hygiene of sexual continence. Each, by mail............10c.

MARRIAGE — As It Was, as It Is and as It Should Be.
By Mrs. Annie Besant. Steel portrait, 50c.; without portrait......25c.

SANITARY-SCIENCE SERIES. (DIME PAMPHLETS.)
By Dr. E. B. Foote, Jr. "BACTERIA IN THEIR RELATION TO DISEASE," presenting the germ-theory, advocating personal and public higiene and opposing vaccination; "HEALTH IN THE SUNBEAM," considering the blue-glass cure—of value to sick and well. Each, by mail...............10c.
"Gynecology or Diseases of Women." Illustrated. Dedicated to sick women; price...10c.

THE RADICAL REMEDY in Social Science, or Borning Better Babies, through Regulating Reproduction by Controlling Conception. By Dr. E. B. Foote, Jr. 150 pages....................25c.

OUR COMPLETE LIST of Books and Pamphlets, in a sixteen-page catalogue, sent free to any address.

www.ingramcontent.com/pod-product-compliance
Lightning Source LLC
Chambersburg PA
CBHW031737230426
43669CB00007B/384